BLADES OF GLORY

THE TRUE STORY OF A YOUNG TEAM BRED TO WIN

JOHN ROSENGREN

SOURCEBOOKS, INC.®
NAPERVILLE, ILLINOIS

Published by Sourcebooks, Inc.
P.O. Box 4410, Naperville, Illinois 60567-4410
(630) 961-3900
fax: (630) 961-2168
www.sourcebooks.com

Library of Congress Cataloging-in-Publication Data

Rosengren, John.
Blades of glory : the story of championship dreams and a young team bred to win / by John Rosengren.
p. cm.
ISBN 1-4022-0047-1 (alk. paper)
1.   Hockey—Minnesota—Bloomington. 2.   School sports—Minnesota—Bloomington. I. Title.
GV848.4.U6R67 2004
796.96'09776'57—dc21
2003005255

Printed and bound in the United States of America
BG   10   9   8   7   6   5   4   3   2   1

For Maria

PHOTOS

ACKNOWLEDGMENTS

So many people lent a part of themselves to this book. A simple thanks doesn't seem enough, but the publisher wouldn't let me put all of your pictures on the cover. Please accept this token acknowledgment and my heartfelt appreciation.

First off, thanks to Tom Saterdalen for allowing me to tag along with his team. Your openness made this book possible. Thanks also to his assistants, Mike Thomas, Barry Karn, Scott Hohag, and Stan Palmer, for your cooperation and insights. Thanks to Bloomington athletic director Joe Dolan for supporting this project from the beginning. And thanks to Bloomington Jefferson's principal, Lyle Odland, for granting me permission to roam the school's hallways.

Thank you to the Jefferson Jaguars 2000–2001 varsity and their parents for welcoming me onto your team, even if you did at times tease me. A special thanks to Michael Bernhagen, Nick Coffman, Matt Duncan, Tommy Gilbert, and Timm Lorenz and their families. I'm grateful for your honesty and candor—your stories bring this book to life.

Thanks, too, to the girls' varsity, especially Gianna Gambucci, Sarah Kraft, Larissa Luther, and Dave Irvin. Congratulations on your state championship.

There are countless others who contributed in many ways to the construction of this book. To detail each of their efforts would make these pages as long as the narrative itself. A blanket thank you to all who spoke with me. In addition, the following should take a bow when your name is called: Tara Barth, John Bianchi, Nicole Black, Madeleine Blais, Buzz Bissinger, Ryan Briese, Herb Brooks, Carolyn Cade, Steve Carroll, Frank Clancy, Ben Clymer, Denny Connelly, Mike Crowley, John Dietz, Jack El-Hai, Jack Falla, Anne Fletcher, William Gildea, Roger Godin, Kevin Harrington, Pete Helberg, Wayne Hergott, Joel Hoekstra, Bobbi Hopkins, Willard Ikola, Cory Jackson, Todd Kennedy, Rob Kinsella, Christian Koelling, Dana Kromer, Roger Mahn, Mike Main, Peter Marshall, Denny May, John Mayasich, Marjorie Miller, Meg and Tom Myers, Lou Nanne, Mark Parrish, Ken Pauly, Michael Rand, Tom Reid, Steve Rushin,

Jason Quehl, Virg Senescall, Glen Sonmor, Pat Sullivan, Mary Turco, Peter Watkins, and Kevin Ziegler. Also, thanks to Mr. Hockey Gordie Howe, Del Reddy, and Aaron Howard. No doubt I've missed someone. Sorry, and thanks.

Thanks to Stephen Bergerson, Deb Orenstein, Sallie Randolph, and Melvin Wulf for the sage legal counsel you lent this effort.

A special thank you to those who endured early, lengthy drafts and offered helpful advice: Matt Callahan, Dale Korogi, Margaret Nelson, Susan Perry, Martha Roth, Dave Shulman, and my wise father, Bill Rosengren. Your patience and comments made this what it is.

Thanks to Del Reddy and Aaron Howard from mrandmrs hockey.com for arraying Gordie Howe's support.

Thank you to Bruce Kluckhohn, the State of Hockey's finest photographer, for expressing with your images far more than I could say with words.

Thank you to Taylor Poole for converting your creative talents into a compelling cover design, and to Amy Reagan for your watchful eye on the manuscript's journey through production.

I am immensely grateful for my agent's early and unflagging enthusiasm for this book. Thank you, Heide Lange.

No book comes to fruition without an editor's guidance. In that regard, I'm doubly blessed. Hillel Black and Todd Stocke combined their extraordinary abilities to offer clear and excellent guidance in the revisions. In twenty years of writing, I've never had such a positive experience as I did working with both of you. Thank you, thank you.

Last, but certainly not least, I thank my wife Maria for her understanding, patience, and support those evenings I skipped dinner to attend hockey games, mornings I fretted over deadlines, and weekends I agonized over what to leave in and what to take out. Thanks, Love.

TABLE OF CONTENTS

JEFFERSON JAGUARS ROSTER
2000–2001 VARSITY

No.	Name	Grade	Position
1	Timm Lorenz	12	Goalie
4	Ryan Van Bockel	10	Defense
5	Brad Peterson	10	Wing
6	Adam Dirlam	11	Defense
7	Jimmy Humbert	12	Wing
9	Nick Dillon	11	Wing
10	Kory Stark	11	Defense
11	Michael Bernhagen	11	Center
14	Justin Wild	10	Center
15	Tommy Gilbert	12	Wing
16	Brian Johnson	12	Center/Wing
17	Eric Lindquist	11	Defense
19	Jeff Rysavy	11	Wing
20	Nick Coffman	12	Wing
21	Bryan Shackle	12	Defense
22	Matt Duncan	12	Center
35	Jeremy Earl	11	Goalie

INTRODUCTION

The average teenage boy thinks about sex once every seven seconds; in Minnesota, he thinks about hockey the other six. The state obsession grips us before puberty. The Farrah Fawcett poster on my bedroom wall was overshadowed by Bobby Orr's autographed likeness, a North Stars pennant, and a pair of crossed hockey sticks flanked by two 8 x 10 color photos, one of my older brother, one of me in my Squirts jersey—a ten-year-old beaming in his Bauers.

I grew up on ice, learning to skate shortly after I could walk. My brother and I waited with eager anticipation for the neighborhood pond to freeze. Soon as the ice could bear our weight, we raced home to grab our skates and sticks. That first game of the year—often played before Thanksgiving—was as exciting as Christmas itself. We skated with the neighbor kids every day after school, even days we had hockey practice or a game that night.

When we weren't playing hockey, we were thinking about it. We would walk half a mile to the corner store to buy a fifteen-cent pack of hockey cards. At Christmas, my parents gave each of us a full box, containing forty packs apiece. We tore off the wrappers, stuffed as much of the stiff bubble gum in our mouths as we could, and traded our doubles. My dad, an artist, made us hockey cards with our picture drawn in color on the front and statistics printed on the back. My mother sewed breezers for our G.I. Joes, and we divided them up into teams that played epic games.

The state high school hockey tournament was the pinnacle of the year. Held the second weekend of March, the Tournament charged the air with a festive holiday atmosphere. The games, played at Met Center, then across the river at the St. Paul Civic Center, always sold out. Not even the governor could get tickets. The Tournament started Thursday, with four quarterfinals played that day, divided into afternoon and evening doubleheaders. Once in a great while, a sympathetic teacher would let us watch the first game, which began at 12:05. Otherwise, we would skip school that afternoon to watch at somebody's house. The final game of the evening session started at 9:45 P.M. In grade school, we struggled to stay awake but usually fell asleep before the first period ended. My dad would soap the final score on the bathroom mirror so we could see it first thing in the morning.

The games—and their players—ballooned larger than life. In fifth grade, I was so impressed by the performance of Dan Mott, the goalie from Southwest Minneapolis High who won a dramatic overtime semifinal to put his team in the championship game, that I wrote him a fan letter. He wrote back. I saved his letter. Still have it, packed in a shoebox along with letters from Jacques Plante, Glenn Hall, and Tony Esposito.

I was partial to goalies, being one myself. I fantasized about starring on that grand stage, leading my team to the title, and becoming the darling of the state. Three other goalies blessed with superior skills in my class at Wayzata High spoiled those dreams. I never played varsity hockey.

But I didn't stop thinking about hockey. I knew those dreams were the stuff of books. So I set out to tell the story of hockey in Minnesota through one high school team.

For this book, I wanted to pick a team that would animate the state's hockey culture. The choice was easy. Through the past two decades, Bloomington Jefferson had dominated high school hockey. There were other storied programs—Edina, Roseau, Hill-Murray, for instance—but none still led by a legend. Jefferson's coach, Tom Saterdalen, was the winningest active hockey coach in the state. He agreed to grant me unlimited access to his 2000–2001 team.

Throughout the season, I attended every team meeting, practice, and game. I rode the team bus, hung out in the locker room, sat in the office when the coaches cut kids, worked out with the team on the ice, talked to the players in school, and watched games in the stands with their families. After games, I hung out at the bar with the parents. These coaches, players, and parents welcomed me as one of their own.

The protocol in press boxes dictates that journalists don't clap. They say we're supposed to be objective. That proved impossible for me. In the time I spent with the '01 Jaguars, I came to care for them. I realized how attached I had become when I found myself laughing at the players' jokes, slapping my forehead at missed opportunities, and second-guessing officials. With time, I couldn't keep myself from cheering their goals. And after the final game of the season, I wanted to cry with them in the dressing room.

It wasn't easy writing this book. I grew attached to these kids, and, as a result, I also grew concerned. Their quest revealed the beauty and goodness of the game I love, and it exposed issues troubling to youth sports. I found it difficult but necessary to examine those delicate issues. Certain details I've included may embarrass those involved, but my hope is that by writing about them, I will bring about a greater good.

For instance, when I discovered several kids I cared about on the team were using a performance-enhancing substance, I wasn't sure what to do. My research revealed that the drug was potentially dangerous. Should I intervene and perhaps change the course of the season's events? Or should I remain silent and perhaps watch one of these kids get hurt? I called my old journalism teacher and mentor. He asked, "How will you feel if you don't say anything, then see one of these kids skate across the blue line, clutch his heart, and collapse?"

I told the players my concerns. I also wrote about it here. Their parents may not like reading about it, but other parents and children stand to benefit by learning about the drug's danger and widespread use. They may be inspired to mitigate the pressure-charged conditions that induce these kids to turn to performance-enhancing drugs for help. Since I made the decision to speak up, three college athletes and two high-profile professional athletes have dropped dead from using the same drug. I tell these boys' stories so that others might revise the endings of their own.

The scenes I observed at the Bloomington Ice Garden are replayed on ice rinks and ballfields across the country. The fervor with which Minnesotans celebrate hockey raises issues about sport and society that transcend Minnesota and reach into communities across the country, wherever kids play and parents cheer them to victory. Kids shiver with early glory and stumble under the expectations placed upon them. It's all there, the thrill of victory, the agony of defeat, every drama human life has to offer played out in the heat of competition. Kids learn lessons about winning and losing, playing under pressure. Valuable life lessons, but ones that one father confided maybe are not necessary to learn at such a vulnerable young age. This book explores those lessons—and the lessons we have to learn from the way youth sports are being played.

CHAPTER ONE

KING SHIT

The boys stripped off their wet gear. Sats had worked them hard in practice. Tomorrow night they would face last year's conference champs, the Eden Prairie Eagles.

"You know why winning the conference is so important?" Tom Saterdalen, still in his skates, glanced around the dressing room as he would his health classroom. His sharp blue eyes measured the faces of the sixteen boys stuffing their soggy equipment into oversized nylon bags. "Bernie, you're the smartest guy in here, you know why?"

Michael Bernhagen, the Jaguars' superstar center, smirked. "You get lots of play."

Sats let it pass. "Those of you who've studied Jefferson hockey history know that every year we've won the conference, we've gone to State—twelve times. Only twice have we gone without winning the conference."

Like every other boy in the dressing room, Tommy Gilbert knew Jefferson had gone to the Tournament fourteen times—more than any other team in the past two decades—and that the Jaguars had come home champions five times. Everybody in the state knew that. The only history that mattered to the Jaguars' 2000–2001 captain was the chapter he and Bernie and the rest of his teammates would write that year. They wanted to win the conference, sure, and make it to the Tournament, but that was only foreshadowing; the climax would come the second Saturday of March when they crowned themselves state champs.

Last week, during his first-period sociology class, Tommy had studied the Minneapolis *Star Tribune* hockey preview. The state's largest daily had ranked his Bloomington Jefferson Jaguars tops in the metro area. Eden Prairie, the preseason favorite, had dropped to No. 4 after losing a couple of key players to injuries. Tommy read his name under the heading "Area's Top Players." His speed, size, and smarts placed him in elite company. He also noted under "Important Dates" December 5, Bloomington Jefferson at Eden Prairie. All eyes in Minnesota would be on the Eden Prairie rink to see which team would position itself as the Lake Conference power.

Matt Duncan, the Jaguars' affable emotional leader and an NHL prospect himself, summed up the significance of the game better than the newspaper or his coach could. Jefferson had started the season with two big wins already, but Eden Prairie was key because the Jaguars' first conference game came against their main rival. Shuffling out of the rink after practice on the eve of the game, his bag slung over his shoulder, Duncs said, "If we lose, people will say we got lucky the first two. If we win, we're King Shit."

The sky surrendered the day's last light Tuesday afternoon when the players showed up at school almost three hours before the 7:30

game. Sats's pregame routine had his boys toss a football in the gym or shoot baskets to tame the butterflies that had swollen during the day with teachers wishing them luck and classmates admonishing them to "kick some ass."

Tommy and Bernie practiced their own pregame ritual. Still in their school clothes, the pair zipped a puck back and forth the length of an empty hallway outside the gym. Each boy recognized the weight of the other's pass on his stick, like knowing the sound of a brother's footsteps on the stairs. On the ice, they didn't have to speak; they sensed where the other would be. Without looking, Bernie could fire a pass onto Tommy's tape. They clicked.

Tommy had blue eyes, short brown bangs, and a big-toothed smile. He often mumbled when he spoke, more comfortable with deeds than words. He had been an All-Conference defenseman his first two varsity seasons, but that year, Sats, needing more scoring punch, had moved his strongest player to forward, reuniting him with Bernie, his superstar playmaker. Tommy, ordinarily reticent, had raced home with the news to call Bernie, who was napping.

"Wake him up," Tommy told Bernie's mom. "It's important."

"You're my center," Bernie heard Tommy say on the other end. He couldn't wait to start skating together again. Three years ago, their last year of Bantams, they had teamed up on "The Magic Line" to score almost two hundred goals. With Tommy back on his wing, Bernie had the only guy on the team he trusted as good enough to play with him. He could make All-State. They could reign as the state's top line.

Tommy banked a pass off the lockers. Bernie caught it effortlessly. Already, in their first two games, they had scored six goals between them. Bring on Eden Prairie.

Sats whistled to his players to get dressed. He walked up and down the rows of blue lockers and doled out sticks of gum from a pencil box held together by white hockey tape. The box held assorted Wrigley flavors. "What color?" he asked each boy. Sats believed chewing gum relaxed his players. Starting his thirty-seventh season, the winningest coach in the state, Sats stuck with his proven traditions. He chewed Jefferson blue.

That fall, Sats had summoned the players returning from the 2000 Tournament to his health classroom. Seeing Tommy Gilbert, Michael Bernhagen, Matt Duncan, Nick Coffman, and Timm Lorenz along with eight other guys seated in the desks of the windowless room, the fifty-eight-year-old coach felt the tingle that had awakened him at 4:15 that morning. He had worked with these boys, excepting Lorenz, since they started skating, watched their talent develop, and eagerly awaited this year. He had not been able to get back to sleep.

"This is the seniors' team," Sats had told them. "People will remember this as the Coffman, Gilbert, and Duncan class." His blue eyes tapped each of the seniors to let that thought sink in. "We'll go as far as the seniors can take us."

Coffman, Gilbert, Duncan, and the rest listened intently. "This is your year." The seniors had heard Sats say that the year before and the year before that, but, finally, this year, he said it for them. This was their team, their time. They felt the tingle, too.

———

The boys pulled on their socks, breezers, and jerseys, piled their equipment bags by the door, and gathered around a green chalkboard in the corner of the school's varsity locker room. Sats had left school during his fourth hour prep period to play squash, something he did every game day to soothe his nerves, then returned before any of his players arrived to write instructions on the green chalkboard. On the left, Sats had written eight instructions for the game: Will fly weak side guy all the time, Love to run off-wing shoot, Look for drop pass in slot....On the right, he had listed the Eden Prairie players by line and jotted notes on each. By Mike Erickson's name, he had chalked: big, strong, hits, goes to net, great shot. Last month, Erickson had committed to the University of Minnesota, the first high school player in the state to sign with a Division-I college.

When Sats got to Erickson's name, he said, "You'll go up against him, Nick." Nick Coffman, seated atop one of the blue lockers in the back next to his buddy Duncs, smiled the warm smile that made his hazel eyes shine. They lit up with the chance to prove himself. This was it.

Nick came from a hockey family. His dad, Mike Coffman, had

starred on the Richfield High School hockey team in the '70s, then played on a scholarship at the University of Michigan. Nick's maternal grandpa had played semipro hockey. Nick's mom, Karen, grew up in hockey skates—she couldn't understand why all of the other girls wore white skates. In high school, where she met Mike, Karen used to cut class to attend afternoon sessions of the Tournament. When a family friend gave Nick a hockey skate planter as a baby gift, Karen believed it foretold his future. "It was inevitable," she said. Hockey was written into Nick's DNA.

His first year of Squirts, Nick played Squirt C, the lowest of the traveling teams. Mike coached him. That year, watching a highlight video of the high school team winning its third straight state championship, the ten-year-old decided upon his life's ambition. The goal created a work ethic. He started working in practice as hard as he could to improve. The next season, he made the Squirt A team.

That year, when Nick was eleven, his parents separated. The following year, Nick's first at the Peewee level, they divorced. Nick and his younger brother stayed with Karen.

His dad remained involved with Nick through hockey. Mike went to games, then called Nick afterward to critique his performance, a practice he continued into high school. During games, he called out to Nick on the ice, "Get over on your wing," or, "Pick that guy up." He watched the game intensely, rarely smiling. "My dad can always find something wrong with what I'm doing," Nick said matter-of-factly. "I can think I've played the game of my life, but then I come home and he's got something to tell me."

Nick was a smart, sensitive kid. He tried to dismiss his dad's criticism as helpful. His dad knew the game, unlike some other hockey parents, he rationalized. "It's like having another coach," he said. But his confidence slumped.

Last year, Nick was one of three junior varsity players called up to join the varsity for the playoffs. When the team boarded the bus to take the Jaguars to Mariucci Arena for the section final, fans in the school parking lot saluted them with honks and formed a caravan that followed the bus to the University of Minnesota campus. After Jefferson won, advancing to the Tournament, those same fans lined up at 5:30 A.M. the following Monday to buy tickets. Nick's mom hung balloon bouquets and good-luck signs around the house. But in their first-round loss, Nick didn't get off the bench. Sats played four defensemen; Nick was the fifth. The Tournament turned into a major disappointment. Getting there had been just a tease.

This year Nick expected that to change. All of his life he had been a third-line player, but he was determined to become a contributor senior year. His teammates had elected him an alternate captain. That gave his confidence a boost. He would do what he had always done—work his tail off—so he and his buddies could go out state champs. He believed that was their destiny. If that meant shadowing the opponent's star, so be it. Bring on Eden Prairie's Erickson.

Sats finished his pregame talk at the board: "If someone were to say you can only win one of the first three, Eden Prairie would be it. This is our first conference game. We haven't won the conference since '98. It's a big game." He clapped his hands. "Let's go."

The boys schlepped their bags up the stairs, across the empty cafeteria, and onto the yellow school bus waiting outside. The mood was loose on the short ride. Bernie laced a skate and pontificated on what he called "the preacher position." The superstar center usually got his way with girls.

The team bus turned right at the driving range, left at the bank. During the '80s and '90s, young money had populated the custom homes that filled out the west side, dubbed "Prestigious West Bloomington." This is George W. country, where residents want to keep taxes down and Washington in its place. The metro area's largest suburb sprawls like a giant park south of Minneapolis, just outside the interstate bypass. Over one-third of its thirty-seven–thousand acres are parks, wetlands, golf courses, ski areas, or preserved forests. Home of the nation's largest indoor shopping mall, the Mall of America, Bloomington is best known in hockey circles throughout the country for its dominant program.

The bus crossed the border into Eden Prairie, and the Christmas lights grew more plentiful as the houses grew bigger. When Prestigious West Bloomington filled out, the new money spilled over into Eden Prairie, which was built big, with "$250K–350K houses a dime a dozen," as one realtor put it. EP was the newer, upscale version of PWB.

While Bloomington's population aged, its student base, divided between two high schools, dwindled. Meanwhile, even though Eden Prairie had maxed out its residential development potential, young families matured and numbers at EP's single high school continued to increase, making it the state's ninth largest. The rise of Eden Prairie's hockey program had followed the suburb's growth and caught Bloomington Jefferson's. When these boys were Peewees, twelve and thirteen years old, "Evil Prairie"—from the lips of some Jags supporters—had toppled Jefferson in the state tournament semifinals. The West Bloomington boys had some history they wanted to set straight.

———

Steve Duncan smoked a cigarette outside the Eden Prairie Community Center, a "smoke-free environment." Duncs's dad pulled on an Old Gold and waited for the Jaguars' bus. He wore what looked like a letter jacket—leather arms, felt chest—with GOP displayed across a large eagle on the back. The bank clock the bus passed read 4°F, and a raw North wind cut through his jacket, numbed his fingers, and made his ears ache deep inside.

When Duncs hopped out the emergency door—the way half of the guys exited the bus—he stopped to talk to his dad. Steve Duncan, who felt much deeper emotion than he let on from behind his walrus mustache, uttered the incantation he repeated to his son before every game: "Give me something to remember."

At the team banquet last year, Sats had announced Duncs as the other alternate captain, along with Nick. Duncs choked up. Despite his talent and charm, he was surprised his teammates had voted for him. Tears of gratitude swarmed his eyes. His teammates had given him a second chance.

They had known Duncs as a punk. His parents had divorced when he was three, and he hadn't taken it well. He threw tantrums and wrecked things. On one tantrum, he heaved a rock through his bedroom wall. Even though his mom, Deb, remarried when Duncs was six and by then she and her ex, Steve, were getting along better, young Duncs hadn't settled down. In middle school, his attitude worsened. He took advantage of others. He stole booze and got drunk with his friends. He smoked dope. That carried over into high school. During hockey season his sophomore year, Duncs kept smoking pot and drinking.

The Minnesota State High School League requires participants in all extracurricular activities to sign an agreement that they won't use tobacco, alcohol, or any other mood-altering chemicals. The agreement covers not just the season but the entire calendar year. Violators risk suspension. For many, signing the agreement is just another hoop, like getting a physical and paying the participation fee.

So it was sophomore year for Duncs and his teammates, a wild bunch. Duncs had partied heavily that summer and fall. When hockey season came around, he hardly slowed down. He got high or drunk almost every weekend. He also chewed, a favorite hockey-player hobby. He didn't think any of that hurt his play. That year, despite a talented team, the Jaguars missed going to State by a game, losing in the section final.

In the spring, Duncs's phys ed teacher busted the sophomore hockey star for chewing in class. Under MSHSL rules, that meant an automatic two-week suspension. The gossip had barely subsided when Duncs got busted again, this time for drinking at a party. The cops wrote up Duncs for consumption of alcohol by a minor. He had to perform community service. Worse, the ticket added a three-week suspension, on top of the first one—almost half of the hockey season.

Duncs went out for soccer the fall of his junior year to serve the suspensions so he would be eligible again once hockey season began. He had never played soccer before, but he knew the coach, who was willing to do him a favor. It wasn't an uncommon practice—single-sport athletes who got busted in the off-season often went out for a different sport before their primary sport season began. The two hockey teammates who got busted drinking with Duncs did the same thing. They served their time on the soccer bench. There were ways to get around the league rules and their consequences.

But Duncs felt like scum. He had trouble facing his friends' parents, the adults who had always supported him. He knew he had disappointed his own parents. They had talked to him in the past, but he hadn't listened. This time, when Deb and Steve sat him down, what they said got his attention. They told him he had to make a choice. He could be a hockey player or a druggie. If he wanted to be a druggie, they couldn't stop him. But if he wanted to be a hockey player, he had to be a leader.

Their message found its mark. Duncs had been playing hockey since he was five. He loved everything about the game, down to the smell of the ice. He quit drinking and drugging. "Hockey meant too much to me," he said. "I wasn't willing to give that up."

He stayed clean his junior year. With a clear head, he took an honest look at himself. He didn't like what he saw. He decided he wanted to be a better person, to treat people kinder. Between a short forehead and a long jaw, he had soft blue eyes that beamed a kind sincerity. He had always been a warm, caring kid, even though he had concealed that during his punk phase. Duncs dropped the attitude; he started to let others see his caring side. A muscular kid with lumberjack strength and schoolyard toughness who played an old-time, bruising style, he became courageous enough to let his teammates see him cry at the banquet, to kiss his mother after games, to tell his dad he loved him. In retrospect, Duncs called getting busted a blessing.

Senior year would be the test. Clean and sober, Duncs had scored eighteen goals last year. Most significantly, he netted many of those in the clutch. He had been the team's go-to guy. This year, as a senior and a captain, he knew his teammates would be looking to him even more as a leader both on and off the ice. So, too, would his parents.

"Give me something to remember," his dad said. "Something good. Something to make me proud." Duncs nodded and headed into the arena.

It wasn't yet 7:00 Tuesday evening, but the Eden Prairie Community Center was already filling up for the showdown between the top contenders of the Lake Conference. The Eden

Prairie band members assembled their shiny instruments from hard black cases. The cheerleaders tied their white skates, smoothed their short skirts, and checked their makeup in pocket mirrors. College and pro scouts lined the glass behind the net to watch warmups. An agent, hot on Eden Prairie's Mike Erickson, chatted with the Phoenix Coyotes strength coach who trained the high school star. Internet and newspaper reporters studied the names on their programs while television cameramen jockeyed with photographers for position to set up their equipment. Parents sipped hot chocolate around the concessions counter.

The boys weaved through that throng to the visitors dressing room, where they dumped their equipment bags on the floor and finished dressing. Goaltender Timm Lorenz followed the same routine he would if he were starting. He tied his left skate first, then his right. He strapped a blue and white Louisville pad to his left leg, then the other to his right. He slipped into his chest protector and arm pads, then pulled his Jaguars jersey over his head. He kissed each piece of equipment before he put it on.

Goalies by nature are quirky. They must willingly face shots traveling the speed of a Randy Johnson fastball, sometimes without being able to see them, and stand their ground while guys bear down on them at twenty miles per hour. Timm fit the profile. With a little flip of closely cropped brown hair at his forehead and a wisp of whiskers on his chin, he looked like a sock-hop kid. He became a goalie because he loved the equipment. Growing up in Colorado, he would come home from preschool, strap on his goalie equipment, and run around the basement pretending to be Chris Gillies, the University of Denver goalie. He slept with his leg pads on. After Timm had fallen asleep, his mother Merrelyn would step softly into his room to lift them off.

————

The pride of Timm's gear was his mask, a five–hundred-dollar, hand-painted *objet d'art*—oil on fiberglass—by Todd Miska, who designed masks for NHL netminders. On Timm's mask, a jaguar snarled at oncoming shooters against a backdrop of Jefferson blue.

On the back, the letter B and a hockey stick formed his father's initials. Bradd Lorenz, who had loved hockey though he never played it, had dropped dead almost five years ago after a workout at the health club. He was forty-seven at the time; Timm was fourteen.

Timm kissed his mask. He cradled it in his lap, leaned his forehead against its forehead, and closed his eyes. He replayed in his mind the section final from last year, the game they won to advance to the state tournament. His body remembered the feel of each save. He visualized his father in the stands, cheering.

The team hit the ice for warmups with the adrenaline rushing through them like the rock music blasting over the public address system. Tommy Gilbert hovered a moment at center ice to chat with Mike Erickson. They had played together at elite USA Hockey Select camps. Both tall and lanky, they shared responsibilities for their teams as captains.

Tommy's teammates had chosen him as their captain because he was the strongest kid on the team, and one of the best skaters, surest stick-handlers, and hardest shooters. The vote had been unanimous except for one. Tommy was the only guy not to pick himself as the team's leader, not so much out of modesty—he believed himself deserving of the honor—but because of the added pressure the role demanded.

In hockey, perhaps more than any other sport, the captain carries the team.

"If no other sport requires such a well-defined leadership structure, maybe it's because no other sport is so dependent on individual displays of physical courage and channeled emotion, the pillars of leadership since the last ice age," Tommy had read in *Sports Illustrated* that fall.

If that were true in the NHL, it was even more so in high school hockey, where surging testosterone whipped emotions into whirling dervishes and boys had yet to define courage for themselves. At Jefferson, the captaincy carried extra weight—far more than organizing pregame spaghetti lunches. Those with the *C* stitched onto their Jaguars sweaters had performed mighty feats that forged the Jefferson tradition, which Tommy was expected not only to uphold but to further. Despite the presence of other talented players on his team, Tommy knew the community would look to him as the pillar meant to buttress the dreams of the '01 Jaguars. More likely to lead by example than impassioned speeches, he feared what it would mean to falter under the pressure.

————

The two teams ran through their pregame drills, then returned to their dressing rooms for the Zamboni to make new ice. Bernie munched a Snickers bar. Sats paced between his players. "Wrist shots, guys, wrist shots….Defense, play good defense."

For more than thirty years, Sats had played out this scene. Next season would be his last. But he still felt the buzz, still wanted each game. He wanted this one especially. He wanted the conference and a shot at another title.

Sats stopped in the middle of the dressing room. "Heads down."

In a singular movement, like a well-drilled military formation, the boys leaned forward, rested their forearms on their breezers, and lowered their heads. No one spoke. The boys could hear the teammates next to them breathing.

Tommy's parents had instilled in him the belief that he had to work hard because of the talent God had blessed him with. "To whom much is given, much is expected." In the silence, Tommy prayed, *This is a big game, God. Help me get through it.*

Sats's fatherly voice punctured the stillness. "These are the games you'll remember for a long time. It's always good to win that first conference game. It's a lot tougher to win the conference title because it means you've got to work hard every game. First shift out there, set the pace!"

Tommy led the boys out of the dressing room. Timm stood by the door; each player punched his blocker glove on the way out. They hopped onto the ice between two rows of Jaguars cheerleaders enthusiastically shaking their blue and silver mylar pom-poms. The Jefferson faithful cheered from the bleachers, which had swollen beyond their 1,200-person capacity. Fans stood in the aisles. The students waved hand-lettered signs: "Go Big Blue," "Tommy is Mr. Hockey," "We Love Duncs." They shouted to their favorite players.

These were their boys. The parents, friends, and longtime Jefferson fans cheered the collegiate Gophers and professional Wild, but not like they cheered their Jaguars. These were the real heroes, the kids who had grown up next door, the kids they cared about—kids like Matt Duncan and Tommy Gilbert who had matured from Squirts with mullet cuts into clean-cut young men. They shared the Gophers and Wild with the whole state; the Jefferson Jaguars were theirs alone to admire and adore.

After the introductions and national anthem, the Jaguars huddled around their goal. "Born to Be Wild" blared over the P.A. system. Duncs spread his arms around his teammates and said, "We can beat these guys. Let's go, boys!"

The Jaguars dominated the opening minutes. They peppered the Eagles's goalie. He turned away their shots, but everyone knew they would score; it was only a matter of time before Bernie, Tommy, and Duncs would do their thing.

Both teams hit hard. The collisions jarred mothers in the stands. Jaguars senior defenseman Bryan Shackle ran an Eagle into the boards and snapped a bone in his own hand. He left for the hospital.

The game got rougher. When the refs finally whistled Eden Prairie for a slashing penalty with fifteen seconds remaining in the first period, Jefferson's chances to score first on the powerplay looked good. Then Bernie took a penalty at the buzzer to negate the opportunity.

Back in the dressing room, the student managers tossed water bottles and oranges to the players. Sats came in and paced amidst the phlegm and peels that coated the floor. "Keep moving. Keep moving….Go to the net. Go to the net." He left and returned a moment later. "We can work a lot harder. That's probably the worst we've worked in any of the three games so far."

The second period started with Bernie in the penalty box. In Bernie's first shift back, Tommy was knocked down, but he muscled the puck forward, launching Bernie on a breakaway. The swift-footed center dazzled the Eagles's goalie with several quick dribbles and slipped the puck past him to put Jefferson up 1–0.

"That's about a 98 percent sure thing." Jaguars assistant coach Barry Karn shook his head in admiration. "He makes me dizzy when he starts moving the puck back and forth like that."

Bernie was a poet on ice. Creative panache defined his play—the impossible pass, the metered moves, the rhythmic stickwork. He stood only 5'9" but weaved freely through much larger players. At times he carried the puck coast to coast; other times he skated circles at center ice to kill penalties. Bernie could read a breakout, anticipate the pass, and step in front to intercept the puck. Like Wayne Gretzky, he seemed to play two or three strides ahead of everybody else. When Bernie took the ice, the game changed.

Two shifts after scoring, Bernie plucked the puck off the side boards and dished a perfect feed to the far side of the Eagles's net— one swift motion, an instinctive pass that couldn't be taught. Brian Johnson touched it in to stake Jefferson a 2–0 lead. "Thataway, Bernie," Sats shouted from the bench.

But Eden Prairie roared back. Three minutes later, Erickson swatted a bouncing puck past Jaguars' goalie Jeremy Earl. The Eden Prairie band struck up the school song. The cheerleaders grooved. The reporters scribbled notes. The players on the ice hugged their captain.

One man standing along the glass turned to his buddy. "This is America, right here."

"It ain't London, I'll tell you that," his buddy replied.

Less than a minute later, the Eagles tied the game 2–2.

Between the second and third periods, Sats yanked Tommy into the hallway and chewed him out. Erickson had nailed him off the puck, and Tommy had let his man go to set up the second goal. Sats wanted Tommy to make his presence felt more. "As the captain goes, so goes the team," Sats told him.

Early in the third period, Eden Prairie banged in a loose puck to pull ahead 3–2. For the first time in the young season, the top-ranked Jaguars had fallen behind in a game. On the bench, Bernie started bitching about his teammates' play. They weren't performing at his level. In the stands, Steve Duncan and the rest of the Jefferson fans mellowed. The Jaguars looked beaten.

Then, at the halfway mark of the third period, 7:28, Jefferson's third line tied the game and revived the fans' hopes. With the clock winding down, the game seemed headed for overtime, a fitting finish for these two skilled squads.

The Jaguars' fortunes reversed in slow motion. With less than two minutes remaining, Eden Prairie broke into the Jefferson zone. A defender took out the puck carrier; Jeremy went down to collect the loose puck, but an Eagle trailing the play poked the black disc forward like a shuffleboard shot. Jeremy's momentum carried him one way; the puck slithered past him the other. That was the goal the state would watch on the evening news.

The Jaguars stomped into the dressing room. "Fuck," Tommy said. For him, that outburst was tantamount to a temper tantrum. Jeremy, a happy-go-lucky kid, hung his head and cried softly. None of the other players could look at him. They felt their own shame. Tommy smarted from Sats's tongue-lashing. Nick knew his dad would point out how Erickson had overmatched him. Bernie was miffed at his teammates. Timm had watched helplessly from the bench. Duncs had managed only three shots on net and let a guy by him for a goal—not what he had wanted to give his dad to remember. Yet, on his way out of the dressing room, Duncs stepped over to Jeremy and rubbed his head.

When the bus got back to school, the cheerleaders comforted the players with hugs in the cold, dark night, but even pressed against the girls' warm sweaters, the December night felt a little colder, a little darker. Since they played every team in the conference twice, the boys would get another shot at Eden Prairie, but that game wasn't for another six weeks. They would have to wait their turn to be King Shit.

CHAPTER TWO

JUDGMENT DAY

Ryan Briese woke on November 13 worried about the pain. It had been a month since he had broken his ankle playing in a fall hockey league, but on his way downstairs that morning, the ankle still hurt. The doctor advised him not to skate until the soreness was gone, but he couldn't skip tryouts. A tall, quiet kid, Ryan wasn't one quick to complain. He was more likely to blame himself than others. He hoped the pain wasn't too much.

When he left for school, it was still dark outside. He could see a wet snow had fallen that night. The street was slicked black, too warm for the snow to stick, but it clung to the bare branches like fuzz on new antlers. During his classes that Monday, Ryan had trouble thinking about anything other than tryouts starting at 2:30. Nine seniors had graduated from the '00 team. There would be spots for guys like Ryan from last year's junior varsity. If Sats did things the way he usually did, he would keep three lines—only nine skaters—and five defensemen, plus two goalies. That didn't leave any margin for error.

Even though last year as a junior Ryan skated three full varsity games in the Holiday Classic tournament when Sats played him on a fourth line, he would have to shine in tryouts to win a spot this year as a senior forward. He could skate with any of the kids returning, except maybe the top three—Tommy, Duncs, and Bernie—yet, somehow last season, his talents hadn't translated into convincing numbers—four goals, eleven assists, and the third lowest plus/minus rating on the team. Sats didn't let seniors play j.v.—there would be no second chances to prove himself. This week was do or die.

The week before, Ryan had gone to see Limp Bizkit, his favorite band, with Duncs and Nick, his two best friends. They had played hockey together since second grade. That night, they talked about how great their senior season was going to be, but Ryan had an uneasy feeling. There was too much hope for him in that kind of talk, not enough certainty. In eighth grade, he had survived the first cut for Bantam As when neither Duncs nor Nick had. Even though he didn't make the final cut that year and they all ended up on the Bantam B team, Ryan had gloated when he had the chance. This time, he didn't feel any of that swagger.

Ryan worried that Sats didn't like him. Several times last season, Sats had ridden him about his play. Then, he hadn't said anything to him. Ryan wasn't sure which was worse, but neither seemed a good sign. Sats had told him to lift weights that summer. Ryan knew he needed to add some meat to his lean frame, but he hardly stepped into the weight room. Instead, he worked that summer building decks with his dad. Going into tryouts, he couldn't shake an uneasy feeling bordering dread.

Ryan wanted to skate with his friends senior year, play before the crowds every Tuesday and Saturday, screw around in the dressing room, earn a varsity letter so he could wear his letter jacket to parties, and go to the Tournament—the whole package.

There was one more thing: Gramps. Last June, the docs diagnosed him with melanoma. The cancer had since spread to his lymph nodes. Gramps and Granny had been to every one of Ryan's games for ten years. It would have been easier on Gramps to go someplace warm in January or February that year, but he hadn't planned a winter vacation. Gramps and Granny wanted to stick around to watch Ryan play varsity. He didn't want to let them down. Going to games would take Gramps's mind off the cancer, make him feel better if only for awhile. Wouldn't it be great to make it to the Tournament and, when he got introduced and the camera was trained on him, say, "Hi, Gramps and Granny." That would make them so proud.

But, first, he had to survive tryouts.

———

Sats hadn't slept well the night before November 13. It wasn't which players to select that kept him awake. He knew as soon as last year's season ended—even earlier in some cases—which players he planned to cut. In that sense, tryouts were merely a formality. They gave Sats an idea of who was in shape and who wasn't, and they helped him experiment with lines and sort bubble players, deciding who was ready to play varsity when the season began and who needed to log more time on j.v. But as far as the players' fates, he had already decided.

No, what kept him awake was having to deliver the bad news. He worried about the reaction. He knew how large their dreams loomed, how big they had inflated by senior year. The kids and their parents never took it easily, especially when he cut a senior. And he planned to cut three seniors.

In 1992, a father had taken out a full page ad in the *Bloomington Sun Current* that questioned the practice of cutting seniors after Sats cut the man's son, a senior. The next year, Sats kept two seniors whom he knew wouldn't play much. He had a highly talented batch of kids, many returning from the undefeated '93 state champion team. At the start of the season, he sat down the two seniors and their parents, explained that they wouldn't play much, but, since they had paid their dues in the program, he offered to let the kids come along for the ride.

Fine, the kids and parents said. Love to. Thanks. Then, as the season wore on, one of the fathers tired of watching his son ride the pine. He groused among other parents. Even though five kids from that team would go on to play in the NHL and almost everybody else went to Division-I college programs, the father griped that Sats wasn't giving his kid the ice time he deserved. Sats led his team to another state title that year with the kids he put on the ice, but the disgruntled father still grumbled. Sats vowed he wouldn't make that mistake again. He would keep the kids he meant to play and cut the rest.

The kids he planned to trim that year could make it easier for him with a poor showing during tryouts, but he couldn't count on it. Their parents wouldn't be satisfied with that as an explanation anyway. They didn't think six days was enough time to pick a team. He would counter that the seniors had had eleven years to try out. He would point to their performance on j.v. the year before. Sats hadn't cut them; they had cut themselves, sealed their own fate. He believed his reasoning solid, but he knew you never won an argument with a parent. Tryouts were hell on him.

It was a long night.

————

In Minnesota, hockey preoccupies the state psyche. One out of every 113 Minnesotans plays hockey, the highest per capita participation rate in the nation. The rest watch. A month before tryouts, on October 11, 2000, 18,827 fans rocked the Xcel Energy Center for the Minnesota Wild's home opener. The following day, the *StarTribune* devoted one-and-a-half pages to the previous evening's debate between Al Gore and George W. Bush and six pages to the Wild opener, including a special commemorative pullout section. Puck eclipsed presidential politics.

St. Paul mayor Norm Coleman, who had championed the return of the NHL, credited high school hockey with putting up the Xcel

Energy Center, the Wild's swanky new home. "I don't think this place would've been built if it weren't for this tournament being here," Coleman would remark during the 2001 Tournament, the first at the Xcel. "The strength of hockey in Minnesota is in high school hockey."

With the largest state high school tournament in the nation, Minnesota hockey is bigger than Texas football, bigger than Indiana basketball. More than one hundred thousand fans attend the annual four-day Tournament the second weekend of March. Another two million tune in on TV. Families argue over who gets to use the tickets each year. Bookies take bets on the games; scalpers include it on their schedules. Just how big is the Tournament? Howard Cosell, the mother of all sports announcers, provided color commentary in the '70s. The erudite sesquipedalian's presence elevated the Tournament to the status of an Ali–Frazier title fight. No other high school tournament can claim that stature.

The Tournament is not only larger than life, it is life. While Canadian kids daydream about hoisting the Stanley Cup, Minnesota boys from the Iron Range in the North to the flat prairies of the South fantasize about playing in the Tournament. Gary Gambucci, who played hockey at Hibbing High and later for the Minnesota North Stars and Saint Paul Fighting Saints, had a singular dream. "Growing up, all I thought about was playing in the Tournament— not even winning, just playing in it," he said. "Getting to the state tournament was my whole reason for existence. It should be that way for every kid. If not, there's something wrong with him."

The late Herb Brooks, who coached the '80 U.S. Olympic team— half of them Minnesota boys—that upset the mighty Soviet juggernaut to capture gold, told *Sports Illustrated* that winning the state tournament was the bigger thrill. As a high school senior, Brooks scored two goals in the championship game to earn St. Paul Johnson High the '55 title. "Winning the state championship with my friends from the neighborhood topped the Miracle on Ice because we had talked about doing that since we were Peewees," Brooks said. "When the smoke clears, your buddies from high school are awfully important, probably more important than anything."

For many boys, the state tournament is simply a fantasy—about as likely as taking Britney Spears to the prom. But in West Bloomington, home of the Jefferson Jaguars, playing in the state tournament is considered a birthright. Winning isn't something Jefferson kids wish for, it is assumed. Led by Tom Saterdalen, the winningest active hockey coach in the state, the Jaguars reached the Tournament more often the past two decades than any other Minnesota high school. Kids coming of age in the Jefferson feeder program expected the chance to live that dream. They watched the older kids win and anticipated their turn to make it to the Big Dance. Tradition was the ticket.

Families with young children moved to Prestigious West Bloomington not for the schools but for the Booster youth hockey program. Parents laid out big bucks for camps, clinics, personal trainers, and equipment to develop their children's talent. As Peewees, kids like Duncs, Nick, and Ryan hung on every word of the Jefferson varsity players, invited as guest speakers to their hockey team banquets. They watched the highlight videos of championship teams in the making with eyes the size of faceoff circles. Parents and kids wanted the chance to perpetuate the tradition. The dream took root and blossomed. "Every kid would give their left nut to play for Jefferson," John Bianchi, Sats's long-time assistant coach, observed. "Every parent wants their kid on that team, wants their kid to have that gold medal around their neck—it's a helluva big loss to a kid or parent if they're eliminated."

Monday afternoon, November 13, hockey teams across the state hit the ice to start the '01 season. At the Bloomington Ice Garden, Ryan, Tommy, Duncs, Nick, Timm, Bernie, and the others skated a few laps to limber up for tryouts before Sats whistled them to the bench, where Tom Thomas and Brad Parker waited. The two middle school teachers had taught all of these boys except Timm, the one Thomas called "Colorado." Many of the players had gone on the pair's Outward Bound–type camping week and felt a special bond with Thomas and Parker. From the time before any of the class of

'01 had been born, tradition dictated that Thomas and Parker inaugurated the season with a pep talk. Dedicated fans, the two of them watched home and away games behind the Jefferson goal. For the Tournament, they sent inspirational telegrams that Sats read aloud in the dressing room. Monday afternoon, Thomas and Parker stood before a large blue sign taped above the bench: JAGUARS 2000–2001 November—Commitment, December—Teamwork, January—Endurance, February—Success, March—Xcel. Love ya Blue, Thomas and Parker.

Once the players had assembled around the pair, Parker, the short one with the brown mustache, said, "You have a unique opportunity to play hockey for Jefferson. Take advantage of it."

Thomas, tall and thin, added in his squeaky voice, "We care about you, and we'll be there to support you."

When they finished, Sats said, "Let's give them three, guys." The players saluted the pair with three quick raps of their sticks on the ice. Before they left, Parker and Thomas hugged Bernie and the other players. The season was officially underway.

Sats sorted the boys into colored-jersey–coded lines and defensive units, and they spent most of the week scrimmaging each other. Sats watched from the stands with Mike Thomas (no relation to Tom Thomas), his assistant coach for the six years since John Bianchi's retirement. Thomas came to Jefferson after being neighboring suburb Richfield's head coach for eleven years and making two state tournament trips. Sats and Thomas scrutinized each move and second-guessed each decision the players made. This wasn't just a scrimmage. This was a chance to see how the players would respond in a big game. That missed pass could be a lost goal against Elk River. That botched backcheck the difference against Eden Prairie.

Ryan, open on the far post, received a perfect pass on his stick but managed only to swipe the puck weakly into Timm's pads. The coaches snickered. "Even I could've made that shot." That could've been a sudden death gamewinner—muffed.

When another player got beaten on a rush, Sats complained the kid was loafing. Thomas defended him. "That's the one thing any kid can do—work," Sats barked. Thomas backed down. Later, when the pace slowed, Sats shouted at the players to pick it up, "Jaguars never stop until they go through the boards!"

Ryan's ankle hurt. Every day that week, he had the trainer at school tape it before he caught the bus to the rink. He popped plenty of Tylenol, but he felt a stab of pain every time he pushed off. The ankle ballooned up inside his skate, and he iced it at night. Ryan's mom had called Sats to tell him about Ryan's ankle. Ryan wouldn't have told the coach himself. But Sats considered the ankle an excuse.

Tommy, Duncs, and Nick weren't worried about making the team. But it was awkward for them around their buddies in jeopardy. Duncs and Nick watched Ryan withdraw during the week, but they didn't know what to say. The sword of Damocles loomed over Ryan's hockey career—and, possibly, their friendship—but they didn't talk about it. They just hoped somehow he would survive the cut.

Before and after the hour-long scrimmages, a current of suspense charged the dressing room banter. The guys sitting in that room knew several of them wouldn't be there next week. Another two or three younger guys would get moved down to j.v. It all depended on how they measured up against each other.

The tension set the tone of the scrimmages. The hits came harder. The sticks came up. Guys jousted after the whistle. They might be friends, but they were still fighting for a varsity spot.

The weather turned cold that week. A mass of arctic air blasted the state and chased the mercury down backyard thermometers. Winds gusting to twenty-five miles per hour whipped the wind chill below zero. Snow sifted across the Ice Garden's parking lot. The ponds behind the rink froze. Nature ordained the time had come to play hockey.

The first snow had come a week earlier, on election day. Throughout tryouts, the presidential election confusion muddled on, with a new plot twist to the Florida tally each day. Even though Sats's task at tryouts wasn't as tricky as that of Palm Beach county officials sorting through hanging and pregnant chads, he faced certain controversy with his decisions. And more personal consequences. Florida Secretary of State Katherine Harris didn't risk running into Al Gore at the ice rink. How would Sats look Jim

Knutson in the eye after he cut his kid? They had known each other thirty years, going back to when Sats was an assistant coach at the University of Minnesota and Knutson was an All-American defenseman. Over the years, Knutson had invested a lot into his son's career. He had served as Booster president, coached youth teams, and frequently defended Sats. The coach still couldn't sleep easy.

————

Sats had scheduled back-to-back scrimmages for Saturday morning against two top twenty teams, Wayzata and Duluth East. The bus left the school at 8 A.M., and most of the players napped on the twenty-minute ride to the Wayzata rink. Before his players took the ice, Sats tried to rouse them with the reminder that tryouts hadn't ended and that he wanted to see them play more physically. "You're nice guys who haven't wanted to hurt your friends this week," he told his boys in the dressing room. "These guys aren't your friends. You can hit them."

The boys' parents, barred from the tryout sessions that week by an unspoken but understood decree, turned out en masse for the Saturday morning scrimmage. Timm's mom was there, sitting with his girlfriend Larissa, a star on the Jefferson girls' hockey team. They watched a groggy performance. Jefferson lost both games, 0–2 to Wayzata and 1–4 to Duluth East. Ryan scored the Jaguars' lone goal of the morning.

————

On the bus ride back to school, Sats told the players he would meet with each one individually in the coaches' office. The office was squeezed between the varsity locker room and the phys ed locker room. Messy and run-down, it reeked of male slovenliness. Small paper circles dumped from a hole puncher littered the rust-colored shag carpet. An old Frigidaire smeared with fingerprints was jammed between desks and file cabinets. Combination padlocks filled a metal basket on one desk. Here, Sats and Thomas would deliver the boys' fate.

They sat at desks opposite one another and munched popcorn. With over sixty years of experience as hockey coaches between them, they had been through this drill before. But it never got easy to swing down the truth and smash fragile dreams to bits. "This is the hardest part about coaching," Thomas said.

Sats nodded, his face tight.

One by one, the kids approached the office through the darkened coaches' locker room and entered the brightly lit office. They sat in a dirty-blue, worn-out desk chair pulled into the open space facing Sats and Thomas.

A senior defenseman sat down. Sats told the senior they wouldn't need him. He reminded the boy how he used to have to fetch him out of the dressing room when he was a Peewee. "If you would've worked harder then, it would be different now," he said. Sats shook the boy's hand and told him to clean out his gear but leave the school equipment in his locker.

After the senior walked out, Sats exhaled. "That went easier than I thought."

Ryan limped through the darkened coaches' locker room. His goal that morning wouldn't save him. Maybe, just maybe, though, added to the goals he had scored the past two years on j.v., it would win him a spot on the roster if not a place in Sats's heart. Maybe. Bullshit. Sats had already decided. Ryan wished he had put more time into the weight room that summer. If he could go back and do it all over again, he would. He really would. He would be there every day, push himself, show Sats. With each step, his trepidation mounted. Ryan slumped into the faded blue chair.

He couldn't look at Sats without tears singeing his eyes. He pulled at his gray Jefferson Jaguars 2000 Hockey T-shirt. The close air in the room smelled of popcorn.

"Coach Thomas and I have decided to let you go," Sats said.

Even though Ryan had expected the news, somehow, once the words hit his ears, the weight of that truth stunned him. Done. Hockey since second grade. Finished. So that's what it feels like when a dream dies inside you.

Just don't cry in front of them. Don't be a pussy. He stood up.

"Want to say anything?" Sats asked.

Ryan turned to the door. "Nope."

Sats didn't have time to tell him to clear out his locker.

The three captains came in last. Tommy looked relieved—one of his buddies had made it; Nick and Duncs looked glum.

Spotting Duncs's shirt—the Budweiser logo inscribed with "Bahamas, King of Islands"—Sats said, "What kind of role model are you?"

Duncs looked at his shirt as though it was the first time he had seen it and shrugged. But he wouldn't wear it again around his coach.

Sats reviewed the morning scrimmages. He asked Nick what he thought of moving from defense to forward. "I'll play anywhere," Nick said.

To Duncs and Tommy, Sats said, "You're not out there to show how good you are, but to show how good our team is. The harder you play, the more times things work out."

Duncs and Nick had carpooled with Ryan and Jimmy Humbert, another good friend and scrappy forward. When the captains walked out of the coaches' office, Ryan sat in front of his locker. "Time to go," Duncs said.

Ryan lost it. The tears crashed down on him. He bawled.

Duncs sat down and put his arm around Ryan's shoulder. Jimmy and Nick huddled around him in the corner. They sat like that for several minutes, Ryan's sobs filling the otherwise empty locker room.

Duncs, Nick, and Jimmy dropped Ryan off at his house. He went upstairs to his bedroom, closed the door, and flung himself onto the bed. He didn't take off his clothes. His buddies were still there with him, pictured on a Wheaties box. Their moms had arranged the photo of their Bantam A team posed on the Zamboni. Ryan smiled from the box with Nick, Duncs, Jimmy, Tommy, Bernie, and all of the other guys who had made the team second year. Nick and the rest had the same Wheaties box in their bedrooms. That Wheaties box was all that Ryan had left of his team. He sobbed.

How would he face people at school? What would he say to Gramps and Granny?

His mom, Laurie, came upstairs. "I'm sorry."

"Leave me alone."

Laurie cried herself. Dougie Stansberry crossed her mind. She didn't want to think of *that*, but she couldn't stop those thoughts. Her gut winced. Ryan had gone to Dougie's funeral. *Please, God, don't let it come to that.*

They had been neighbors. Dougie's mom, Bobbi, had taken care of Ryan. The two families had been close.

Five years ago when Dougie came home the Saturday of tryouts week, Bobbi waited with balloons to celebrate. After playing j.v. the year before, he had made varsity his senior year. But the instant she saw him get out of the car in the driveway, she knew something was wrong. The kid who was always smiling wasn't smiling. The kid they called "Tigger" because of the bounce in his step sagged into the house.

"What's wrong," Bobbi asked. "What's wrong?"

"I got cut," said Dougie, his face white.

"You couldn't get cut," she said. "You already made the team."

"I got cut." He went upstairs and locked himself in his room.

Dougie wanted to make the Jefferson varsity in the worst way. His family moved to Bloomington in part so he and his younger brothers could play hockey at Jefferson, where his father, Doug Sr., and Bobbi had gone to high school. Dougie had an early brush with stardom, playing an extra in the original *Mighty Ducks* movie and a skating double in the second and third movies. Even though the parts were anonymous, it still sounded good at school to say he'd been in the movies. But being one of the mighty Jaguars would be better than anything Hollywood could dream up. By the fall of 1995, Dougie's senior year, the Jefferson tradition was at its zenith.

His dream didn't seem so farfetched. Dougie had played Bantam A with the group that would be seniors. If he worked hard, the summit seemed within reach. That summer, he shot buckets of pucks in the garage. He Rollerbladed with ankle weights up and down the hills by his house. He pictured himself in the Jaguars jersey.

Two weeks before tryouts began, Sats handed out copies of the season schedule at his meeting with returning players from the varsity and j.v. Dougie took his copy home and taped it to the refrigerator. He dreamed about playing those games. "He idolized that piece of paper," Bobbi said.

Dougie scored a hat trick in the Saturday scrimmage, but afterward his world collapsed.

Stansberry was small, only 5'8". He didn't have Bernhagen-caliber skills to compensate for that size deficit. He played center. In Sats's system, the center was the most skilled player on the line. On a talent-rich team, Stansberry didn't crack the top five in the depth chart. Being a senior became a liability; there were younger players to develop. Sats cut him.

Dougie refused to come out of his room for two days. He didn't go to school Monday. Tuesday, John Bianchi called to check on him. It was Bianchi's first year not coaching, but he couldn't stop caring about the kids. He was the Jefferson principal that year. Kids respected him. He convinced Dougie to come back to school.

Dougie played Junior Gold hockey along with other kids who hadn't made the varsity, but it wasn't the same. He still wished he were a Jaguar. On their game days, he left school early. He couldn't bear seeing the Jefferson hockey players hanging out in Jock Hall wearing their Jaguars jerseys. Bobbi feared he was missing so much school he might not graduate.

During the Jaguars section playoffs, Dougie came to Bobbi's room in the middle of the night. The 175-pound boy crawled into his mother's bed and curled into the fetal position. "I want to kill myself."

She held him through the night. The next day, Bobbi took him to a psychologist who prescribed medication and saw Dougie regularly for a month. Tigger bounced back. "Luckily for us, Jefferson didn't make it to State that year," Bobbi said.

Dougie graduated. He got a job in a group home for autistic kids and liked the work. He was a compassionate kid, always taking care of someone, always looking out for the underdog. Before he moved to Bloomington, his parents had divorced and his mother remarried. The fall after graduation, he moved in with his dad.

Doug Sr. called Bobbi Sunday morning, October 27, 1996. She had known something was wrong even before the phone rang. She just had a feeling. She spent the night on the couch, unable to sleep. She had talked to Dougie that Saturday. They made plans to have lunch that week and go shopping. He needed boxer shorts. Then the phone rang. She heard her ex-husband say, "Bob, some kid called and said Dougie hanged himself."

Call-waiting beeped on his end. It could be the police. He would call back.

Bobbi took out the phone book and started dialing through the list of hospitals. She was frantic to know what happened. An hour later, her ex called back. It had been the police. With the awful news.

Dougie had been at a party Saturday night in downtown Minneapolis. Friends said he had been drinking. He argued with his girlfriend. Back at her apartment, she fell asleep. He scribbled on a Post-It note: "Sorry for fucking everything up, but I guess that's the way you always wanted me to feel. Love you, always will, Dougie"— his mother has memorized this. Dougie left the yellow paper in his sleeping girlfriend's hand for her to find when she woke up. He went out to the back hallway of the old apartment building where the brick walls and stairwells were painted a dreary gray. He snaked a shoelace out of his boot, knotted one end around the gray bannister overhead, and looped the other end around his neck. Within seconds, the nylon lace tightened against the carotid artery and shut off the oxygen supply to his brain.

They buried him two weeks before tryouts began for the coming hockey season.

———

Dougie had been clinically depressed. He had stopped taking his medication. He was a victim of depression, not a coach's decision. "We know a single life event doesn't cause someone to kill themselves," said one counselor from the Bloomington school district. "Depression does."

But his mother couldn't hear that. She had just buried her son. "Why?" she cried out, but the question rang vacantly against the marble vault of her despair. She wanted an answer. She wanted someone to blame. Her grief-stricken gaze landed on Sats.

Bobbi thought Sats had led Dougie on, held out the false promise that he could play varsity. When Dougie came home and taped the schedule to the fridge, his family thought he had made the team.

In hindsight, one sees that was premature. But she is not convinced. Perception is reality. Dougie believed he would wear the Jaguars sweater. "It was like giving a child a piece of candy, then turning around and saying, 'No, you can't have that,'" she said. "That is a really vulnerable age for kids, especially boys. It's wrong to play with teenagers that way. Their lives are just too precious."

Five years later, when she heard Ryan got cut, Bobbi's anger bubbled up once more. Sats hadn't learned from Dougie's death. Ryan was a better player than some of the younger kids Sats had kept. He could have let Ryan play varsity his senior year, she reasoned, and given the younger boys their chance the next year. After the time he had put into the program, Ryan, like Dougie, deserved that. "To take that away from a senior who is a better player—that's wrong," she said.

———

The coach who is in it for more than one year must have an eye to the future. True of hockey, true of any sport. Given two players of even talent, most coaches go with the younger one. It's a wash for that season, but by the time the younger one is a senior, he will have developed into a better player than the senior cut to make room for him. That is the theory, anyway: sacrifice one boy for the greater good of the team's future. Do it in the name of development.

"But just what is being developed?" asked Al Horner after his son got cut senior year. He claimed to have received more than fifty responses to the full-page ad he ran in the fall of '92 asking that question. He reported that 95 percent of those people said the primary purpose of the hockey program should be to teach good values and offer growth opportunities, and that an older player should not be cut in favor of a younger one when all else is equal.

"Taking the younger kid to develop the team puts winning first," Horner explained. "If you have a senior and sophomore and their abilities to contribute this year are equivalent and you keep the senior, you put that kid's growth and interests at the top. If you pick the sophomore, you put the future development and a winning record at the top. When you place the value of a possible future winning record over the experience of that child and rewarding a senior for his commitment, loyalty, and hard work, that's the wrong choice. Kids grow up with the dream to play their senior year. To deny that dream shows misplaced priorities, and that's the essence of the problem. Sats wants to win. He's a competitive guy. There's nothing wrong with that. My only criticism is that winning should be subordinate to the growth and development of young people."

Horner took his cause to the principal, then the athletic director, then the school board. At each step, his audience listened but didn't offer to make any changes. The system, he concluded, was too caught up in winning, too willing to grant Sats free reign to chase a perfect record (which he accomplished that season, going 28–0). Winning, for better or worse, was endemic to the Jefferson tradition.

What troubled Horner was the damage done in the name of winning. He said he received letters from men in their late twenties and thirties who wrote that they still carried scars from playing for Jefferson. He read stories of teenaged boys crying on the bench, victims of what they called "mind games." Their letters were painful to read. "The system as I saw it was structured to teach these kids to win," Horner said. "The clear lesson was to do whatever it takes to win."

Sats is quick to point out that Horner's boy had grown up in the cross-town Bloomington Kennedy Booster youth hockey program, attended a private school his freshman year (where he played varsity), then transferred to Jefferson his sophomore year. He wasn't a kid who had paid his dues in the program, not one deserving to be rewarded for his loyalty. Sats also points out that he tried keeping seniors who didn't play one year, and it was a disaster for him.

The Saturday Ryan and two other seniors got cut, Sats kept fourteen sophomores on the two teams, several of whom he planned to try at varsity. That was the most sophomores he had kept since the closing of Lincoln, the third Bloomington high school, brought fifteen sophs to Jefferson in 1983.

Jim Knutson, father of one of the seniors Sats cut Saturday, wrote a letter of complaint to Sats. He referenced a speech Sats had made to the Booster Club about loyalty, then wrote, "The non-verbal message you sent isn't about loyalty or character, it's about winning. If you really were committed to developing character, I do not think you would cut seniors who have given endless hours to the program....I think it was pretty clear—loyalty is a one-way street when winning is concerned!" Later, Knutson explained, "I'm calling his bluff, saying, 'You didn't do what you've spoken about.'"

But Sats countered that he couldn't keep kids to reward parents for volunteering in the Booster program. Ultimately, the kid's attitude became the determining factor. "If you're hiring someone to work for you and you know that their parents have never had any discipline, going through school he's never been on time and never done his job, and the dad comes to you and says, 'Hey, we're friends, could you hire him?' and you've got another kid who's really a good kid and really a hard worker, which one do you hire? You know which one you hire. That's what happens all the time," Sats said.

Bianchi, who coached twenty-one years with Sats, said he admired Sats for his willingness to do what he believed was right. "You make a decision based on what's best for everybody, not just what's best for one kid or one family or one year or whatever; it's a big decision, so I respected him and admired him for that more than anything."

There were times, of course, when Sats cut kids for reasons the Monday morning quarterbacks weren't privy to. A kid's drug use, bad attitude, or even pushy parents could be the *x* factor to alter the equation when talent between two players remained equal. Other times, a kid's talents may have plateaued already by senior year, rendering his skills unequal to those of younger players, though parents were often unlikely to recognize that. The critics didn't always see what he saw behind the scenes.

The kids who didn't survive tryouts, for whatever reason, had to find a way to trudge on through their shattered dreams, knowing their lives would never be the same. The father of a player on the '01 varsity observed one night before his son played, "I imagine that the kids who don't make the team spend their entire adult lives dealing with that failure."

Or, worse, they can't deal with it. "This is high school and this is a game, but is winning everything?" Dougie's mom asked. "If anybody would get to the point of doing what Dougie did, what have you really won? People are more valuable than winning a state championship."

————

Saturday afternoon, Nick's mom, Karen, called the Gilberts from the grocery store parking lot to find out what had happened to Ryan. Bernie answered. He told her Ryan hadn't made the team. Karen started crying.

Karen, Bernie's mom Nancy, and Ryan's mom Laurie were good friends. Karen knew it would be hard on Laurie. For ten years their social lives had centered around their sons' hockey. They banded together in the cold bleachers of rinks across the state. They traveled to tournaments in Canada. They volunteered at the concession stand. They formed a book club. They drew names to exchange Christmas ornaments. Suddenly, Sats's decision booted Laurie out of the sorority.

Karen drove over to offer Laurie support. Nancy was already there. They had a good cry together. Nancy coaxed Ryan from his bedroom. He talked some. She hugged him and told him she was sorry. Other family friends called. Some sent cards to express their condolences.

Ryan was too embarrassed to break the news to Gramps and Granny. He could overhear his mother crying on the phone with them.

That night, the kids who made the team went to the girls' hockey game together. Then Duncs, Nick, and Jimmy came over and picked up Ryan. They went to Jimmy's house, ordered pizza, and watched *Dumb and Dumber*. They laughed, and Ryan felt a bit better. But it was tough going to school Monday. Even though people were trying to be nice when they said they were sorry, that he should have made the team, it didn't change anything. The season would start without him.

CHAPTER THREE

PASSING THE TORCH

To you from falling hands we throw the torch; be yours to hold it high.
—inscribed on the dressing room wall of the Montreal Canadiens
(John McCrae, "In Flanders Fields")

*Being a member of this team is an honor, makes you a 'little' special,
and also means you have reached a goal you have always wanted....
Remember, if we all work as hard as we can, we will uphold
the rich tradition of the Jefferson Hockey Program.*
—excerpt from the letter Sats sends to boys who make varsity

The week of Thanksgiving, red Salvation Army buckets resumed their posts outside Bloomington's grocery store entrances and the bells jingled across the parking lots, where Boy Scout troops stacked Christmas trees and wreaths in makeshift retail outlets. School children repeated stories of Native Americans sharing food with pilgrims. College kids returned home. And, Thanksgiving Eve—as sure as there would be turkey on the table tomorrow—Jefferson High played the twenty-eighth annual Blue–White game.

Where other schools scheduled preseason exhibitions against one another, Jefferson played this intrasquad scrimmage, a tradition Sats established when he arrived in 1973. The Blue–White game focused Jefferson upon itself. The preview gave Jefferson faithful its first impression of this year's crop and the chance to see how these boys measured up to past Jaguars talent. The teaser reminded them of the excitement absent in summer, set the mood for high school hockey to resume, and jolted them with Jefferson pride.

In the lobby outside Bloomington Ice Garden's Rink 1, Karen, Nick Coffman's mom, the '01 Varsity Social Director, arranged a buffet of brownies, blondie bars, and cookies on a banquet table set in front of a crowded trophy showcase. Other parents, still in their bulky winter coats, checked the film in their cameras and remarked on the day's mild weather, when sunny skies coaxed temps over 20°F. They also talked about the prospects for this year's team, shaped by the previous Saturday's cuts. On their way in, they picked up a program to see how Sats had divided the lineups and figured Duncs and Tommy gave the Blue squad a slight advantage over the White.

Meanwhile, the boys milled about the school locker room, split into white home and blue away jerseys. Sats walked out of the coaches' office in a black sweatshirt emblazoned "Jefferson Hockey." He chalked the outline of a rink on the green board and whistled the players to attention. Talking fast, he diagramed the Jaguars' forecheck and other game logistics. Then he wiped the board with a rag and faced his players.

"Tonight is an exciting time." His voice slowed to a tone serious as a priest celebrating mass. "When we started this twenty-eight years ago, [assistant j.v. coach] Stan Palmer was a sophomore.

Nobody knew what the Blue–White game was, but it wasn't long before we had almost one thousand people there.

"I know some of you guys have been waiting all your life for this. We have fourteen sophomores this year. If you don't take advantage of this, you might not make it as a senior. But if you do, there's no reason you can't be winning your third state championship as seniors. Wear those jerseys with pride."

They boarded the bus for the mile ride from school and unloaded at BIG's front entrance. To reach Rink 1, the boys passed through the Bloomington Hockey Hall of Fame. They had toted their equipment bags through this corridor outside Rink 2 since the days their bags outweighed them. Maybe a hundred times each year, they had passed under the 2' x 3' photos of Bloomington's glorious past, one of each team that had made it to the Tournament. Over the years, the '01 Jags had watched the Jefferson team photos accumulate on the walls and felt the tradition seep into them.

When the boys reached the Rink 1 lobby, the fans lining either side cheered at the first sight of them in their new varsity jerseys. The flashbulbs winked. The Jaguars marched the length of the rink, passed a third trophy case, turned right, and disappeared into the dressing room under the five state champion banners.

––––––––

Tradition formed the bedrock of Jefferson success. Sats served as creator and curator of that tradition. Upon it, he founded a dynasty.

When Tom Saterdalen arrived at Jefferson in 1973, the high school was only three years old; BIG had just one rink. The hockey team had never finished higher than fifth in the Lake Conference. Bloomington was just another Minneapolis suburb.

Sats got busy building his legacy. He took over the Jefferson Booster youth hockey program, the high school's feeder system, and quickly put an end to the practice of parents coaching their own kids. He set up off-season clinics for the younger kids so he could have a hand in their development from the beginning. And he immediately demanded hard work and team focus from his players. Hot-dogging was anathema. When one of his star players in those early years made a trick shot on a breakaway with his stick between his legs, Sats berated him. "I scored, didn't I?" the player shrugged. A junior, he led the team in scoring, but Sats kicked him off the team the next year. The message was clear: my way or the highway.

Sats's way didn't play with all of the parents. When he first arrived, some tried to curry his favor with gifts. One parent who owned a liquor store delivered bottles of expensive cognac to the Saterdalen home. Another pulled out his checkbook to write the program a ten-thousand-dollar donation. Sats refused their gifts; he wouldn't be bought. His refusal punched the would-be gift horses in the mouth. They organized. His second year at Jefferson, a band of disgruntled parents presented the principal with a petition calling for Sats's head.

Herb Brooks, Zeus among Minnesota's hockey gods, was among those who defended Jefferson's new coach. Then the University of Minnesota coach, Brooks wrote a letter to Jefferson's principal urging him to give Brooks's former assistant a chance to revamp the school's hockey program. The principal stood by Sats. He told the complainers to go to hell. They didn't go that far, though some did take their kids out of Jefferson and put them into other schools. Sats stayed. He had won an important early victory and secured the cornerstone of his legacy.

By the '01 season, Sats had built Bloomington Jefferson into a high school hockey powerhouse respected throughout the United States and Canada. He had won more games than any other high school hockey coach active in the state. His 501 victories at Jefferson trailed only Willard Ikola (616, Edina, 1958–91), Larry Ross (566, International Falls, 1954–85), and Cliff Thompson (534, Eveleth, 1926–58) for most hockey games won by any high school coach in the state's history. Sats had won five state championships in Minnesota and two in Wisconsin. His program had placed more kids on Division-I college and NHL teams than any other high school in the state. His success had reserved him a place in Minnesota hockey history among the august company of Ikola, Ross, Thompson, John Mariucci, and Herb Brooks. "When you talk about great hockey coaches, you've got to mention Tom Saterdalen," Brooks confirmed.

Bloomington Ice Garden has its Hall of Fame; Jefferson High has B202. Sats's office adjoining his classroom is a museum of Jefferson history as much as it is a personal shrine. Five Christian Brothers hockey sticks hang on the wall above his desk, one for each of the Minnesota state titles Sats has won, each signed by that year's team. Another wall is covered with medals, plaques, photos, framed newspaper articles, and other miscellaneous mementos. An oak case houses twenty-six pucks, one for each of the conference titles and state appearances—each with the score of the section final game that got them there inked on it. Another puck commemorates Sats's 500th win at Jefferson.

One wall features boys' tennis, which Saterdalen has coached for twenty-one years with characteristic success. Several hockey photos spill over onto that wall, abutted by metal shelves weighted with hockey scrapbooks. There's a scrapbook from each season, assembled by the parents of the varsity scrapbook committee. Almost lost among the hockey clutter, several 3" x 5" color photographs of Sats's wife and grandchildren are taped above his desk—and above a framed 5" x 7" photo of Sats with John Bianchi. Saterdalen is a grandfather, father, husband, teacher, and coach, but his life clearly revolves around hockey.

Sats's personal scrapbook, a three-ring binder thick as the Oxford Shakespeare, stands proud upon the metal shelf. His two student teaching assistants earned credit over eighty hours last year spent carefully inserting articles and photographs into clear plastic pages. There's a black-and-white shot of the Bemidji State University hockey team Sats captained in 1964. To the far right, second row from the top, No. 4 sports a buzz cut and exposes a line of big teeth. Sats squints at the camera through thick black glasses. Turn the page to another black-and-white team photo, this of the 1964–65 Cloquet High pucksters on a snowy outdoor rink, Sats, the assistant, in the same black glasses, his mouth again slightly open. Another shows him in a Gophers warmup jacket with the University of Minnesota team he helped coach from 1970–73. In between, from 1966–70, in his first head coaching job, he led the Superior High hockey team to two Wisconsin state championships, the first team not from the capital city of Madison to win the title. In the early photos, like the one in the Superior gym telling boosters how his team pulled off its repeat, Sats looks surprised. Any one of the shots could have been lifted from his driver's license.

It is not until 1981, when holding his first Minnesota state champion trophy with his team around him, that Sats smiles. Finally, he had arrived. Sats told the throng of newspaper reporters gathered outside the Jaguars dressing room, "This is the biggest thrill ever. Nothing I've experienced has come close to approaching this." For the Minnesota high school hockey coach who has devoted his adult life to this pursuit, winning the state championship is the biggest thrill conceivable.

By the 28th Annual Blue–White game, Sats had experienced that thrill five times. He wanted it again. This year might be his last chance. He had announced his retirement after next season, the '02 campaign, but this year's team—with Duncs, Tommy, Timm, and several other key senior role players—gave Sats his best shot to hang another banner at BIG. He wanted that to cap his legacy.

————

Separated into the home and guest dressing rooms, the Blue and White squads strapped on their gear to fill out their jerseys and met on the ice. The public address announcer introduced each player, and the boys skated out to their respective blue lines. They left their helmets on the benches. Their parents trained video cameras on their sons' faces to immortalize the moment.

The squads stood in two lines for the national anthem, one wearing crisp white jerseys and socks, the other sharp blue jerseys and socks, looking proud as marines in formal dress. For two weeks, they had drilled in mesh practice jerseys, old breezers, and torn socks— but suddenly their new uniforms transformed them from a ragtag group into two respectable teams. They stood taller and skated bigger in their Jaguars sweaters, like those they followed.

————

The teams hanging in BIG's Hall of Fame wore white home jerseys. Among the names printed underneath, several families appeared prominently—Anderson, Dahlberg, Gess, Kranz, Petersen, Skogland, Sullivan, Trebil—those families had written themselves into Jefferson history. But no family had shaped the Jefferson tradition more than the Bianchi clan.

Everybody loved John Bianchi. The wise-cracking Bianchi patriarch who had coached alongside Sats from 1974–95 endeared himself to kids and parents with his warmth and genuine concern. They looked up to him even though he stood barely 5'4". He retired from the Bloomington School District after thirty-seven years as a teacher, counselor, administrator, and coach. His round head held less hair than it used to, and a bad hip caused him to waddle, but his charismatic presence remained irresistible.

John's three boys each played on Jefferson Tournament champion teams. In fact, the Jaguars had won all five of their state titles with a Bianchi boy leading them; Jefferson had never won a championship without the Bianchis. Jefferson's reputation grew up with those boys. Such was the Bianchi Blessing.

The oldest, Steve, was a sophomore center on the team that pioneered the Jaguars' first trip to the Tournament and a 5'5" junior on the '81 team that won the school's first title. Getting there made Jefferson respectable; winning made them champions. "When we won the state title that year, those guys set the stage for every other Jefferson kid that plays hockey in our program," John Bianchi said. "They all wanted to be a Jaguar. They all wanted to play in the state tournament. They all wanted to win the state championship. It was infectious."

Tony Bianchi was a ten-year-old stickboy in 1980, so small he could only carry half-a-dozen sticks at a time, but he dreamed big. Seeing the team go crazy on the bus ride following the team's opening-round win at the '80 Tournament, he thought, "I'd do anything for this."

By 1989, Tony's senior year, he captained a resilient bunch that survived personal difficulties and came together as a team. Like his older brother, Tony could put the puck in the net and craft scoring plays. At 5'6", he had maybe an inch on Steve and was beefier and gifted with better hands. With Tony leading the way (setting a school record for most points in a season: sixty-seven), the '89 Jaguars stormed through the Tournament. Tony scored the tying goal in the final that they won in overtime.

The youngest Bianchi, Joey, watched Steve's team win the '81 championship from section 128 of the Civic Center as a five-year-old who already understood the game. He was thirteen and coming into his own when Tony's team won the '89 title. His time came sophomore year. Joey led the '92 Jaguars in scoring and to the Tournament, where his pure hat trick in a 4:52 span of the first game broke the mighty John Mayasich's forty-one-year-old record. Jefferson beat Moorhead 6–3 for its third title, and a new era dawned in Bloomington.

Joey's junior year, the '93 Jaguars sailed undefeated to their second straight state title, only the seventh school in Minnesota history to post a perfect season. The cover of the February '93 issue of *Hockey* magazine featured the familiar image of Joey Bianchi with his stick raised and the caption "Best Prep Team Ever?" John Gilbert—Minnesota hockey's Grantland Rice—thought so: "These Jags move with amazingly coordinated smoothness and grace. They not only beat opponents, they do it with speed, finesse, effective bodychecks, and an incredible unselfishness that seems to guide each player to make the best play, free from hot-dogging or point-seeking."

Senior year, Joey captained a team that started the '94 season on a fifty-game undefeated streak. On December 17, 1991, the Jaguars had lost to crosstown rival Kennedy 2–1. They wouldn't lose another game for three years and sixty games, until Blake surprised them 3–2, ten games into the '94 campaign. After that upset, they won their next game 7–1 over Kennedy and the rest of their games, cruising to their third title by outscoring opponents 130–20 in the balance of Joey's senior season.

During Joey's three varsity seasons, the Jaguars had gone 79–3–2, been invincible for sixty games, and played perfectly in the Tournament, hanging three straight banners in BIG. Only two other schools—Larry Ross's International Falls and Cliff Thompson's Eveleth—had won three consecutive titles in the Tournament's fifty-six-year history. Joey scored thirty-one goals and forty-three assists to pass his older brother Tony as Jefferson's all-time leading scorer. A Mr. Hockey finalist, Joey was edged out by his teammate Mike Crowley, who, as an offensive defenseman, registered three more points than Joey on the season. By the time Joey and Mike graduated in 1994, they had elevated the Jefferson tradition to its glorious pinnacle, establishing a dynasty the likes of the Eveleth Bears of the late '40s or the Montreal Canadians of the '70s. Jefferson hockey would never be the same.

In those days, at the dynasty's peak, you couldn't find a seat for the Blue–White game. You couldn't even find a place to stand. Fans eager to glimpse the coming season's glory filled the spaces behind the nets and stood several deep in the lobby, craning to see the action on the ice. Kids clambered outside to find a peephole in the fire exit doors' strip of wire-thatched glass.

Growing up a pint-sized shooting guard in the hockey town of Hibbing (a year ahead of a shy kid named Bob Zimmerman, who would later change his last name to Dylan), John Bianchi never imagined that hockey would bond him with his sons and become the way he would reach out to hundreds of other young men. But then he met Tom Saterdalen at a Bloomington coaches meeting. When the call had gone out the year before for volunteers to coach Steve's Squirt team, John had responded. He could hardly skate and knew little about hockey, but he understood people and cared about kids. Sats could see Bianchi would be an excellent coach and asked him to be his assistant. They formed a perfect match, high school hockey's Starsky and Hutch.

Sats was the mind, and Bianchi was the heart of Jefferson hockey. Sats would tell the boys what they had to do; Bianchi would get them to do it. As head coach, Sats got his name engraved on the awards, but those in the know recognized Bianchi as the unsung hero, the emotional guru and motivator behind the program's success. "If someone made Bloomington hockey, it was John Bianchi," said one past Jefferson Booster president. "He was a blessing to Bloomington—both sides—we owe an awful lot to him."

Another past Booster president went so far as to say Sats couldn't do it without Bianchi. In his letter after Sats cut his son, Jim

Knutson wrote, "If you look at your record since John Bianchi's departure, maybe the lack of commitment to truly developing character and loyalty from players and coaches is the heart of the problem." In the five years since Bianchi's retirement, Sats had compiled a 115–33–3 record, or a .762 winning percentage; in Bianchi's last five years, Sats went 108–15–2, an .864 winning percentage. Most significantly, he hadn't won a state title since Bianchi left. Knutson wasn't the first to point out the six-year drought. Sats knew the rap against him. He wanted to win another one to shut up the critics and polish his reputation. The Bianchi Blessing had become his curse.

The Blue–White game started for the players with a photo shoot in the school gym. A professional photographer snapped team and individual portraits for that year's glossy cover team yearbook, which included school records and an honor roll of alumni who had played college hockey. It was the first time that year the boys posed in their new jerseys.

Team manager Kelly Bergmann, who dated one of the prettiest girls in school, arrived early to unload two cardboard boxes safely stowed in the equipment room. One box held the blue jerseys, the other the white. He unpacked the new jerseys, individually wrapped in plastic, and sorted them by number, one to thirty-five. The dazzle nylon material shimmered under the bare bulbs, a definite upgrade over last year's mesh. This year's V-necked jerseys featured a snarling, green-eyed jaguar on either shoulder and a Lake Conference patch on front. "Jaguars" ran in royal blue script across the chest. Playing on the Booster teams growing up, the boys wore jerseys that said, "Jefferson." Not until they reached high school did they become Jaguars.

Trimmed in royal blue and silver, the Jags' defining color was a powder blue, the only team in the state to claim that color as its own. Listed officially as "Columbia blue," the shade lay somewhere between the North Carolina Tarheels' light blue and the Duke Blue Devils' royal blue; it was close to L.L. Bean periwinkle or Crayola sky blue. But *not* baby blue—that description upset Sats. When asked if he had ever thought of changing the jersey color from baby blue to a more intimidating color, say, black, he snapped, "You think when our guys go on the ice that doesn't intimidate opponents?"

Whatever the opponents felt upon seeing the Jefferson blue, the players felt a sense of inherited pride and the weight of tradition when they wore those sweaters. Alumnus Dave Hergert told the *StarTribune*, "Every game you put on that jersey, you're putting on tradition. You never want to have a bad showing because you worry about what players from past teams would say. That makes me go out and try harder. I get enthused by it."

They might as well be wrapped in Old Glory. Mark Parrish, '95, now of the New York Islanders, summed up the pride he felt playing in the Jaguars jersey: "It almost felt like I was fighting for my country when I played for them."

Sats distributed the jerseys ceremoniously. He called the players into the equipment room one by one, starting with the captains, then the returning lettermen, next seniors, juniors, and sophomores new to varsity. Kelly handed them the number they selected. Sats passed them two pairs of socks—one home whites, one away blues— and a gray cutoff T-shirt to wear underneath their jerseys. On the front, it read "JEFFERSON HOCKEY," and on back, "Energy and Persistancy [sic] Conquer All Things."

Duncs took No. 22, same as last year—two was his lucky number. Looking to improve his luck, Nick picked No. 20, having worn No. 4 last year. Timm took No. 1, same as junior year. Bernie again laid claim to No. 11, already known as his number. To Tommy, Sats bestowed No. 15.

That was the Bianchis' number. Steve, Tony, and Joey had all worn No. 15. No one else had worn that number since Joey graduated seven years earlier. Sats didn't believe in retiring high school jerseys, but he had wanted to save No. 15 for the right player. He figured Tommy, captain his senior year, was that player. For the first time in twenty years, a kid not named Bianchi would wear No. 15.

The number's significance was not lost on Tommy.

When Tommy was three years old, his family moved next door to the Bianchis. He quickly learned to skate and to idolize his neighbors.

Some nights after Joey got home from practice, he came over and played hockey with Tommy and his younger brother Cory on the rink their father flooded in the back yard. "That was the coolest thing that ever happened in my life," Tommy said.

Joey gave Tommy his old Christian Brothers blades. Tony had given his younger brother sticks, and Joey figured he should pass on blades to his young admirer. He also gave Tommy a blue Easton aluminum shaft. Joey had anointed that stick with his own hands, used it in high school games to win glory and fame. On the cover of *Hockey* magazine, he had raised his stick proudly. Now he passed it to Tommy as though he passed him Excalibur. Tommy treasured that stick. He used that lucky stick through Squirts and Peewees until he outgrew it. He started to dream about playing in the Tournament like Joey had. Other kids wanted to be a doctor when they grew up, a lawyer maybe, or a movie star. Tommy Gilbert wanted to be Joey Bianchi.

At the team banquet last spring, Tommy had inherited another stick from the Bianchis. Tradition had the outgoing captain pass a floor hockey stick painted Jefferson blue and signed by previous captains—including the three Bianchi boys—to the newly announced captain. The '00 captain passed the stick to Tommy, who signed it himself and kept it in his family room, right by the answering machine, where everyone would see the Jaguars captains' baton.

Now, Tommy wore No. 15 with the *C* stitched on his chest. Pulling the sweater over his head for the first time, he felt the weight upon his shoulders.

———

The Blue–White exhibition had all the trappings of a real game: cheerleaders in full uniform waved their glittery pom-poms, a garbled recording played the national anthem, guys skated hurt, stat girls tallied shots, the P.A. announced goals, parents yelled at the striped-shirted referees, fans crowded the concessions stand between periods while the Zamboni resurfaced and students razzed their friends on the ice.

Alumni scattered about the stands sought out Sats to say hello. One clump of the most recent alumni, the Class of '00, back from college for the Thanksgiving holiday, watched the action from behind the Jags' home net. For them, the Blue–White game jarred loose painful memories of the overtime Tournament loss that ended their hopes senior year. "Not a day goes by that we don't think about that game," said Christian Koelling, the Jags' leading goal scorer last year who netted Jefferson's first goal in that game.

When they went to the Tournament as sophomores, Sats had read a letter in the dressing room that Joey Bianchi had written them. "Soak this up," Joey wrote. "Never again will you play in front of a crowd this big."

Up at University of Minnesota–Duluth, Koelling didn't even try to explain to people he met what it had been like to play for Jefferson. "There's no way they can understand," he said.

"That's right," Chris Lindahl, a 210-pound high school defenseman now a full-time student at Boston College, which would win that year's NCAA hockey championship. "They think they've got big crowds at B.C. No one can understand we played in front of bigger crowds."

But it had all gone by so fast, they hadn't soaked it all in, not like they wished they had. "You don't appreciate it until it's over," Lindahl said.

"I hated practice all season," chimed in B.J. Lange, a winger home from Gustavus Adolphus College. "But that Monday after the season ended, I would've done anything to practice again."

It hurt, but they couldn't stay away. Now relegated to spectators out of the spotlight, they had joined a larger fraternity, the ranks of alumni who shared a special bond strong as war veterans. "I wanted to see how the boys are doing," Lindahl said.

————

Graduation affected the boys' parents in a different way. When hockey ended, they had to find a replacement for their social lives, but they were able to enter BIG without the stress. One alumni mother remarked, "It's like withdrawal when you stop coming." Another commented over the buffet of bars set up in the lobby that she could finally enjoy the game without worrying about the politics of ice time. She, too, had entered a new phase of life.

Ryan Briese sat in the last row of the stands, his best friend Matt Duncan's three-year-old brother on his lap. His face glum, Ryan looked neutered in his street clothes, not the way he usually dressed for these hockey games. He should have been out there, he thought; he was better than half the guys that dressed for this game. He didn't understand why he should be sitting with the ordinary public when he belonged on the ice. Between periods, he wished he could've been in the dressing room joking with his buddies, but that was suddenly off limits to him. Sure, he could walk in there if he wanted; no one was going to physically stop him. But he couldn't face those guys dressed as he was. His pride banned him.

A group of Peewee players followed the action intently from one corner of the rink. The young boys still watched with innocent visions of themselves one day wearing those jerseys. Maybe one of them would be the next to wear No. 15.

————

It ended in an upset: White 2, Blue 1. The players lined up to shake hands, engaged in some good-natured shoving, then ducked into the dressing room to change before heading out to the lobby, where they would revel in their friends' and parents' comments. Bernie hustled Adam Dirlam out of the dressing room. Last year, as the two youngest players on the team, they had to sweep the dressing room after everybody else left. They could leave that to this year's sophomores: Justin Wild, Brad Peterson, and Ryan Van Bockel. "Come on, now we can go talk," Bernie urged Adam. "We don't have to clean the dressing room."

Outfitted in their new Jaguars jerseys, sneakers, and baseball caps, Bernie and the other players descended upon the bars and cookies Karen had assembled and chugged the colored varieties of Gatorade. Ryan Briese made plans to meet up with Nick and Duncs, but felt conspicuously out of place in his Polo shirt and tan field jacket.

————

Sats walked the length of the empty stands from the dressing room to the lobby as the rink maintenance staff swept the bleachers littered with popcorn boxes and Styrofoam cups. He wasn't smiling. Despite some physical play—including a check that sent flying a man's coffee cup set on the edge of the boards—Sats wasn't satisfied with the effort. He had reason to be concerned. The boys had played politely instead of with tenacity. The stands had been less than half full. Sats had a lot of work ahead of him if he was going to bring this team up to the level of his dynasty teams. Duncs, Tommy, Nick, Timm, and the rest were nice kids, skilled kids, but not dominant. They didn't play physical. They had dropped the two Saturday scrimmages with a lackluster effort, the first time that had happened since 1975, which embarrassed Sats. Then they put on this mediocre exhibition less than a week before the regular season started. The coach's frown deepened. "We've got a long way to go," he said. "A long way to go."

CHAPTER FOUR

YOU'VE GOT TO WANT IT

The Monday following Thanksgiving, Sats had the boys name their goals. They returned to school after practice, showered, and headed up to Sats's room, B201. In the hallway outside, several chatted briefly with the cheerleaders painting signs that advertised Tuesday night's season opener. They ducked into B201 through Sats's office, passing under the five championship team sticks hanging over the doorway like a hunter's guns, and picked up one white and one purple three-by-five-inch note card.

Sats trotted out the tradition to inspire them. He handed each player stat sheets with season totals from last year's team and from a half dozen Tournament years, with team bests highlighted in powder blue and team worsts in pink. He also handed out sheets listing Jefferson career and season records. "Here are some things you can aim for in your goals," he said, walking among the rows of desks.

Timm, Duncs, Tommy, Bernie, Nick, and the other players seated in the desks studied the sheets and commented on Kelly Hultgren's 157 takeouts in '89, Mike Crowley's +79 on-ice value in '94, Jeff Heil's .945 save percentage, also in '94. Junior defenseman Adam Dirlam, a Division-I college prospect, asked about Ben Clymer, '96, Most Career Takeouts: 248. "He was just called up to the Tampa Bay Lightning," Sats said. "You could go for that, Adam."

Sats leaned against his desk in the front of the room. "We've got enough guys who can achieve some of these records," he said. "I hope this turns you guys on."

A week earlier, Sats had prepped them with another meeting. He quizzed the players on which of the eight principles of goal-setting displayed by the overhead projector was the most important.

"Be ready to make a behavior change if necessary," Duncs said. Not an A student, he had learned that lesson from personal experience.

After hearing from several other players, Sats said, "I agree with Duncs. You must be willing to change behavior to make your goals happen." He spoke slowly with deep emphasis, wanting his point to find its mark. "To be a winner, you have to be willing to make a behavior change."

Reminding the boys of those principles, Sats instructed them to write their team and individual goals on both of the note cards. They would turn in the white card and keep the purple one.

The boys did not peek at one another's cards, just focused on their own. Senior wing Brian Johnson chewed his nails. The mood was as studious as if they were writing an essay exam on "How I Can Contribute to the Jefferson Tradition." The minutes ticked by while they reflected and wrote in silence.

Tommy printed in red ink: "Force myself to skate hard every shift, be a good leader, and don't get selfish."

Duncs wrote in all caps, "USE MY SIZE AND STRENGTH, SHOOT WHEN POSSIBLE, AND KEEP TEAM MOTIVATED NO MATTER WHAT."

Nick printed neatly in blue ink, "Compete for the team lead in takeouts, block at least one shot per game, and play hard defensively as well as offensively."

Timm wrote with a black felt pen, "Work as hard as I can all the time, save percentage over 90 and GAA under 2." Sats had pointed out that Timm and Jeremy's combined goals against the average of 2.59 last year had been the third worst in Jefferson history.

Every boy in the room included as a team goal to reach or win State.

Bernie was the only one to list individual honors among his goals:

1) All-State;

2) Tournament team;

3) Get single season point record, goal record, assist record;

4) Get best faceoff percentage of all time;

and, as though an afterthought,

5) Give everything I've got every shift and do whatever it takes to win every game.

Five minutes passed. Finally, Bryan Shackle stood up, gathered his books and skates, and placed his white card on Sats's desk. Tommy followed, then Jimmy Humbert and Brad Peterson. Sats, seated at his desk, read their cards as they turned them in. It was another five minutes before the rest of the players finished. Kory Stark, a junior defenseman, was the last. He folded the purple card and slipped it into his billfold.

Sats was pleased they had taken the exercise seriously. Earlier that afternoon at practice, he hadn't liked what he had seen on the ice. He whistled sharply to interrupt the drill and blew a gasket. "How many of you guys know we have a game tomorrow?" he shouted. The boys looked back at him mutely or stared at the ice. "There's no intensity out here. How can you play hard if you don't practice hard? That goes for every guy out here. You've got to want it all the time!"

When all of the players had left his room, Sats pulled on his coat and gloves and headed out to his car. It had been twelve hours since he had parked it in the lot. "These kids have no idea how hard they can work, what they can do. They've got to want it. Bob Beamon was able to do what he did [shatter the world long jump record at the '68 Olympic Games in Mexico City] because he wanted it." He paused. "I've seen teams, guys, play the best they ever have at the Tournament." He smiled. "They'll never play better in their lives.

"I love to yell at them. It gets them going." He picked his way across the snowy path to the parking lot. "Some of these kids resent us because we push them. But they realize ten years later what we did for them. They wish they had a boss who pushed them. A Bernhagen might come back and say thanks."

––––––––

Tuesday afternoon Emily Finley, a senior varsity hockey cheer-leader, stopped into Cub Foods, down the hill from Jefferson High, to buy Mountain Dew for that night's bus ride. Tradition had the cheerleaders host a party on the ride back to school, serving pop, candy, and homemade treats. The cashier ringing up the twelve-packs spotted the crossed hockey sticks on Emily's powder blue letter jacket. "Big game tonight," he said. "I've been following the team for years."

By late November, Bloomington eagerly anticipated the Minnesota high school hockey season opener. Nobody was more eager than the players. They had been skating since the second week of September—first captains' practices, then tryouts, practices, and scrimmages. They itched for the real thing. Tonight, they would get it.

In the school locker room, the anticipation hummed underneath the pregame routine. Nick slipped a new blade on his shaft and melted the glue with a handheld torch. Sats weaved his way through the players and doled out gum.

Kelly Bergmann laid Tommy's stick across a bench and sawed off a half inch. The move to forward placed new expectations on Tommy's lumber. On defense, his Easton aluminum shaft with the big curved Koho blade had tied up guys in front of the net, swiped pucks away from attackers, sparked offensive breakouts with crisp passes, corralled the puck in the offensive zone, and blasted slapshots—he had needed the extra length. Now, Tommy needed increased maneuverability to stickhandle past swiping defensemen, to work the puck in tight corners, to steer close to the net, and to fire wrist shots. The shorter stick would give him that.

After a quick talk at the board—"Let's go out there, lay our ears back, and have fun"—they boarded the bus for the long ride across town to meet Hill-Murray on its own ice. The seating hierarchy reserved the back of the bus for the captains, then the seniors, each to his own seat. Bernie and Adam sat next to the seniors, then the rest of the players doubled up in the rows up to the two statisticians and six cheerleaders, whose perfume filtered the sweat from the equipment bags shoved several deep into scattered seats.

The bus was as quiet as a church. Only Sats and Thomas traded whispers up front in their seat by the door. Ranked sixth in the preseason metro poll, Hill-Murray was good, the first of three tough opponents in three away games that opened the season. The private Catholic high school in suburban St. Paul had its own proud hockey tradition, making its eighteenth Tournament appearance last year, boasting two state titles, and fielding a perfect team (28–0) in 1983. The Pioneers claimed many distinguished alumni, including Dave "Moose" Langevin, who wore four Stanley Cup rings from his days with the New York Islanders. Tommy and friends stared out of the windows and meditated on the challenge ahead of them.

The route to Aldrich Arena cut across downtown St. Paul. Through a veil of thick snowflakes, Tommy could see the red letters—Xcel Energy Center—glowing like a beacon atop the Wild's new rink where the Tournament would be played. The red letters beckoned.

After the third line scored an early goal, the night belonged to Tommy Gilbert. Hopping over the boards in the first period, the Jaguars captain picked up a loose puck at center ice and sped in alone with his trademark long and efficient strides. He faked to his forehand, slid the puck to his backhand, and flipped it into the net. Credit an assist to Kelly for taking that half-inch off Tommy's stick.

Less than four minutes later, Tommy dug for a rebound in the Hill-Murray crease while getting mugged by the Pioneers defense.

The 6'2", 185-pound forward held his ground and muscled the puck into the net. His lean basketball player's build belied his heavy-weight wrestler's strength.

Halfway through the second period, Jefferson whipped the puck around on the power play—Bernie to Duncs to Tommy, who snapped a wrist shot from inside the blue line. When rubber hit mesh, hats littered the ice. Tommy had tallied a pure hat trick less than twenty-three minutes into the season to put Jefferson up 4–0. The last two years, he had proven he could play varsity defense; now he was flaunting the full package of skills that had NHL scouts taking note. Most importantly, Tommy was doing the jersey proud, living up to the No. 15 on his back and the *C* on his chest.

Hill-Murray managed a couple of goals, but Bernie sparked Tommy's magic to seal the game in the third. With a scrum in front of the net, Bernie picked the puck out of his skates and slid it to Tommy. No. 15 banged it home. Looking for more scoring punch, Sats had moved his team leader to forward. Tommy, with his four goals, made his coach look like a genius.

The reporters in the dressing room all wanted a piece of Tommy. The quiet captain appreciated the attention but felt more comfortable letting his stick do the talking. He told them, "It was awkward going from defense to offense, getting back into it." Wait until he found his stride.

The next day, when Tommy walked into his first-period sociology class, classmates hailed him "Mr. Hockey." If he continued to play like he did Tuesday night, Tommy was a cinch to join Mike Crowley and Nick Checco as Jaguars honored with the state's top individual title.

———

Thursday, November 30, two days after the Hill-Murray game and two days before Elk River, Bernie paused over his lunch in the school cafeteria and remarked to the friend sitting with him, "A year ago at this time, I was in jail."

Playing Trojan Ball in phys ed class, Bernie had lunged for a loose ball. Another sophomore going for the same ball kicked his hand.

Bernie pushed the kid. The teacher separated them. Bernie reached around the teacher and sucker-punched the kid. Blood gushed from the boy's face. It would take several thousand dollars' worth of dental work to set his mouth right.

The school's police officer arrested Bernie for felony-level assault. She cuffed him and led him outside past the cafeteria crowded with students. At the station, the police booked him, fingerprinted him, and snapped a mug shot. While his classmates attended their fourth-period classes, abuzz with gossip of the fight, Michael Bernhagen sat on a metal grate bench in the holding cell at the Bloomington P.D. and waited for his mother.

The Jefferson administration moved to expel Bernie. Not all Jefferson students who fought in school got kicked out, but the administration deemed grounds for expulsion Bernie's disregard for the teacher trying to restrain him and the severity of the injury he inflicted. Two boys were expelled the same year for relentlessly kicking another student after a teacher told them to stop. But the administration's decision to oust the hockey team's superstar sparked a controversy that divided the community.

In Bloomington's grocery store aisles and church parking lots, residents traded strong opinions over Bernie's crime and punishment. One segment took a zero tolerance stance on violence, calling for Bernie's expulsion. In a land where varsity hockey players were revered as deities, that faction worried that Bernie would be granted favorable consideration. They wanted fair treatment, the same as would be given their kid. Those who took Bernie's side saw him as a victim of his status. They accused the administration of acting harshly, overreacting in its effort to appear impartial. They suspected those resentful of the hockey program's success would revel in seeing it dealt the blow of losing its superstar. In effect, Jefferson hockey was on trial, with Bernie involuntarily cast as its sacrificial lamb.

Bernie's mom, Nancy, requested the matter be settled by mediation. A hearing date was set over Christmas vacation. In the meantime, the school kept suspending Bernie in five-day increments, the maximum length allowed. Bernie was ineligible to play hockey until his case was decided.

The fight happened the day of the season opener. Bernie missed the team's first nine games. The Jaguars managed to skate to a 7–2 record over that stretch, but Sats did not want to lose his most talented player for the season, perhaps forever. He initiated a grassroots effort to reinstate Bernie and vindicate his program.

A local attorney came to Bernie's aid. A groundswell of Bloomington residents telephoned the school board and district officials on Bernie's behalf. The callers weren't arguing Bernie deserved the chance to study Chaucer at Jefferson; they wanted to see No. 11 back in the Jaguars lineup. In the end, when the mediator had listened to the attorneys, administrators, and witnesses, he decided that the time Bernie had already served fit the crime. The superintendent admitted Bernie back into school—and onto the hockey team.

The day Bernie returned to Jefferson and walked into Sats's health class, the students applauded. Bernie soaked it up. He didn't let on to any remorse. Sats may have felt like clapping himself, but he had a deeper understanding that Bernie's presence could also be a grave liability. Sats knew the team's fortunes were likely to go whichever way Bernie went.

To crown his sophomore season, Bernie scored the goal that put Jefferson in the '00 Tournament. The Section 5AA final game against Holy Angels was tied with seven minutes left in the third period. Both goalies had played well, with Timm kicking out every shot but one. The game was tight and tense. Then Bernie sashayed past both defensemen and ripped a wrist shot the Holy Angels goalie had no prayer to stop. With characteristic panache, Bernie's shot knocked the goalie's water bottle off the top of the net and sent Jefferson to its fourteenth state tournament appearance.

Even though Bernie catapulted the team to the Tournament, the fight sullied his reputation. Fall of his junior year, he took out the assistant superintendent's daughter. The first thing she said when she got into his car was, "I told my mom I was going out with you. She knows who you are." Bernie didn't like that sort of notoriety. He wanted to be adored for his exploits on the ice. He was determined to have the season of his life to make others forget about the fight. The '01 campaign was to be his season of redemption.

On December 1, the day before Elk River, Bernie's twelve-month probation expired. His teammates still teased him about getting sent to jail, but he was a free man. He had submitted to a month of anger counseling and performed thirty hours of community service. His mother and her new husband, whom she married two weeks after Bernie returned to the team last year, had paid more than two thousand dollars in restitution. Bernie had cleared random urine checks and cooperated with his probation officer. The question was, had it made any difference?

Sats remained doubtful. He figured it would take more than peeing into a cup and picking up trash alongside city roads to tame Bernie's temper. During the summer, Sats had met with Bernie, his mom, and Bernie's grandpa, who had helped raise Bernie. Sats told Bernie he could be as good as he wanted to be if he stayed out of trouble. If not, Sats said, Bernie would screw himself out of a Division-I scholarship.

But Sats didn't expect his words to carry much weight; he placed his faith in peer pressure. It would be up to his teammates to keep Bernie in line.

The night before the Elk River game, Bernie's first that probation didn't require he comply with Bloomington's midnight curfew, his friends headed to a comedy club—without him. He went home, watched the Gophers hockey game, and was in bed by midnight. "Last year, I would've been out until 1 A.M.," Bernie admitted in the locker room as he dressed for Elk River. "This year, there's too much on the line. This is too big a game to stay out late."

During the hour-long bus ride up to Elk River, Bernie bridged the gap with the seniors, chatting in the aisle with Tommy. Timm sat alone, two seats behind the cheerleaders. At practice Monday, Coach Thomas had pulled the two goalies aside and told them Jeremy had played better, so he would start against Hill-Murray, and Timm would play Saturday against Elk River. They would rotate until Christmas, then see if the coaches could pick a No. 1 goalie. That hadn't surprised Timm. He had alternated with Jeremy all of last season. Sats liked to rotate his goalies to push them to play their best. Elk River would be Timm's first battle in the fight for starting honors.

Timm Lorenz loved hockey as much as any Minnesota kid. He started skating when he was three, and for as long as he could remember, his life had revolved around hockey. He had played baseball and lacrosse for a year each, but those sports didn't excite him the way hockey did. His parents, Bradd and Merrelyn, both University of Denver alumni and season ticket holders, took Timm to UD hockey games. Bradd nurtured Timm's love. He bought a pitching machine, sawed off the legs, and set it up in the garage. He stuffed it with whiffleballs and shot on Timm, who developed a quick glove hand. Timm's older brother, Matt, would grab a stick and whack at the rebounds. Bradd had played football himself, but he was a big hockey fan and wanted his sons to share his affection for the game. They did. Bradd had pushed Matt, the older boy, but learned to back off with Timm. Timm's love for the game blossomed uninhibited.

The problem was that Timm grew up in Littleton, Colorado. In Colorado, hockey flew coach. It wasn't even a varsity sport. Timm's high school didn't have a team. The local option was to play Midgets, the equivalent of Minnesota's Junior Gold, where the kids who got cut from the high school varsity played. That wasn't good enough for Timm. He had played on the best team in Colorado— they had won four straight state championships through Peewees, Bantams, and his first-year Midget. Colorado high school kids who wanted to play top-level hockey beyond Bantams could strike out for Canada to try their luck in the junior leagues. Living away from home didn't appeal to Timm, but for a kid who couldn't imagine his life without hockey, he didn't see many other options.

Then Timm learned about Minnesota high school hockey. When Timm was a Bantam, his brother Matt returned from a visit to Minnesota, where he had watched a Jefferson hockey game. He sounded like Marco Polo returned from exotic lands, detailing amazing sights unimaginable in his native town. "It was incredible!" Matt said. "You wouldn't believe the people. There must have been over a thousand there. At a high school game. They had cheerleaders. The band played. It was amazing." Timm listened with wide ears. Show him the way to Minnesota. That's where he wanted to play hockey.

Then his world turned upside down. April 5, 1996, Bradd collapsed in the health club locker room after a workout. At fourteen, Timm suddenly lost his father, his friend, his biggest fan. Just like that. Gone. Two days after his father's funeral, Timm traveled to Ohio to play in the national Bantam tournament. He figured his dad would have wanted him to take advantage of the once-in-a-lifetime opportunity. He had lost his father but still had hockey.

His father's heart attack may have shown Timm the way to Bloomington. Two years after Bradd's death, Matt had matriculated at the University of Denver, and Merrelyn entertained the idea of moving to Minnesota to give Timm the chance to play high school hockey. Since her husband's death, Merrelyn had isolated herself from friends. Minnesota hockey might help Timm heal, and the change of scenery might be good for her, too. She saw the land of ten thousand frozen lakes as the tonic to their grief.

The summer before Timm's junior year, Merrelyn and Timm packed his red Dodge Dakota Sport truck with the "Happiness is ice hockey" license plate border and headed north. They kept the house in Littleton, where Matt lived with several college buddies, and rented a townhome in West Bloomington. Merrelyn found work as an elementary school substitute teacher. In Colorado, she had run Bradd's veterinarian office until his death, then taught. Timm enrolled at Jefferson High, immediately eligible to play varsity hockey under the state's liberal transfer laws.

The day of Bernie's fight, Timm had started the team's first game of the season against Elk River. The Bloomington Ice Garden was packed. Timm couldn't believe it when he stepped onto the ice and saw the seats filled on both sides of the rink. There must have been two thousand fans crammed into them. It was even bigger than his brother Matt had described. Until that night, Timm had played only in front of small crowds of parents clustered together in mostly empty bleachers. It was a home game for Jefferson, but Elk River's notoriously boisterous fans made it sound like Jefferson was on enemy ice. Before the game even started, when a puck got by Timm during warmups, the Elk River faithful jeered him, "Sieve, Sieve, Sieve." His nerves never recovered. He gave up eight goals. Jefferson lost 3–8.

This year, he would seek his revenge, though he would have to do it on the Elks's turf. Jefferson had never beaten Elk River in this arena. The last time the team traveled there, two years ago—when Tommy, Duncs, and Nick were sophomores, Bernie a freshman, and Timm was playing midgets in Colorado—on a snowy winter evening, the bus skidded on a patch of ice and struck another car. No one was hurt, but the team arrived a half hour late for the game. When the Jaguars finally took the ice, the Elk River fans booed lustily. The boys' concentration, already rattled, collapsed. The Elks humiliated them 7–0.

The Elk River Arena was a wild place to play hockey. The "Elkoholics," as they called themselves, reigned as the state's rudest and nastiest fanatics. Intimidating last year at BIG, they were downright threatening at home. The rink's design accompliced their rowdiness. On one side, aluminum bleachers rose steeply above the team benches, stacking the fans on top of the players. A catwalk ringed the rest of the rink, with standing room above and below, a metal cage or a thin sheet of Plexiglas all that separated the Elkoholics from the ice. During stoppages of play, acid music, amplified at rock concert decibels over speakers bolted to the low metal ceiling, whipped the dense assembly into delirious indecency and contributed to the rink's claustrophobic stranglehold on opponents.

The small arena afforded only a meager minority of support. The 250 tickets allotted to Jefferson that went on sale Friday were quickly snatched up before the school day ended. The week leading up to the game, several Jaguars fans played their connections with Sats to secure tickets. Saturday night, the Elk River Arena was crammed to its cacophonous capacity.

Bernie thrived on the pandemonium, but the rink could play hell on a visiting goalie. The rowdiest Elkoholics—teenaged boys drunk on testosterone—headquartered behind the visitors' net. Among them, on the catwalk directly behind Timm, eight guys wore bandit ski masks, looking like they had just bumped off a 7-Eleven. The hoodlums lit into Timm as soon as he started stretching in the crease during warmups.

"You suck."

"Go back to Colorado."

"My sister could score on you."

"You're so ugly, you give sperm a bad name."

Once the game started, their verbal battery intensified. At each whistle, they took up the "Sieve" chant. That didn't let up. Try as he might, Timm couldn't block them out. They were too close, too loud. He heard every word they said. The barrage stoked his ambition.

In the dressing room, with Nick's headphones blaring Limp Bizkit from across the room, Timm had put his head down, forehead to his mask, and visualized last year's Holy Angels game. He replayed his big saves, imagined the feeling of his mind locked on the puck, his body moving quickly in front of it. He heard the crowd's friendly cheers. He pictured his father alongside his mother in the stands.

Timm used to check the stands for his dad's reaction. Bradd would flash him signs—point to his eyes, *watch the puck.* When Timm wasn't looking at him, he could hear his dad yelling at the refs or cheering his saves. His forehead pressed to his father's initials on his mask, Timm heard his father again. *Play well. I'm with you.*

He knew he would need all the help he could get against Elk River, ranked No. 2 in the metro area. The Elks had graduated last year's Mr. Hockey, Paul Martin, to the University of Minnesota, but had perhaps an even stronger team this year, bolstered by a handful of transfers, including goalie Dusty Hall. Sats called the Elks's first line perhaps the best in the state—a direct challenge to Tommy, Bernie, and Brian "B.J." Johnson.

The raucous fans booed Jefferson during introductions. One fan waved a sign behind the Elk River net: "Home Grown in North Dakota (No. 33)" for senior wing Darin Ciavarella, who had transferred from Bismarck. On the ice, the student mascot, outfitted in an oversized elk's head, glared down the Jaguars as their names were announced and rapped their sticks with his.

Early in the game, the Elks's coach threw out his first line at Jefferson's third line. The mismatch pinned Jefferson in its own end, where the Elks's best pressured Timm. Merrelyn clenched her hands to her face. Timm knew his mother suffered through every one of his starts. In the bleachers to his right, he could see her seated next to Jeremy's mom, where his dad should have been. He managed to make two tough saves and freeze the puck, which brought the Jefferson section to its feet. The hoodlums behind the net taunted him.

The well-rested Bernie scored the game's first goal halfway through the opening period.

Duncs's line followed Bernie's. Catching a long pass up the middle, Jimmy wedged himself between the Elks's blueliners and beat Hall to the stick side, putting the Jags up 2–0. The goal sparked a flurry of high-fives among the Jefferson parents and a rowdy outburst from the students clumped in the Jags' section. An armed police officer picked his way through the students crowded on the steps to collar one boy and warn him not to bang on the glass. Elk River's blue turned a blind eye to the bandits behind Timm.

In the dressing room after the first period, Bernie fired his endless stream of banter, one part motivational speaker, one part sergeant, and many parts irrelevant: "The singular is *el* agua, but the plural is *las* aguas—figure that one out." When Bernie interrupted himself with a coughing fit, Adam Dirlam remarked, "That's God's way of punishing you for talking so much."

Timm stared at the floor in front of him and pulled on his fingers.

Bernie, Tommy, and B.J. jumped on the Elks to start the second period, but the Jags' top line couldn't maneuver a clean shot. Frustrated, Tommy took a high-sticking penalty at the end of the shift. On the powerplay, Elk River cut Jefferson's lead to 2–1. "SIEVE, SIEVE, SIEVE" rained down on Timm.

The Elks came out flying in the third period, skating only two lines and digging deep. Five minutes into the period, the Elks's star walked in behind the Jefferson defense and faced Timm all alone. Merrelyn gasped. Timm threw himself in front of the shot, and Jefferson clung to its slim lead.

The Elks took a penalty, but twenty-two seconds into the powerplay, Bernie's temper surged. He took a retaliation penalty to snuff out the advantage.

The third period action raced from end to end with mounting intensity. With only 2:45 remaining, the refs called Adam for interference when he flattened an Elk skating underneath a puck flipped in the air. "Homer!" the Jefferson parents shouted. The Elkoholics on the catwalk above the penalty box banged on the metal cage in front of them. Merrelyn looked like she was about to get sick.

Timm stopped a deflection and turned away a rebound attempt. Jefferson cleared the puck down to the Elk River end, and Bernie gave chase to forecheck. He anticipated the breakout pass and picked it off. Breaking in from the left, he whistled a wrist shot between Hall's legs. With only 1:14 remaining, the score was Jaguars 3, Elks 1. Emily Finley and the rest of the Jefferson cheerleaders broke into a "We're No. 1" chant, and one student flaunted a cardboard sign, "Sucks to be No. 2."

After Elk River pulled Hall to gain an extra skater advantage, Duncs flipped the puck from center ice. It bounced, rattled off the pipe, and landed in the empty net. Elk River didn't let up, tipping in a wrist shot from the point with only ten seconds left on the clock to narrow the score to 4–2, but it was too little, too late. Jefferson finished on top.

Coming off the ice, Timm finally smiled. His girlfriend, Larissa, the standout on the girls' hockey team, was on a recruiting trip out East, but one of her teammates wrapped Timm in a bear hug outside the dressing room. "Way to go, man."

The Jaguars had played like No. 1. Bernie's responsible shuteye netted two goals, including the short-handed gamewinner. Timm had added another highlight to his pregame visualization reel. He had maintained his composure under the Elkoholics' barrage. His seventeen spectacular saves earned him Varsity Online's Spotlight Athlete of the Week honors. Dad would have been proud.

Come Tuesday, the Jaguars headed to Eden Prairie.

Jefferson blew an excellent opportunity to put away its opponent on the ropes. Injuries sidelined several top Eagles, and the starting goalie didn't play, suspended for drinking. The goalie's suspension reminded Duncs what could happen to him. He had been there, busted twice. He didn't want to go back.

But fast-living, thrill-seeking hockey players were vulnerable to illicit vices, underage consumption among them. That, too, had been part of the Jefferson tradition, a part Sats had tried to change—with mixed success.

In the late '70s, Jefferson came close to the Tournament, losing the section final three years straight. Frustrated, Sats and Bianchi puzzled over talented players who couldn't pull it off as a team. Sats, the health teacher, and Bianchi, the school's drug counselor at the time, suspected they had players partying during the season, which handicapped their play and poisoned the team dynamics. They turned to Carolyn Cade, the district's chemical awareness coordinator. Together they developed a leadership program for captains of all sports and activities that trained and supported student leaders to stay clean and apply peer pressure to positively influence their teammates. In 1980, three of the hockey players they confronted moved out of the area, and a fourth transferred schools. Despite losing those regulars, the clean team won the section final, and Jefferson reached the Tournament for the first time.

The hockey team's success and respect for Sats and Bianchi firmly established A Positive Peer Leadership (APPL) program across all extracurricular activities at Jefferson. Before the program's inception, Jefferson teams had won three state titles in ten years. After 1980, it won thirty-six in eleven different sports. Word got out, and soon schools across the state had started similar leadership programs. Cade, along with coaches like Sats and Bianchi, lobbied the MSHSL to revise its policies on chemical use, making the league a pioneer in fighting adolescent chemical abuse. Cade found herself speaking to the National Federation of High School Activity Associations, and Bloomington's APPL program became a national model, with some version of it adopted in all fifty states. Kids still drank and they still smoked dope—witness Duncs sophomore year—but there was more support for them to stay sober through extracurriculars.

Nationwide, three out of ten high school seniors had downed five or more drinks in a row within the past two weeks, according to the University of Michigan's annual study released a week after the Eden Prairie game. Over one-third had smoked pot in the past year. Eight percent had tripped on ecstasy in that period.

Bloomington ran slightly ahead of the national curve in its student chemical consumption, according to a 1998 survey, the district's most current data. The school's police officer acknowledged students dealt drugs in the classrooms and drank in the school parking lot. It wasn't unusual for Jefferson's full-time liaison officer to confiscate alcohol from cars during the school day. Ecstasy tablets were found on a table in the school lunchroom. In prestigious West Bloomington, kids were as likely to spend their discretionary income on alcohol and other drugs as they were on clothes and CDs. Two-thirds of Bloomington's seniors believed their school had a drug problem. "If I wanted a bag [of marijuana] third period, I could have it by fourth," one hockey player said matter-of-factly.

On weekends, Jefferson students partied at hotel rooms where older siblings signed the register, at houses where parents were out of town (or predictably stayed upstairs), in cars, parks, college dorms—basically, wherever they could. Alcohol, pot, and ecstasy—in that order—provided their preferred altered states.

It wasn't easy hanging out with friends when they sought fun on a different plane. It was tough to go to a party and clutch a Dew while everybody else pounded brew. The deck was stacked against Duncs.

He had all the incentive in the world to stay clean during hockey season his senior year, but, as a kid from a divorced family who had started drinking and smoking dope as a young teen and who had already been busted twice, he was high-risk. Kids in Jefferson's Jock Hall still called Duncan "Drunken." If he wasn't careful, he could end up suspended like Eden Prairie's goalie, only in Duncs's case, his third violation would carry a twelve-game penalty. A lot was riding on his ability to just say no again and again until March 10.

————

Following the Eden Prairie loss, Sats gathered his players down in the drafty school locker room. The 5–2 romp over Hill-Murray was an early sign of the team's might, and the 4–2 victory over Elk River an indication of its grit, but Sats wasn't satisfied with the boys' losing effort. Standing in front of the green board still chalked with his pregame exhortations, Sats reprimanded them for not passing to the open man, for bitching on the bench. "You guys have the chance to be state champs, but you're not going to get there if you play like you did tonight. I know what it takes to get there."

Tommy would have to skate as hard every shift as he had against Hill-Murray, Duncs would have to stay eligible to use his size and strength, Nick would have to make his presence felt both offensively and defensively, Timm would have to compete as consistently as he did against Elk River, and Bernie would have to stay out of the penalty box so his talents would outweigh his temper.

Sats surveyed the beaten bunch, already bitten by their own self-recriminations. "Tomorrow we're going to work hard in practice."

They wanted the same goal, but not all of his boys were with him. Headed to the shower, a towel in hand, Duncs shook his head. "I don't think it's anything we can fix in practice. Maybe we got too high on ourselves. It's mental."

CHAPTER FIVE

FRIENDLY CONFINES

On the Jaguar hockey schedules posted about town—over gas station registers, on restaurant doors, and in shop windows—fans noted three home games followed the three away games that opened the season. Bloomington Ice Garden, home of the Jefferson Jaguars and Kennedy Eagles, was a low-slung, brown-brick building located midway between the two high schools. BIG was Bloomington's version of the town square. Deliberately situated in the heart of the city, BIG occupied a significant place in the hearts of Bloomington residents.

Inside, no rock music blared over the P.A. During warmups on Saturday afternoon, December 9, the scrape of blades, the crack of sticks, the thump of pucks into goalie pads, or the thwack against glass composed the BIG soundtrack. Art Seplak, the rink announcer who doubled as a Jefferson English teacher, did his part to pump up the players and crowd. His voice boomed off the large, earthtone sound panels behind the bleachers, "Welcome to the friendly confines of Bloomington Ice Garden."

That description rang true for the hometown fans who had crowded Rink 1 for thirty years and for the boys who had played hundreds of games on this ice, but it didn't feel like such a friendly place for the Rosemount Irish, perennial Lake Conference cellar dwellers. Like other visiting teams entering BIG, they had to walk the gauntlet down the Hall of Fame and the countless trophy cases. Standing at attention to face the Star-Spangled Banner draped by the five state-champion banners, they felt the eyes of the Jaguars lined up on the blue line behind them hot on their necks. By the end of the first period, Jefferson led 5–0.

The game had started the way Jaguar home games had for the past twenty-six years. "The Voice of Bloomington Ice Garden—Mr. Michael Posch" sang an off-key rendition of the national anthem. Wearing his navy blue parka with the furry collared hood and large snow boots, Posch stood in the penalty box with Seplak holding a tape recorder playing a scratchy accompaniment. When Posch warbled what sounded like "land of the *brie*," Duncs's stepdad Dave Irvin cracked, "He thinks we're in Wisconsin."

Irvin stood with Steve Duncan and the other dads behind the moms, grandparents, and siblings. Although tickets were general admission, the seat assignments in the bleachers were as regulated by habit as those on the team bus. The families sat above the Jaguars player bench. To their right, students and alumni filled the vocal section closest to the Jefferson net. To their left sat regular fans like Jim Splinter, who had missed only three home games since the school opened with his son on the varsity. Farther down, Diane Saterdalen, the coach's wife, distanced herself from the parents, often joined by her daughter, Paige, and two grandchildren. That's also where Kevin Bernhagen and Mike Coffman sat, distancing themselves from their ex-wives with their new husbands.

In the Diane Saterdalen section, Krishna Ramalingam, '91, shepherded a group of maybe ten students from the Montessori school his parents ran. Mike Crowley had gone to the small Ramalynn Montessori school in the old Lincoln High building, and so had junior Nick Dillon from this year's team. Ramalingam, who taught fourth through sixth grades at the school, rewarded students for completing their homework with trips to home games.

The son of Sri Lankan immigrants, Ramalingam caught Jaguars fever when he was in sixth grade. That year, the Jags' opening round game of the '85 Tournament against Minnetonka was suspended after three overtimes and resumed at 9 A.M. the next day. The Jags plunked in the winning goal 2:21 minutes into the fourth OT of the historic two-day contest, the longest Tournament game in thirty years. The young Ramalingam was amazed that a group of teenagers dominated the news and packed a professional arena. "Finding out they actually went to school was a surprise," he said.

By the time he reached high school, Ramalingam had become what John Bianchi called the Jaguars' "best fan of all time." He didn't miss a game and became the team manager his senior year. Now, he cultivated that awe in his students, who asked the high school players for autographs. "They don't look at these players as fifteen-, sixteen-, or seventeen-year-old kids," he said. "They look at them as Minnesota Wild players."

Wes Hermann was there, too. A mountain of a man with thick glasses and a brown moustache, Wes unloaded trucks at the Sysco Foods plant and ran a french fry stand at the Minnesota State Fair, but he had an insatiable appetite for high school hockey. The forty-something fan rode city buses all over the seven-county metro area to feed his craving. A regular at Jefferson games, Wes often wandered into the dressing room afterward or stepped onto the bus to bark platitudes. At opening night, he wore the relic Jaguars jersey with his name printed on the back that Sats had given him at the Eden Prairie game, and he clutched his ubiquitous bag stuffed with newspaper articles. "This is as stunning entertainment in hockey as I've ever seen," Wes growled.

For the students, BIG was the place to be for home games. Girls with freshly mascaraed faces huddled under blankets and whispered through one another's ear muffs; boys with baseball caps turned backwards shouted and shoved one another. The school's social elite came together to cheer their friends and make plans to party that night. They punched their cell phones to hook up with other friends unable to switch their work schedules or stuck at a family function. Those unfortunates would have to catch the game's replay on Channel 14, Bloomington's "Station of Champions."

Right before Posch started the anthem, Scott Davis, a junior, yelled, "Earl the Squirrel!" Scott and Jeremy had been buddies since fifth grade. They played baseball together on summer teams, Scott pitching to Jeremy. Scott wore the No. 35 jersey Jeremy had given him. Last year, he had painted his face for games. This year, he quit the j.v. basketball team because the team's schedule conflicted with hockey games.

Just as Jeremy's mom sat next to Merrelyn at games, Scott sat next to Brian Mylerberg, Timm's designated fan. Wearing a No. 1 jersey, Brian yelled, "Timm Dogg," and the fans answered with barks.

Once the game started, the cheerleaders exchanged their skates for sneakers and occupied the front row of the student section, several hundred strong. Emily and the other girls clapped their white mittens knit with blue Js. They named Pat Gibbs the ultimate fan of the game. The senior, who had been the team manager with Kelly last year, kept up a clever running monologue during the game, entertaining those around him. In appreciation for his outspoken enthusiasm, the cheerleaders gave him a lime-green T-shirt that read "Ultimate Jaguar Fan 2000–2001."

Gibbs and the boys banged on the glass and yelled.

When a Rosemount player fell: "Hey, that ice is slippery!"

When the ref whistled questionable coincidental minors: "This is hockey, not tennis."

When the ref stumbled: "One step at a time, Ref!"

They improvised a cheer not approved by the National Cheerleader Association: "Give me a *C*. Give me an *O*. Give me an *N*. Give me a *D*. Give me an *O*. Give me an *M*. What's that spell? Condom! What's that mean? DEFENSE!"

These were the moments they would recall at their reunions.

On his second shift of the game, Eric Lindquist won a trip to Perkins. The junior defenseman blocked a Rosemount clearing attempt up the boards, skated the puck around the net, and stuffed it unassisted. Sats took any player who scored on a wraparound out to breakfast. After the game, he would flip Eric a puck to commemorate his first varsity goal and invite him for pancakes.

Jefferson scored in such a flurry that Seplak couldn't keep up. While he was announcing one goal, Jefferson scored another.

Nick Dillon brought the Ramalynn Montessori students to their feet twice in the second period. The small but crafty wing didn't score often, but when he did, it was usually pretty. Two minutes after netting a slick wrist shot, the Ramalynn Montessori alumnus slithered through the defense, wiggled around the goalie, and slipped the biscuit behind him. The move was ESPN-Play-of-the-Day caliber.

With Jefferson up by more than six goals, they played the last fifteen minutes running time. The Jaguars quickly sent home the hapless Irish 8–2 losers.

———

That week, a blast of arctic air shoved temperatures below zero. The *high* Tuesday, the day of the Eagan game, was -1°F. That's cold, even by Minnesota standards.

In that kind of cold, cars don't start. AAA Minneapolis received more than eight hundred calls—*triple* its normal volume—reporting dead batteries.

In that kind of cold, exhaust freezes on roadways in "black ice." Hundreds of spinouts and accidents extended rush hour traffic reports.

In that kind of cold, exposed skin freezes quicker than a minor penalty expires—in less than two minutes. Meteorologists issued frostbite warnings, and the Salvation Army shortened shifts for bell-ringers.

In that kind of cold, it's cold inside, too. Especially when you forget to turn on the heat. Tuesday night, BIG was an icebox. The coils in the suspended heaters that usually glowed a comforting red stared blankly down on the bleachers. Even after the rink manager discovered his mistake, the fans, bundled in their puffy coats, complained more about the cold than about the officiating and consumed bucketloads of hot chocolate from the concessions stand.

Students in the pep band warmed their mouthpieces in their hands so the metal wouldn't stick to their lips. They played when the

Jags hit the ice. They backed up Mr. Michael Posch on the national anthem. They performed the school fight song, set to the University of Michigan's tune, when the Jags scored—seemingly continuously during Jefferson's 9–1 romp over Eagan. That night, the kids standing in the far left section didn't get much rest.

The Jaguars so tamed the Wildcats that even with Nick Coffman in the penalty box, Eagan couldn't break out of its own end. When the announcer reported, "Jefferson full strength," Adam Dirlam's mom said, "I'd forgotten we had a penalty."

Back at school, before the game started, Sats had stung Nick with his comments at the board. Nick had already perused the stats posted in the equipment office window for both the Rosemount game and the season to date. His on-ice value—zero—ranked lowest on the team and put his name at the bottom. When Sats said, "Be proud of your plus/minus rating," Nick winced.

Sats had paired Nick on a line with Duncs and Jimmy but didn't think Nick would be able to play to their level. He figured Nick would finish the season on the third line, like he always had. Nick desperately wanted to bring up his play. He cranked his favorite tune, Limp Bizkit's "Livin' it Up," for inspiration.

It worked. In the first period, he punched in a one-timer from Tommy on the powerplay to put Jefferson up 3–0. He was on the ice for four of the Jaguars' goals. Finally, he felt like he was contributing.

After singing the national anthem, the Voice of Bloomington climbed the bleachers on the visitors' side and watched the game alone. Posch pulled a pair of large field glasses from the faded canvas Adidas bag he carried and tried to pick up the action.

Only forty-five, he was plagued by a nursing home's worth of physical ailments. His vision was failing—"I'm legally blind," he told anyone who crossed his path in the lobby before the game. He also had a brain cyst, asthma, diabetes, and heart trouble, he mumbled. Short and balding, Posch wore bushy sideburns and thick glasses.

He worked part-time at an engineering company doing menial office tasks and lived by himself. Sats asked him to sing for Jefferson varsity games after hearing Posch solo at a Thanksgiving tournament. The hockey games had become his social life.

A 1974 Lincoln High grad, Posch had tried out for the hockey team as a goalie his sophomore year but was cut. These days, he bowled and pitched horseshoes. He also wrote original songs that he performed at community talent shows and carved rink-shaped wooden trophies for the Booster program's Silver Stick Tournament. His lifelong ambition was an 11 x 6–foot plywood board he envisioned with 360 lights arranged in the image of the American flag. He dreamed of the giant Stars and Stripes being wheeled out to center ice on a cart when he sang the anthem.

John Bianchi organized Posch Appreciation Night last year to honor the loyal singer for his dedication and commitment in supporting Bloomington hockey. The mayor presented him with a plaque. A picture of Posch clasping a microphone now hangs in the Hall of Fame.

Halfway through the second period, Posch slipped from the stands and headed for the front door where his mother picked him up at 8:30. He missed both of Duncs's goals in the period's final five minutes. Between the second and third period, Sats told his top two lines that they would skate one shift each then sit the third. Enjoying a 7–0 lead, Sats didn't want to risk injury to his top players. In the first period, an Eagan defenseman had cross-checked Duncs in the throat.

On the first shift of the third, the same defenseman blind-sided Duncs, sticking out his leg when Duncs skated back to the bench. Duncs lay face down on the ice. The trainer and Sats skidded out to him. Duncs clutched his leg above his left knee. In the stands, Steve Duncan grimaced.

Jimmy helped Duncs off the ice. Deb Irvin, Duncs's mom, scrambled down to the dressing room. The trainer told her he had a bruised thigh. The hit had pushed the pad in his breezers inside-out. He was lucky it hadn't caught him an inch lower, or he would be headed to the emergency room for knee surgery. As it was, Duncs spent the third period in the dressing room with a bag of ice on his left thigh. Limping out afterward, he politely thanked the trainer for her attention.

"See why we sit the third period?" Sats said afterward. "They start taking cheap shots—everybody wants a piece of us."

———

Later that week, the mood was upbeat after practice. They had finished with "Stanley Cup," an everyone-on-the-ice, just-for-fun scrimmage, managers included. In the dressing room, Sats playfully flicked some snow off his skates at Bernie. Then, he made the mistake of bending over to slip on his shoes. Bernie packed a slushball with snow collected from half-a-dozen teammates and beaned his coach with a cheap shot. The dressing room erupted in laughter.

————

It snowed through the night. Saturday morning, Bloomington woke up to six inches powdering the lawns. The snow capped swingsets, barbecue grills, and mailboxes with white fluff. Any toys left in the yard created lumps in the otherwise even coating. While Tommy still slept, Kelly Gilbert welcomed the chance to fire up his new snowblower and clear the snow from his driveway.

Bloomington declared a snow emergency. Strict parking restrictions—violators were towed—opened the city's 360 miles of streets to make room for long yellow tractors with wheels as tall as Jimmy Humbert and blades almost as wide as the team bench. The city's twenty-five–ton dump trucks with blinking blue lights followed, spreading a salt and sand mixture behind them. Outside Jefferson High, a Bobcat fitted with a plow and a front-end loader heaped huge mounds of snow at the edge of the lot.

Minneapolis canceled its downtown Holidazzle parade for only the sixth time in its history, but they played hockey in Bloomington. From the metro area's southwestern edge, the Chaska Hawks rode a school bus to the Saturday night conference contest at BIG.

Inside, rink attendant T.J. Gannon pushed the nets back into place. The Zamboni had cleared the layer of snow that collected during the final period of the j.v. game and spread a thin film of water to start the varsity game on fresh ice. Before the home opener, Seplak had acknowledged T.J. and mentioned that after seventeen years, BIG almost lost T.J. to a Supervalu job. The fans applauded T.J.'s decision to stay on as swing shift supervisor. T.J. starred in a suburban legend about BIG's Zamboni that reflected the machine's mysterious allure.

The Zamboni maxes out at a top speed of about eight miles per hour, but its aura surpasses that of a NASCAR Chevy. No other sport has anything that can touch its large physical and metaphysical presence. Not the artificial turf vacuums nor the infield tractors dragging chainlink. The Zamboni stands alone, unique to hockey as the ice itself.

Ice defines hockey. The frozen sheet gives the game its smell and complexion. Ice provides the source of its speed—with players skating on metal blades faster than any other team sport played in America. Combined with the players' speed, the unforgiving surface adds an element of danger that ups the ante on the sport's excitement. Ice also adds a degree of difficulty to the game. Hockey is one of the few sports for which participants must master a prerequisite skill—skating—before they can play. The game is not the same when played on a field of grass or a varnished floor or even a paved street. Ice hockey is what it is because of the ice.

The ice—and the game—wouldn't be what it is without the Zamboni. During the dozen minutes it takes the Zamboni to do its thing, fans—without a game to watch nor officials to harass—scrutinize the job as scrupulously as IRS inspectors. They boo a driver for missing spots and criticize him for laying down too much water in spots.

No one watches the Zamboni slowly spin its mesmerizing loops without falling under its spell. Young and old, they want to get behind its wheel. Minnesota native Martin Zellar, as lead singer of the Gear Daddies, captured that universal urge in his cult anthem:

"Now ever since I was young it's been my dream
That I might drive a Zamboni machine!
I'd get the ice just as slick as could be,
And all the kids would look up to me."

BIG's rink manager Denny May sometimes played Ricardo Montalban to those dreams. When a disc jockey on the Twin Cities's most popular radio station, WCCO—"the good neighbor"—confessed on the air that she had always wanted to drive the Zamboni, Denny made it happen. A man who had rented BIG ice to shoot a commercial blindfolded his wife, brought her to the rink, and, for her thirtieth birthday present, Denny let her drive the Zamboni. A Bloomington woman arranged for her husband, one of BIG's scorekeepers, to fulfill his private desire: he zammed.

Which loops us back to T.J. Jefferson hockey players tell the tale that one day, not that long ago, T.J. fired up the Zamboni and drove it down nearby France Avenue, the main drag between BIG and Jefferson High, until the police pulled him over. Denny says it didn't happen. But T.J. insists it did, that he made it all the way through the McDonald's drive-thru, where he ordered the #2 value meal.

While fans debated the Zamboni legend, the home team had its way with Chaska that snowy December night in the friendly confines. Over and over and over, Seplak announced, "Scoring for Jefferson, Gilbert from Bernhagen." Another hat trick for the captain, another creative playmaking performance from the poet.

Before faceoffs, Bernie briefed Tommy on what he planned to pull off. Tommy towered a helmet taller over Bernie. His game was strength, Bernie's finesse. He had speed, Bernie quickness. Tommy seemed a stranger to the spoken word, Bernie never had an unspoken thought.

Those differences had caused friction in the past. During tryouts, the two scuffled over a seat in the dressing room. Bernie ended up on top of Tommy. Someone joked, "I'm calling the cops, Bernie. You're going to jail."

But once paired together on the same line, they seemed to put their differences behind them. They found their old magic. Their line had scored over half of the team's goals, averaging better than three a game.

Their favorite play went like this: with the puck in their own end, Tommy slipped behind the opposition defense and angled across the neutral zone like a split end running a deep-post pattern. Bernie lobbed the puck just below the rafters onto Tommy's stick—voilà, breakaway. The play looked simple the way they executed it, but Bernie's precision pass synched to Tommy's timing pattern made it work.

It would've worked against Chaska, but Tommy got tripped from behind. No matter—while the ref had his arm in the air to call the delayed penalty, Adam scored. When it was over, Jefferson had blanked the Hawks 5–0. Timm had earned his first shutout with some quality stops.

Duncs played, but was frustrated by his slow start. He hadn't picked up where he had left off last season. He wasn't living up to his expectations. He wasn't giving his dad much to remember.

When Sats paired Tommy with Bernie and B.J. and put Duncs between Nick and Jimmy, Duncs was bummed. Even though Nick and Jimmy were his best friends, the combination demoted him to second line status. Sats rotated starting lines, but Duncs had taken it personally. Sats, knowing Duncs's faith, counseled him, "You're where you're supposed to be right now. This must be God's plan for you."

Friday afternoon, with talk of weekend parties in the air, Duncs wasn't a firm believer. Sitting in the cafeteria before heading to practice, he asked his teammates, "Why aren't we out getting drunk?"

After home games, parents gathered at Billabong on "the Strip," a string of hotels, restaurants, and bars that stretched westward from the airport along Interstate 494. Billabong, an Aussie grill and pub next door to a Mercedes dealership, claimed in its Jaguars 2001 yearbook back-page ad, "There's no place else to go!" Not for Jaguar parents, anyway.

The captain's parents, Mary and Kelly Gilbert, served as de facto hosts of the post-game gatherings. They pulled together several tables in the bar. Mary, a manager for a medical device manufacturer, was fun-loving and gregarious. Kelly, a salesman for a paint distributor, was friendly but introverted. Tommy had his mother's big-toothed smile but his father's reticence. Mary and Kelly had both graduated from Kennedy, then upgraded to West Bloomington when they bought the house next to the Bianchis. Mary quickly adapted to the rigors of being a hockey mom, complete with predawn practices. "Getting up at 5 was a blast," she said. She was serious.

Tommy's election as captain rewarded their sacrifices. "To have your son be captain of a team at an elite school is a good feeling," Kelly said.

Mary sat next to Nick's dad and teased him about a previous girlfriend.

Mike Coffman, a salesman for Capital Fleet, fit the salesman mold: charming, talkative, strong-jaw-handsome—i.e., one of the guys. He ordered two Mooseheads as soon as he sat down. Before he finished the beer in his hand, he ordered another, same as the chain smoker who lights a fresh cigarette with the one he is finishing. Mary also joked about him getting tossed out of some of Bloomington's other watering holes.

Mike preferred to talk about his glory days at Michigan, where he ran with a crowd that included Steve Howe, the pitching sensation who had been the rookie of the year with the Dodgers in 1980 but repeatedly suspended by Major League Baseball because of his drug use. When Mike's Wolverines hockey team came to town to play the Gophers, players from the two teams partied together after games. Upset that his players showed up at practice hungover, "Our coach skated us hard so we would sweat out the alcohol," Mike said with a laugh.

The bar was Mike's turf. Karen, the '01 Varsity Social Director, and her new husband skipped the Billabong gatherings.

Deb Irvin's new husband, Dave, though not so new anymore after twelve years of marriage, took the boys home after the game so she could enjoy a night out. Duncs's mom, with a small gold cross hanging around her neck and pretty brown hair pulled back by a headband, looked every bit the Catholic girl grown into the respectable suburban mom, but she nurtured a wild side she had passed on to her son. That spring her graduation present to him would be a tattoo. She had one herself, a discreet likeness of Piglet.

Deb still talked every day to Steve, her ex. Sometimes they both showed up at Billabong. Dave, too. It wasn't unusual for Steve, who hadn't remarried, to attend Dave's family events. Duncs alternated weeks between his father's and mother's houses. They were one big, blended extended family.

It would take some time before Merrelyn Lorenz remarried. After her husband's death, she had gone into seclusion. The move to Minnesota had pried her out of her shell; Jaguars hockey had reignited her social life. She and Jeremy's mom, Debbie Earl, had become fast friends. As mothers of goaltenders, they shared a special bond.

Merrelyn was short, with frosted blonde hair and sad blue eyes that looked ready to smear her mascara at any moment. "This has been a good move for us," she said over her drink. "It has made me stronger, happier. For Timm, it has helped to have hockey in place of his dad."

They all owed something to hockey, Jefferson hockey in particular. They couldn't imagine their lives without it. Saturday night, after a game at BIG, it truly did seem there was no place else to go. They toasted their boys proudly.

CHAPTER SIX

A JAGUAR IS BRED

On the first Sunday of Advent, the parking lots are full at St. Stephen Lutheran, West Bloomington Evangelical Free, and Calvary Christian Reformation, three France Avenue churches on the way to BIG, where the lot is also nearly full. It's Blade Day, when the crosstown rival Jefferson and Kennedy Booster programs face off at their various age levels, Mites through Bantams. Fifteen minutes before the puck drops for the Squirt A game at 9:45 A.M., fans line the railing above the rink. Never mind the neighbors at church; these parents wouldn't miss this game for all the Advent wreaths in the world.

Rink 2 is decorated for the occasion. Hanging from the glass in one corner, a banner crafted with all the care of one hung over an altar displays the names and photos of the Kennedy Squirt A team. A felt Jefferson banner hangs in the opposite corner. Parents sport buttons bearing photos of their players. The Kennedy parents carry stiff pennants fashioned from navy blue and yellow felt on a stick, each decorated with a different player's number and topped by a jingling bell. One mother stayed up until three o'clock to finish the crafts that would do Martha Stewart proud.

The players hit the ice to applause, ten- and eleven-year-old versions of the high school players they aspire to be. Clad in socks, breezers, and jerseys with their names on the back, these Squirts play like pint-size incarnations of their older counterparts—they go down to block shots, clear the puck off the glass, and change lines on the fly. Between shifts, an assistant coach on the Jefferson bench diagrams a strategy for playing the puck high in the defensive zone. Tony Bianchi, the former Jaguar standout who now coaches the Jefferson Squirt A team, shouts directions to his players.

On the railing, the Jefferson and Kennedy parents are split like Lutherans and Catholics, Jefferson to the left, Kennedy to the right. They holler encouragement to their side. But when a Jefferson player walks into the Kennedy zone and cuts in front of the net to score, putting his team up 3–0, a sharp-jawed man in Kennedy navy shakes his head in disgust. "Come on, coaches, fire them up," he yells.

After the game, one Jefferson mother admits she never thought she would be spending Sunday mornings at the ice rink. But her family got hockey like some folks got religion: "We said we would never do this because of the schedule, but now we are into it hook, line, and sinker."

———

Blade Day in Bloomington was a don't-stick-your-tongue-to-the-flagpole cold morning, the sun white in a clear sky—the kind of day when kids used to skate on frozen ponds and shoot on goals fashioned from a pair of boots. Not so anymore. Hockey has grown up, lost its innocence. It got organized.

The creativity required to stickhandle through twenty guys on an outdoor rink or find an open teammate to catch a pass is stifled by the structured systems coaches impose—lost with it is the freedom to play the game with individual style and spontaneity. Kids come of age in a program, not in their neighborhood.

No longer do they race down to the pond after school—they follow a strict schedule dictated by ice-time availability. They skate indoors on artificial ice manicured by Zambonis and edging machines, ringed by designer boards and tempered glass. It could be January, could be July—they skate in comfort at either extreme. The move indoors changed the game's climate. It shifted from a way the rugged survived long, cold winters to a pampered pastime.

The preference for artificial ice placed a premium upon availability. Ice became a political issue. When girls and women took to hockey in the '90s, the limited supply couldn't keep pace with the expanding demand. In 1995, the state legislature passed the Mighty Ducks Bill, which provided three hundred million dollars in emergency ice relief, but the question of whether to build another ice rink divided communities. Instead of picking teams, the kids found themselves choosing sides.

The adults have shown up. Coaches with hours of training under their belts and clipboards in hand. Referees blowing whistles to resolve disputes kids once sorted through themselves. Parents with opinions about how their children should play. It used to be that the only spectators were younger kids begging for a chance to get into the game. Now the adults are telling the kids what to do.

In Minnesota, it starts at age five with Mites, then Squirts (ages ten to eleven), Peewees (twelve to thirteen), Bantams (fourteen to fifteen) and, for those who don't play high school hockey, Junior Gold (sixteen to nineteen). In some programs, the girls play with the boys. In those like Bloomington's, where the numbers are greater, the girls play in age divisions—Under Ten, Under Twelve, and Under Fifteen—then junior varsity and varsity at the high school. The most talented players are selected to play on traveling teams beginning in Squirts, while the rest of the kids play in "house" or recreation leagues with less rigorous schedules.

Bloomington has organized its traveling youth hockey teams into the Jefferson and Kennedy Booster programs along the high school borders. The Jefferson Booster program was in its infancy when Sats arrived. He invested himself heavily into its maturation—for obvious reasons. Youth program mission statements may read that they provide opportunities for youth to compete at the appropriate skill levels, but their bottom line is clear: to groom varsity hockey players. "It is the feeder system, the bread and butter of our program," Sats said.

The desks in B201 are filled with the Booster volunteers on a late September evening. After a full day teaching and two hours on the ice with junior varsity hopefuls, Sats snarfs down a quick McDonald's dinner in his office, then addresses the heart and soul of his feeder program. In a '94 Jefferson Hockey T-shirt, Columbia blue sweats, and very worn Docksides, Sats diagrams drills on the board and pulls a puck from his desk to demonstrate how to tie up the opposing center on a faceoff. At 8:45 P.M., he is still answering questions, his voice charged by the subject.

The group is not a bunch of hockey neophytes. Many of them played Division-I college, some played pro. Yet they are eager to hear what Sats has to say on various points of strategy and overall philosophy. He tells them they don't have to use his systems, but they will. When the University of Minnesota has adopted a high school coach's penalty kill system, as it did with Saterdalen's, most Squirt and Bantam coaches figure it is good enough for them, too. Sats reminds them how important their role is in the Jaguars' success: "It's not my team, it's *our* team."

Booster teams play the Jefferson varsity style; they are strong-skating quads that can move the puck. The Phoenix Coyotes skating coach tutors the Mites and teaches their coaches skating drills. Jefferson teams are characteristically disciplined and hard-working—ready to play for Sats when they reach high school. It is no coincidence that the first Jaguars team to make it to the Tournament—Steve Bianchi's 1980 team—was the first group to have come of age in Sats's youth program.

The Booster kids bent under the weight of their hockey bags pass nearly daily through BIG's Hall of Fame. The Jaguar teams hanging on the wall keep before them the youth program's ultimate objective. "It's what you're bred for," explained one Booster project whose face is on that wall. "From the first level all the way up, you're here to play in the Tournament for Jefferson—and to sacrifice everything to get there."

———————

Varsity tryouts begin in Squirts. Watch Tony Bianchi's Squirt A squad, and you could be previewing the Jaguars '07 varsity. Every October, coaches sort kids into A and B teams from Squirts on up. Despite Sats's assurances that anything can happen—kids' skills develop at varying rates, their bodies mature at different ages—parents fear at each tryout that their kid's future is on the line.

With so much at stake, it's inevitable that politics come into play. Steve Duncan, who coached his son's Mite team, said the whole program is "as political as the goddamn Soviet Union." And at no time more so than during tryouts.

The hopefuls drill and scrimmage under the watchful eyes of coaches and volunteer evaluators, who anonymously rate each child's quickness/speed, skills, hockey sense, and aggressiveness either excellent, above average, fair, or poor, then assign each player an overall grade. Some communities, to squelch suspicions and accusations of unfair judgments, have hired independent evaluating firms to assess abilities. Others employ computer programs to objectively tabulate skill assessments. Bloomington relies on its own volunteer ranks. At BIG, the parents in the stands eye the evaluators as closely as they watch the kids on the ice.

In the end, the coaches select their own teams. The forms, one Jefferson tryout evaluator confided, are just for show. "They're a backup for when the coach gets called onto the carpet by the parents if their kid is cut," he said.

Second-year kids have to outperform first-year kids at each level. Even though the Jefferson Booster guidelines state that if two players are close, coaches should select the older one, it doesn't always work that way. A father whose second-year son was moved down to the Squirt B team complained his son hadn't been treated fairly. "It's a select program," Squirt A coach Tony Bianchi responded. "It's not a city-run, full-participation program."

Kids in private schools—or suspected to be headed to private schools that older brothers or sisters already attend—get short shrift. Or so the perception goes. One mother, who thought her son a superior goalie to a boy who made the team, complained that Sats ignored her son, a private school student. "Sats gives preference to kids in the Jefferson program," she charged.

Parents fear if their kid doesn't make the A team, he'll get labeled a B kid, a second-rate rap hard to overcome. They also fear their own status is at stake. Tryouts establish that season's caste system. Come the final cuts, they'll either be A parents or B parents. "It's a status symbol, like wearing a Polo shirt, to be able to say, my kid's on the Squirt A team," Tony Bianchi said.

———

October had been the toughest time of year for Karen. When Nick's parents divorced, Mike paid child support, but Karen raised the boys. Tommy Gilbert was always a given on the A team. But not Nick. Despite his genetic predisposition, he was not loaded with talent. Each year was dicey.

Karen did all she could to help. Before tryouts, the slender mother with the knockout smile strapped on goalie equipment and let Nick and Ben shoot foam rubber pucks at her in the basement. When the boys got bigger and shot harder, she bought them a shooter tutor, a goalie outlined on a board. Their target practice freckled the basement wall with black marks.

When tryouts began, Karen gave Nick and Ben each a card wishing them well and enclosed a good luck token, like a cloverleaf penny she purchased at the drugstore. The family enacted an annual ritual. Together, they watched the *Mighty Ducks* movie and ate pizza. Before heading to the rink, Karen cranked the Jock Rocks CD, a collection of pumped-up tunes played during stoppages of play at the North Stars games.

The boys were pumped, but their mother was a nervous wreck. "I hated driving to the rink the first day of tryouts," Karen said. "It was always so tense." She sat in the bleachers with other parents and tried to gauge Nick's skills against the other boys'. She drew up possible line combinations with the best players to see if Nick fit among them. The prospects weren't always promising. Nick played Squirt A, but it wasn't until his second year of Bantams that he again made an A team.

Karen and the boys survived the cuts just like they survived the foot of water in the basement, an oven fire, and that first winter when she didn't have a clue how to start the snowblower. With characteristic resilience, they kept showing up.

But life didn't get easier for Karen after October. With both boys on different teams playing as many as seventy games apiece and practicing most every day in between, just getting Nick and Ben to and from the rink became a nightmare. Forget the Christmas parties, the Holidazzle parade, or dinner with the girls, she hardly had a moment to breathe after work and hockey. It was a challenge to squeeze in a trip to buy groceries or get skates sharpened. Some nights, she watched part of Nick's game then drove thirty miles across the metro area to see the last half of Ben's. She had to post sticky notes on her dashboard to remind her where the boys had to be and at what time. Sometimes snowy roads made her late. Others, when trying to find an unfamiliar rink, she got lost.

Karen traveled to the tournaments in Rochester, Saint Cloud, Hastings, Duluth, Fargo, Grand Forks, Port Huron, and Sarnia, but one year she had to put Nick on a bus alone because she couldn't afford to go. Her flight attendant's salary only stretched so far. She split the annual $1,600 basic hockey expenses for each boy with Mike but was on her own for the rest. She agonized over money. Pay the phone bill or buy Nick a new stick? She hoped Ma Bell didn't cut off her service. Sure, she could have sold the four-bedroom house where the boys had grown up, but after the divorce, she had determined to give them what stability she could. "I was trying to have their lives as nice as their friends' lives, even though they were not the same," she said.

So she scrimped and saved where possible. At one tournament, the other parents complained that Karen—always the social director—had made reservations at a cheap hotel, but it was the best she could afford. Another year she returned the Christmas gifts she had received so she could travel to a tournament in Duluth. At the tournaments, Karen took the boys out for dinner one night, but for the rest of the weekend she ordered KFC in bulk. Mornings they ate cereal with milk she kept chilled in the snow outside the room.

Karen dismissed her brother's suggestion she move to a community that was more affordable. "You wouldn't leave because of hockey, right?" he asked.

"Right," she said. "Bloomington has always had such good hockey programs. It was important to us, and we knew it."

Right before Nick's senior year, Karen married Mike Bender, a high school boyfriend also divorced and with two boys. They bought a house behind the Minnesota Valley Country Club in Wexford Estates, a newer neighborhood where Karen used to take the boys to look at the fancy Christmas decorations. Curled up on the couch of her dream house with the *tannenbaum* in the front window rising two stories, those struggles seemed long ago. What with Nick now an alternate captain and Ben taking the year off from hockey, there wouldn't be another October like those she had known alone. Still, Karen beamed that warm smile with the deep dimples and said she would do it all over again. "Nobody would spend this much time and money if they didn't really love their kid," she said.

———————

Competition to make the team has kids skating year-round. Not wanting to get left behind, kids quit playing football, baseball, tennis, or whatever, so that they can focus on hockey fall, winter, spring, and summer. If they shag flies while their teammates skate circles, they fear they won't make the A team next October. That is how you come to find thirty nine- and ten-year-olds skating inside at BIG on a sunny July day with the smell of mown grass hanging in the air and other kids running through sprinklers. For two hours, they drill and scrimmage under Sats's tutelage. Barely reaching the height of the net, they are split into blue and white squads with their last names taped to the front of their helmets. On the final day of the five-week clinic, parents clutch Sats's evaluation forms like report cards they have picked up at parent-teacher conferences, eager to discuss with their son his strengths and areas for improvement.

At three hundred dollars per kid, Sats's summer clinics give the coach a chance to pocket a little extra cash, but his primary objective is to get to know the kids. He is able to learn their personalities, gauge their hockey sense, and assess their abilities. He knows where they live, how they are doing in school, what church they attend, whose parents are divorced, and which ones have drinking problems. By the time they are Peewees, Sats pretty much knows where they stand.

"It impresses me that Tom has called my son by his first name since he was six years old when he saw him at Cub Foods, in the hallway at BIG, wherever," said Denny Connelly, whose son is now a Bantam with a varsity future. "When the high school coach is calling him by his first name not once, not twice, but every time, you get the sense you're part of the family."

To be welcomed into the family, a kid has to start skating early. Bob Lange feared his son had gotten off to a late start—B.J. Lange didn't start playing hockey until the ripe age of nine. His father wanted to help him make up for lost time. The Bloomington personal injury attorney hired Dennis Maruk, a former North Star, to put B.J. on a crash course to catch up to the other kids. Lange rented early morning ice at BIG, where Maruk gave B.J. private skating lessons. Summer vacation and weekends during the school year, Lange had his son on the ice at 4:30 A.M. "Everybody thought I pushed him, but the little guy wanted to do it," Lange said. "He would wake *me* up."

Squirt A teams like Tony Bianchi's play more than forty games and log upward of two hundred hours of ice time October through February. During that stretch, they will rarely have two consecutive days off. As Peewees, they will add another twenty games and a month to their schedule. By Bantams, they could play more than seventy games and average only four or five days off per month. Kids forego birthday parties and sleepovers so they are rested and prepared for games.

"Sure, they don't have a whole lot of time for anything other than homework and hockey, but that's the sacrifice you have to be willing to make to play at the A level," said Denny Connelly, who is also Jefferson's Peewee A coach.

When their son is picked for the team, parents sign a consent form agreeing to have him at all the games unless he is sick or has a church function. Several years back, when one Peewee A player missed a Thanksgiving tournament to attend a family reunion, the coach, one of Connelly's predecessors, made the boy perform community service.

If a kid is serious about hockey—and the coaches are serious about him as a prospect—he will have to commit to hockey as early as Peewees, where college scouts will come to watch him play. Just as German kids are placed on different education tracks at fourteen, most American kids by that age have committed to a single sport track to earn a varsity letter and perhaps the prize of a college scholarship.

They must specialize not only to commit to their development but to avoid injury. Sats discouraged varsity prospects from playing rougher sports like football. Ben Clymer, '96, now of the Tampa Bay Lightning, had skied competitively four years, but his Peewee coach told him he had to give up his second sport.

Parents looking to give their kid an edge ship them off to summer hockey camps, sign them up to play in elite off-season leagues that promise thirty games, and enroll them in power-skating schools. They experiment with plyometrics, dryland workouts, and personal trainers to better their son's chances. "They're looking for a gimmick, whatever they can find," said physiologist Kevin Ziegler of Innovative Sports, which had trained scores of Jefferson hockey players.

The rigors demanded of young hockey players—pushed to specialize, pressured to play, prodded to succeed—can rub out the fun of playing a game. They burn out. There are those for whom love of the game will last a lifetime. But for others, when pressure erases the pleasure, hockey becomes a chore about as fun as cleaning the litter box. So they quit.

"I would be willing to bet not all of the kids are having fun because they've lost perspective of fun," says Richard Weinberg, Ph.D., a professor at the University of Minnesota's Institute of Child Development familiar with the rigors of youth hockey. "There are too many other layers of issues placed on them: the competition and confrontation and pushing of their skills and parents' expectations and losing out on other aspects of their lives all counters the fun. It's pretty hard to have fun doing something that's overwhelmingly stressful."

Some kids would quit, but feel they can't because their parents have invested too much in their young hockey careers. Not all, but some fathers and mothers live vicariously through their child's ice exploits. When their child does get cut or quit, they experience a personal withdrawal. "The kids feel guilty if they don't pursue sports because they see how much their parents are getting out of it," Weinberg said.

Most parents start with the best of intentions, seeking for their child the benefits of playing organized sports, but somewhere along the way their perspective slips. "Parents want their children to be involved in youth sports for positive reasons, but they lose sight of those when they start challenging kids, pushing them beyond their limits, and setting unrealistic expectations," Weinberg said.

Worst case: they push their children over the edge. Carl Bloomberg Jr.'s photo hangs in BIG's Hall of Fame. The All-State goaltender steered Bloomington Kennedy to the consolation championship in the '76 Tournament. He led the state with the lowest goals against average and set a school record for most career shutouts (nine). Yet parents rush their children to practice past Carl's photo outside Rink 2 without a thought to the pressure that killed him.

Carl sits front row, far right. The enlargement of the photo has slightly blurred his features, the feathered blond hair and wide smile. Handsome and successful, Carl was the kid others admired and wished they could be. They didn't see what it was like from the inside. Driving to the rink, Carl had to grip the steering wheel tightly to steady his shaking hands. A teammate had to tie his gloves. Before taking up his position between the pipes, he puked in the toilet stall. The skills that let him star on that frozen stage won him rich praise, but he worried they would fail him, render him worthless.

Following one game when he played poorly, Carl searched out his father's face in the crowd. Carl Sr. shook his head disapprovingly.

After graduating from Kennedy, Carl played Division-I hockey at St. Louis University, then toured Europe with the USA national team. He planned to return to college to play out his remaining eligibility, but St. Louis U cut its program. When Carl lost hockey, there was nothing left.

In November 1980—just four years after his Tournament of Glory—Carl snuck out of his parents' house late one night. He let himself into a former girlfriend's apartment. She wasn't home. Carl put a shotgun to his head and pulled the trigger.

On a nationally televised special about pressure parents place on their children, Carl Sr. shakes his head again, this time at himself. "We could've de-emphasized the importance of athletics." Pause. "The sport was for fun."

"There's more to life than sports," adds Carl's mother. "Let the child do what he wants to do. Don't force sports on them."

Sats shows that tape to parents. He wants them to keep things in perspective—to learn the lesson that Carl's parents learned too late. But they may be so caught up in their child's hockey—hook, line, and sinker—that they can only recognize the warning signs in another, not in themselves. Like a gradual sight loss, they don't realize how blurred their vision has become until they put on a pair of glasses.

"Maybe there's too much emphasis on winning, since the beginning," Karen reflected after Nick's senior season had ended. "Before we got wrapped up in this (hockey) twelve years ago, I was not sure this was the way kids should be. I thought life should be more relaxing, not do or die. Now, I can't even remember that attitude."

———

Some kids show early signs of genius. Mozart composed his first works at four; Bobby Fischer whupped the nation's top chess masters before he was old enough to drive a car; Argentine Nobel laureate Bernardo Houssay entered college at nine. Bernie started playing hockey in kindergarten. He made the Jefferson varsity in ninth grade, one of only two players in the school's history to do so. (The other, Toby Petersen, played for the Pittsburgh Penguins in the 2000–2001 season on a line with Jaromir Jagr.) Even among elite company, Bernie was head of the class. Sats anointed him the most talented Jaguar he had coached.

Kevin Bernhagen couldn't help but spot young Bernie's talent. Kevin, who played football at Jefferson High School in the mid-'70s and recreational hockey growing up, used to take his five-year-old stepson with him to play pickup hockey at the park. They skated full days, up to eight hours. Within a month, Bernie could move with uncommon grace and maneuver the puck on his stick like a maestro. "My jaw dropped," Kevin said.

Days Kevin couldn't skate himself, he dropped Bernie off at the Bloomington city park and paid the Parrish brothers, Mark and Gino—both of whom would go on to play professional hockey— twenty dollars to let young Michael skate with them. Bernie honed his skills against the older kids and learned to play tough to keep up with the big boys. "That was the best hockey camp he ever went to," Kevin said.

Despite his enormous talent, Bernie was small for his age. He needed more strength to compete against larger kids. When Michael was eight, still in second grade, Kevin enrolled him at Innovative Sports, the personal fitness center that specialized in training professional athletes.

Framed photos hanging in the stairwells and on the walls of the otherwise nondescript tan brick building on the northern edge of Bloomington testify to dreams come true. The Olympic and professional athletes thank strength coach Kevin Ziegler for their success. Above Ziegler's desk, there is a framed photo of eight guys from the '93 Jefferson team dressed in black tuxedos and holding hockey sticks. Joey Bianchi, Mike Crowley, and some of their teammates were so devoted to their trainer they had stopped in on their way to the prom.

In another photo, eight-year-old Michael Bernhagen in skates and a T-shirt sits on a bench, his blades barely reaching the carpet. He sips a Gatorade. The boy with the short brown hair carries all the innocence of his youth, but his success came at a price.

Bernie skated on plastic ice, lifted weights, and did plyometrics. He worked on specific skills, like catching passes off his skates. Kevin Bernhagen was proud of his budding superstar. Even though he had not been able to legally adopt Michael, he thought of him as his son. When he married Michael's mother, Nancy, Kevin had given the three-year-old Michael his last name. The goal was for Bernie to play varsity hockey for Jefferson, then see what opportunities waited beyond that. Problem was, as a bricklayer, Kevin sometimes had trouble covering the twenty-five dollar fee for each hour-long session, even with all of the extra Saturdays he worked.

Nancy had been reluctant at first even to let Bernie play hockey because of the time commitment. Among other things, she hadn't wanted him to miss church because of games. Kevin had to convince her that Bernie had unusual talent and deserved the chance to play.

They argued about more than hockey. One day when Bernie was ten, he came home from school to find out his stepdad had split.

––––––––

It costs about six hundred dollars to launch a kindergartner into hockey. On top of annual registration fees starting at two hundred dollars, he must be dressed for the occasion. You can outfit the Mite in full equipment for about two hundred dollars, but he'll outgrow that in a year or two. Trading in used equipment at season's end for another kid's used gear a size larger will help manage costs but still set parents back at least a C-note.

Skates run extra. They are hockey's showcase equipment, the rink's equivalent to the basketball shoes worn at the playground: Nike, meet Bauer. One sporting goods store owner tells of parents who insist on spending $460 on the top-end adult skate, even though he advises them their little tyke would do just as well in the $129 children's model. "They don't want to hear that," he laughs. "They drive up in their Lincoln Navigator and want the Lincoln Navigator skate for their child."

Call it vicarious status. If Johnny looks good, Daddy looks good.

Nothing buys status like winning. Each Thursday, parents arriving at BIG grab the fresh issue of *Let's Play Hockey* and turn to page ten to check the rankings, Peewee through NCAA. They want to see where their team stands, if anything has changed based on the past week's games. They want to see if their stock has risen or fallen.

With all that they have invested, parents demand a lot of the volunteers who have donated countless hours to coach their boys. You would think that with his team riding *LPH*'s No. 1 slot since Thanksgiving, Jefferson Peewee A coach Denny Connelly would enjoy a reprieve from criticism. Not so. A high-profile team raises everyone's expectations. Parents want their son to play a high-profile role. "They don't think the third line's their place," said Denny, who manages a Kmart distribution center in his off time. "Their emotional attachment blinds their perspective."

You might notice parents in the stands working the stopwatches whenever Johnny begins and ends a shift. They complain their son isn't getting enough ice time. After shelling out big bucks, parents want their child to be able to play x amount of time with the value of x directly proportional to the parent's perception of their son's ability. Most find the value of x slightly greater than the value of y, which represents the actual amount of time their child is playing.

In West Bloomington, coaches like Connelly find themselves in the unfortunate position of having to explain the discrepant values of x and y to parents like the one who also happens to be the top scout for an NHL team. "He expects his kid to be as talented as he was." Denny shrugs. "It must be frustrating that he's not."

Last year, the parents of a Peewee B team petitioned Sats to remove the coach. They complained that he wasted precious practice time talking to the players about things he could've gone over in the dressing room. They criticized him for running simplistic drills the boys had done as Mites and Squirts instead of teaching systems. They accused him of playing lane hockey instead of the varsity's cycling game. They worried he wouldn't raise their sons' skills to the A level. In December, less than two months into the season, Sats gave him the hook.

———

Fast forward to the third Sunday of Lent, March 18, 2001, and a Blade Day rematch for the Peewee A state championship. This time, when Jefferson and Kennedy face off at Charles Schulz Highland Park Arena, they are playing for more than bragging rights around Bloomington; they are playing for the state title. A half hour before game time, the closest parking spot in the St. Paul neighborhood where the creator of the *Peanuts* strip grew up playing hockey is more than a block away on side streets, where a winter's worth of melting snow runs in rivers.

In the dawn of the 21st century, the Peewee A state tournament has become a small scale version of the high school tournament played the week before at the Xcel Energy Center down the road. Charles Schulz Arena fills quickly. Fans stand several deep in the landing above the bleachers. They include reporters, scouts, and both Bloomington high school coaches. Little girls have painted their faces with powder blue Jaguar paws. The players take their places on the blue line when their name is announced over the P.A. and stand at attention for the national anthem. The television cameras are replaced by parents with video cameras and Nikons outfitted with telephoto lenses. A fog horn blasts for each goal, just like at the Xcel. The most notable difference is that the parents are younger—they tote car seats with napping infants.

On their way into the rink, the players carry their jerseys in blue garment bags past a dancing Snoopy statue in the lobby. The pup's carefree, light-hearted jig seemed fitting upon first impression, given Schulz's boyhood love of the game. But scratch the surface and you see these twelve- and thirteen-year-olds are anything but carefree, skating under the watchful eyes of high school coaches calculating where the boys will fit into their plans. They are playing their sixty-third game of the year that day not just for a championship but to further their hockey careers. The mood feels Lenten.

Jefferson's Peewee As were the Booster's showcase team for the '01 season. They won the Blade Day matchup against Kennedy and every other time the two teams met, six total. The only game they lost all season was the Silver Stick Tournament final against a Littleton, Colorado, team coached by Kent Murphy, formerly a Jefferson Booster coach. Jefferson had been ranked Minnesota's top Peewee team since Thanksgiving, and nobody in the arena doubted that is where they would finish.

But Denny Connelly wanted to be sure. He had coached eight years but hadn't won a championship. If he could snag this one, he would make Jefferson one of only three programs in the state, along with Edina and Grand Rapids, to have won four Peewee A titles. This year's Peewee As, the best since Tommy Gilbert's Peewee team, had brought him within a game. That weekend Denny planned to play a card he had pulled out of Sats's sleeve. "One thing I've got over every other coach this weekend is tradition," Denny said the day before the final. "I can use that."

Right before they headed to the Charles Schulz Arena for Sunday's game, he showed his team the '94 Jaguars' highlight tape.

In the dressing room, Denny stands before the boys in his black Bauer Jefferson hockey jacket. "This is our last day together. It has been a memorable season, the thrill of a lifetime for me. Make sure it's the thrill of yours."

It works. The last strains of the national anthem still linger in the rafters when Jefferson scores. Barely thirty seconds elapse before Peter Mueller jams home a rebound. No surprise. Jefferson's leading scorer had already netted ninety goals that season. He would score a hat trick before the day was over.

A muscular twelve-year-old with streaked brown hair and a mischievous smile, Mueller is the best player on the ice. He is fast, strong, and physical. He has soft hands and 20/15 ice vision. He hustles and works hard—backchecking, digging in corners, and leading the breakout. He makes Sats smile.

Especially once he put on a Jefferson jersey. Until this season, Peter had worn a Chaska sweater. The folks back there are still sore the kid skipped town.

Peter Mueller wasn't the first hockey player to move into Bloomington. The Jefferson tradition was padded with relocated kids. Randy Koeppl, goalie on the '93 state champions, came from Minnetonka as an eighth-grade Bantam. Chris Hanson, '96, had moved all the way from Grand Rapids. Ben Clymer's parents wanted to buy a house in Hopkins, but the eleven-year-old vetoed the move and insisted on West Bloomington for its hockey. Ian and Toby Petersen immigrated from Mound as Peewees and Squirts respectively. Goaltender Jeremy Earl moved from the Kennedy Booster to the Jefferson Booster his first year of Bantams, one of many players to move on up from the East side.

Some who didn't move claimed they had. District officials had not caught any kids lying about their age the way Little League officials kept busy, but they had busted parents for fudging their addresses to get their son onto a Jefferson team. The Booster program, feeder for Jefferson's varsity, attracted families to West Bloomington like a magnet school. "Let's face it," said Bob Lange, a past Booster president. "Nobody moves to Bloomington because they sweep their streets cleaner—it's for the amenities." Namely, hockey.

Peter Mueller wasn't the only Peewee new to West Bloomington that season. But Peter's situation was sticky because the Mueller family hadn't actually moved when the season started.

Under the rules of Minnesota Hockey, governing body of the state's youth hockey associations, kids have to be a resident of the area where they play. When Denny was picking his team in October, the Muellers still lived within Chaska boundaries. They had signed a purchase agreement on a West Bloomington house with a December 20 closing date, but for Peter to be eligible for the Jefferson roster sooner, the Chaska Youth Hockey Association had to waive rights to him. That meant saying good-bye to the boy who, in his first year as a Peewee, had scored 110 goals for Chaska's A team. Some suspected the family was simply trying to upgrade their son's hockey team with no actual intention of moving. Chaska wasn't home to a proud hockey tradition, but Chaskans still had their pride.

There is a December 31 deadline beyond which teams cannot make roster changes. Chaska feared losing Peter even if the house deal fell apart. Should Chaska give its blessing, he feasibly could play the season for Jefferson without ever moving. The Chaska Association president wanted to place a contingency on the house purchase: if it didn't go through, Peter would quit playing at the end of December. Randy Mueller, Peter's dad, took the matter over their heads to the Minnesota Hockey District 6 director, who approved Peter's Jefferson eligibility.

The situation rubbed even some Jefferson parents the wrong way. As always, when an A-caliber kid moved in, he bumped another boy down to the B team, who in turn bumped yet another boy off the B team. In Peter's case, he also took away coveted powerplay and penalty kill time from skilled A players. The parents gave Denny an earful. "Do the names Toby Petersen and Ben Clymer sound familiar?" he shot back. "They both moved in, yet their names are synonymous with Jefferson hockey. We're not going to lock our doors at this level."

Meanwhile, Chaskans were hopping mad. Chaska is a small town with suburban aspirations. No doubt, there were those who begrudged the bigger, better suburb for plucking its rising star. But the resentments ran personal as well. Randy Mueller, Peter's father, had been heavily involved in the Chaska hockey program, lending a hand to the community's construction of a new rink. They felt he had betrayed them.

Those hard feelings spilled onto the ice when the Jefferson Peewees played Chaska. Randy heard adults on the Chaska side yelling, "Take Peter out!" and, "Get Mueller." The rough play claimed casualties on both sides. But that didn't faze Denny. An unseen intensity smolders beneath his drooping brown moustache and soft eyes. In his pregame speeches, he exhorts his "warriors" to do "battle." After his team won the violent Chaska game, he said, "I loved it."

Meanwhile, back at the state final, Jefferson is slapping Kennedy silly. Peter scores his second goal of the game. The father of another boy whose future Jefferson varsity career seems secure remarks, "That sure was a nice Christmas present to have him move in."

By the time Peter completes his hat trick, there's 2:30 left. Jefferson is up 12–0. The Kennedy kids skate hard until the end, but they are hopelessly outclassed. As the final twenty seconds tick off, the Jefferson fans rise to their feet and applaud. The first sticks and gloves fly skyward before the final buzzer, and the boys bury their goaltender in the traditional, happy hog pile.

They sort themselves out to receive their individual medals and dump a water bottle on their coach. With the backwash from a blue Powerade bottle, they baptize Denny into the elite legion of Booster coaches who have garnered state titles. When he started this odyssey over six months ago, wanting this moment kept him going. The hundreds of hours he had logged on the ice, in the dressing room, and behind the bench; the countless more he had scouted each team they played; the road trips and tournaments; the sessions with Sats, seeking advice and direction; even the complaints he had endured—all that distilled to this moment on the ice with these boys and the water trickling into his shorts and the medals wrapped around their necks. "This feels fantastic," he says, his breath visible in the frosty air. "We're the only team that set our goals this high that reached them."

When the Jefferson captains are summoned to collect the first place trophy, the entire team lunges as a group for the hardware. Giddy with the moment, they all want to lay their hands on it, like the faithful clambering to touch a saint's relic. The rock band Queen belts out the universal winner's anthem over the arena loudspeakers: *We are the champions, my friend.* The Jefferson boys skate over to the stands with their prize borne aloft for their parents to photograph. The Peewee A champions will have their picture published in the *Bloomington Sun Current* and *Let's Play Hockey* alongside articles detailing their accomplishment. *We are the champions, we are the champions.* Elsewhere on the ice, the Kennedy players, seventeen boys who have yet to suffer their first pimple, stand in sweaty hockey equipment that's quickly chilling and watch the Jefferson revelry as helplessly as they did while the clock was still running. Their shoulders slump. *No time for losers, 'cause we are the champions.*

CHAPTER SEVEN

HOME FOR CHRISTMAS

Timm went home for Christmas. To Colorado.

His original plan had been to catch the late-night Saturday flight, December 23, after the Grand Rapids game he was scheduled to start, then return Christmas night in time for the Holiday Classic tournament the following day.

Merrelyn planned to fly home Monday, almost a week before Timm, to put the house in order. Timm's older brother, Matt, a senior at the University of Denver, stayed at the house where the boys had grown up. Merrelyn wanted to allow enough time to clean and decorate for the holiday.

When love soured, their plans changed.

The day after Timm's shutout against Chaska, he broke up with Larissa, his girlfriend of seven months. He had found the resolve to do so in a long talk with his mom the afternoon of the game. Since his father died, he and his mom had grown tight—even more so with just the two of them sharing the townhouse in Bloomington. He had been able to tell her what he couldn't tell anybody else. She was glad to listen, even late on a weekend night when Timm woke her up in a chatty mood after coming home. Tired as she might be, she happily propped herself up and welcomed the chance to connect with her son. She knew he missed his father as much as she missed her husband. She wanted to be there for Timm in every way Bradd couldn't. Fatigue seemed a small price to pay for the bond that developed between them.

Saturday afternoon, December 16, they talked for two hours. Timm told her everything that had gone wrong with Larissa. Initially Timm had been attracted to her strong personality and lean, muscular body. She had transferred to Jefferson to play hockey the same year Timm did—they had that in common. Things had gone well at first, but he thought she had become possessive. It seemed like she wanted to control his life. He felt suffocated. Merrelyn listened patiently. Having unloaded his heart, Timm felt like he had stripped off the 25 pound weight vest Sats sometimes had them wear in practice. That night he played a solid game.

But the breakup didn't go well. Timm tried to tell Larissa over the phone that they were finished, but she didn't believe him. He went over to her house to convince her he was serious. She became very upset.

Concerned, Merrelyn didn't want to leave Timm alone. If Sats was willing to switch the rotation to let Timm play Tuesday night against Eastview, she and Timm could fly out together on Wednesday. It meant Timm would miss the Grand Rapids game, but Sats might understand. She talked to him and explained the situation, adding that her father was sick. He'd had a series of heart trouble and his faulty valve was causing problems. Sats agreed, and she changed their tickets.

Merrelyn had helped Timm as best as she could but figured he needed a man to support him. She sent him to Sats, who was accustomed to guiding his players through personal issues. They talked. Sats encouraged him to lean on his teammates. He called in Nick and Duncs, told them their friend needed support. Timm was grateful for Sats's understanding.

That Monday afternoon, December 18, Bloomington snowplows worked overtime to clear six inches of fresh snow off the roads. At practice, Coach Thomas pulled Timm and Jeremy aside to explain the adjustment to the rotation. The pair would switch their starts, with Timm playing Tuesday against Eastview and Jeremy Saturday against Grand Rapids. Sats, meanwhile, told the team in the dressing room that Timm's grandfather back in Colorado was very sick. He also mentioned that Timm was having some trouble with his girlfriend, which wasn't news to them. He explained that Timm had arranged to go back to Colorado a little early and in the meantime needed their support.

While they practiced on the ice, Larissa showed up. They saw her standing behind the glass in the concessions area outside the rink. Standing and waiting. Timm saw her, too.

After practice, Larissa cornered Timm in the lobby. The two spoke in hushed tones. Timm leaned on his goalie stick. She brushed a tear from her cheek and pressed a note into his hand. The other guys watched out of the corner of their eyes while they waited for the bus, which seemed to take forever in arriving. She wasn't going to make it easy for him to say good-bye.

Before Tuesday night's game against Eastview, Timm was a wreck. After school he shaved, like he did every game day—all except the wisp of light brown whiskers on his chin. He ate the ribs and brisket at Famous Dave's Barbecue with his mother, their regular Tuesday ritual, but his stomach was in knots. His mind was scattered; his emotions strained. He finally settled down some at school before the game when he slipped on his headphones in the locker room and dressed. Metallica's head-banging sounds soothed him.

He took his regular spot on the bench before the board, front row, center, and chewed his gum—blue for Jefferson. He spun his blue wool cap on his hand while Sats talked. On the bus ride to the

Eastview rink, Timm sat alone behind the cheerleaders and stared straight ahead. During heads down, he prayed he would play well. He touched his forehead to his mask. The rituals provided some comfort, but his hands still shook. He worried that he would be too distracted to stay in the game.

Timm hit the ice with a couple of running strides, skated a hard lap, and kept that momentum. Early on, he made a nice save with his right leg pad on a shot from low in the slot. His teammates helped, spotting him to a 3–0 lead. Eastview scored late in the second period with less than two minutes remaining to draw within 3–1. The Lightning gained some momentum and pressured the Jags' goal, but Timm made two big stops in the next minute.

He gave his mother a scare in the second period when a blocked Jaguar shot bounced out to center ice, setting up a potential Lightning breakaway. "Oh my god," Merrelyn exclaimed. Opting for a line change, the Eastview forward rang the puck around the boards, and Timm scrabbled to cut it off. It was often a nervous proposition when Timm, a somewhat shaky stickhandler, left the net to play the puck. "No, Timmy, no," Merrelyn shouted. But he escaped without incident.

Timm shut down a breakaway in the third, and the game was theirs 6–2, behind Bernie's goal and two assists. The two goals Eastview did score came on slick passing plays that left Timm—or any goalie, for that matter—vulnerable. They hadn't been his fault. It helped that his mother was there in the stands rather than already back in Denver. And, thank god, Larissa didn't show up.

After the game, Coach Thomas slapped Timm on the shoulder and told him he had played well. Timm wasn't completely happy. He chided himself for giving up too many rebounds, but at least he had proven to himself he had the mental tenacity to play through the bewilderment of heartbreak.

The next day, he and his mom flew to Denver, home of Timm's beloved Colorado Avalanche and favorite player, Patrick Roy, the Avs's All-Star netminder. Another future hall-of-famer dominated sports-page headlines in the papers aboard the flight: Mario Lemieux had returned from his three-year retirement the day of the Eastview game. That excited Timm almost as much as his trip home. He would catch an Avs or University of Denver hockey game if he could that weekend. He looked forward to that and the chance to chill away from Larissa. It would be good to see Matt and Grandpa and the rest of the family. It would be good to be home.

————

Against Eastview, Timm hadn't been the only hockey import on the ice. Opposite him, a kid from California started in the Lightning net. After watching last year's Tournament, Orlando Alamano fell under the spell of Minnesota high school hockey. At seventeen, he bid adios to Fresno, his mother, younger brother, and a '72 Ford Maverick, and headed north to seek his hockey fortunes. Eastview coach Mike Gibbons arranged for the eleventh grade goaltender to stay with the parents of a Lightning hockey player who had graduated the prior year. Like Timm, Orlando planned to return home for Christmas, though for him that meant a reunion with his mother, who couldn't afford the trip to Minnesota.

Orlando had picked Eastview, a startup high school without a hockey tradition, with the help of Darin Olver. The two had played together on the same team in Fresno. When Olver's dad took a job coaching the Idaho Steelheads of the West Coast Hockey League, Darin knew he wouldn't further his own hockey future in Boise. John Olver contacted Gibbons, whom he had known from the minor league hockey circuit and thought had the potential to make something of the Lightning. Gibbons arranged for Darin, a fast-skating sophomore forward who could break open a game, to stay with the family of another Eastview forward.

Against Jefferson, Olver set up a goal, but Alamano struggled. Gibbons yanked him after the Jaguars' sixth goal. Still, Gibbons was glad to have the pair of transfers, who added depth to his young program. He welcomed the out-of-towners to Eastview.

Four years earlier, Gibbons and Sats had nearly come to blows when the Eastview coach accused the Jefferson legend of recruiting. They were in St. Cloud coaching at the annual USA Hockey Select summer camp. Following a night of drinking, the group of coaches wound up at Perkins in the early hours of the morning. Jefferson had just graduated a group of NHL-bound seniors, and talk turned to the Jaguars' future without the illustrious pack. "That's all right," Sats remembers Gibbons saying. "You'll just go out and recruit another group of talent."

That touched a raw nerve. "You don't know what the fuck you're talking about," Sats retorted. "Don't ever say that about our program. We'll win or lose with our kids."

That was a point of pride with Sats. His Booster program was so good, he didn't have to recruit. If the kids moved in, it was before high school, anyway. Once they were there, they were his kids, and he didn't think it right to displace them for a high school transfer.

Gibbons backed down.

Sats had stuck with his own kids until Timm showed up, even though it meant displacing Brett Shelanski.

———

When his parents divorced, eight-year-old Brett and his mother moved to Bloomington from Binghamton, New York, where his dad did play-by-play for the local American Hockey League team. Already a hockey fan, Brett immediately adopted the Jefferson dream after watching the Jaguars win the first state tournament he ever saw in '94. He hadn't made the Booster A teams, but played j.v. as a freshman and dressed for varsity games as a sophomore. By his junior year, Brett expected to split the goaltending duties with Jeremy Earl. Then he heard about some kid from Colorado moving in. He couldn't believe it. He didn't think it was fair. "Colorado" hadn't grown up in the Booster program. He hadn't worn the Jaguars jersey. Junior year, Brett wound up back on j.v. He felt shortchanged of the chance he deserved.

Sats didn't think it was fair, either. Although he frequently received calls from parents wanting to move into the area or have their kid open-enroll at Jefferson to play hockey there, he routinely discouraged them. He told one father who had already made a down payment on a house in West Bloomington that his kid wouldn't play for Jefferson. The family forfeited its escrow money and bought a house in another district.

Sats had been burned once before. In 1981, Adam Glickman of Skokie, Illinois, had moved in with a Bloomington host family to play at Jefferson. Sats had met Glickman five years earlier at a hockey school he ran with Herb Brooks. Adam's high school in Skokie didn't have a varsity hockey team. Brooks encouraged him to attend Jefferson. The sophomore defenseman made the varsity, bumping a Bloomington native down to j.v. That boy's mother called the state high school league to complain. The MSHSL investigated and discovered that the Jefferson principal had failed to apply for a waiver required by league policy. Midseason, the high school league ruled Glickman ineligible and converted Jefferson's six wins with him to forfeits. Adam returned home to Skokie. Even though Jefferson won the state tournament, the Glickman affair tainted the season. "I learned my lesson," Sats said.

"Never again," he said. With one brief exception in 1986—the year after Sats had graduated fifteen seniors—he had stood firm on his no-transfer policy. Until he met Timm Lorenz. Sats knew his team was weak in goal the year Timm wanted to transfer. He didn't discourage him. The kid came with an impressive résumé: four consecutive Colorado state championships and a glowing recommendation from Steve Duncan (Timm's outstanding play in a Bantam A Thanksgiving tournament had beaten Duncs's team). Sats told people Timm's mom was from Bloomington, that her parents still lived in the area. He said Timm's dad told Sats if he ever needed a goalie, let him know; they would move there. Then, when Bradd died, Merrelyn naturally decided to move back home. That was the spin Sats put on it, anyway, when Timm became the first kid in almost fifteen years to play varsity without coming up through the ranks.

Merrelyn, in fact, grew up in Colorado. Her parents had grown up in the Rocky Mountain state, and so had their parents before them. She was a third-generation Coloradan.

When Sats welcomed Timm, a fourth-generation Coloradan, to Jefferson, that put Shelanski out in the cold. As a concession to Brett, Sats offered him the chance to play j.v. and letter since he was a senior. He could also come along to the Xcel Center. He wouldn't dress for Tournament games, but he could stay in the hotel and take part in the festivities. Brett considered playing Junior Gold instead. It was a buzz kill as a senior not to skate varsity. "That's why you play—to make it to that level," he said during tryouts. After thinking it over, he decided to play j.v. to keep alive his varsity hopes in case either Timm or Jeremy got injured or suspended for some reason. "It was the better move for my career," he said.

———————

After hearing her son Matt's initial tales about Minnesota high school hockey, Merrelyn had learned more about the state's hockey scene from fathers of teams Timm played against in regional and national tournaments. She got to know Steve Duncan and found out that Jefferson was short on goalies. Timm's sophomore year, mother and son went to Minnesota on a fact-finding trip. They visited several schools with reputable hockey programs and attended a couple of high school games, which were every bit as exciting as Matt had described. That sold them. Merrelyn couldn't give Timm his dad back, but she could give him hockey. They just had to pick a school.

Timm and his mom narrowed the decision down to two schools, Jefferson and the Academy of Holy Angels, the Catholic high school coached by former Jefferson Booster coach Greg Trebil. Timm had learned about the school from another Littleton kid who had moved to Minnesota to play hockey there. Coach Trebil took Timm and a few other kids interested in Holy Angels to lunch. Timm liked him and was impressed by his success. That year, his team beat Jefferson in the section final to play in its first state tournament. But as a Lutheran, Timm didn't feel comfortable when he toured the Catholic school, with its crucifixes on the walls and nuns at the blackboard. "It was like walking into a church," he said. "It was creepy."

He felt more at home in Thomas Jefferson High, which reminded him of his high school in Littleton, the rival to Columbine High. The single-story modern brick schoolhouse, opened in 1970, had a carpeted main hallway lined with eighteen flags representing the countries of foreign exchange students the school had hosted. But Jefferson was unmistakably suburban. A student passing two others speaking Russian in the hallway admonished them, "Speak English." The administration didn't allow students to wear caps in the building—an issue students had protested with a walkout that year—but didn't seem otherwise unduly harsh. They didn't have to wear uniforms like at Holy Angels. Jefferson students dressed casually in name-brand clothes—during passing time, a slow-moving stream of logoed sweat-shirts and labeled jeans flowed through the hallways. They were Abercrombie kids without seeming stuck up. Classrooms had a laid-back air. During study halls, kids listened to music on headphones or napped at their desks. They carried cell phones in their backpacks, which were supposed to be turned off but occasionally rang during class, annoying teachers and amusing students. Hockey players were easy to spot: the kids in gray hooded Jaguars sweatshirts with their number on the shoulder getting the most nods walking down the hallway. Between the lunchroom and the gymnasium, there was a dis-play case filled with wooden state championship trophies, thirty-six from girls' basketball to boys' gymnastics. The five hockey trophies—more than any other sport claimed—lined the top shelf.

Timm met Coach Saterdalen briefly. He was low-key, didn't make any promises. In fact, Sats seemed indifferent whether Timm moved to Minnesota or chose to play at his school. Based on first impres-sions, Timm liked Trebil better than Saterdalen. What tipped the scales in favor of Jefferson was that Holy Angels had a goaltender who would be a senior next year and probably play ahead of Timm. The nets at Jefferson, on the other hand, were relatively wide open, waiting for him to stake his claim.

After Timm's first season, Merrelyn renewed the lease on their Bloomington townhouse for another year. They would stay through graduation and the open house parties. Then Merrelyn would move back to Littleton, and Timm would wind up playing wherever he could land an offer.

———

Back in Colorado, Timm was glad to have some time with Grandpa. It was also good to hang out with his old friends, though they still couldn't understand what it was like to play high school hockey in Minnesota without having experienced it for themselves.

He celebrated Christmas with his family. The relatives came over to the house Christmas Eve. Timm got a University of Maine baseball cap, which was almost a perfect Jefferson blue. His mom gave him some cash. He also got some shirts, sweaters, and other warm clothing he desperately needed, having moved to Minnesota without the right winter wardrobe. But he felt a palpable absence. Christmas had been his dad's favorite holiday.

On the flat, windswept prairies of Minnesota, Timm missed the mountains that defined Colorado. He missed UD hockey. He missed his dog, Tiffany. Most of all, he missed his dad. Back home, he missed him even more.

When Timm got home, he went to see him. He headed out to the cemetery, down the long drive lined with American flags snapping in the winter breeze. He parked and walked to his father's bare tombstone: Bradd Lorenz, 1948–1996. He stood there, alone in the flat cemetery that seemed as big as Denver itself, sprawling across the open acres with the mountains looking down on him. And he talked to his dad.

We beat Elk River this year. There. You should've seen it. The rink was crammed. They were on me from the start. But I shut 'em down. You would've loved it.

Saturday, I shut out Chaska. I'm 4–0, have a 1.50 goals against.

We've lost only one. We're tight. Tighter than last year. I think we can go all the way.

He talked and kept talking through the tears. He wanted him to know.

————

Timm flew back to Minnesota Christmas night in time for the Holiday Classic to begin the next day. He hadn't told his dad about Larissa. Hadn't wanted to trouble him. For six days Timm hadn't talked to her. In Colorado he had been able to breathe again. When he returned to the townhouse in Bloomington, he found the earrings he had bought her for Christmas still on top of his dresser, right where he left them.

CHAPTER EIGHT

FALLEN ANGEL

Art thou that traitor Angel? art thou he,
Who first broke peace in Heaven and faith…
—*Paradise Lost*, Book II: 689-90

There. See the handshake? That says it all.

Stop time. Rewind the tape of last year's section 5AA final. In front of the Jefferson net, Bernie intercepts a pass and clears the zone to finish off the clock and the Academy of Holy Angels. The Jaguars celebrate, the Stars slump. The coaches meet. Sats the victor, Trebil the loser. The roles reversed from the year before when Trebil went to the

Tournament, and Sats went home. The two coaches meet on the ice in their street shoes, between the players, in front of the empty benches.

There it is. Trebil squeezes Sats's hand. His expression strained. He looks beyond Sats, avoids his eyes. Sats turns away, avoids Trebil's eyes. It's quick, over in an instant, but in that moment you can count the years of love lost between these two.

As the Jefferson Bantam A coach for nine years, Greg Trebil was Sats's top lieutenant. He put the final shine on the Jefferson talent before it stepped up to the varsity. Including four years coaching Squirts and Peewees, Trebil established a 538–73–30 overall record in the Jefferson Booster program. He sent three sons Sats's way; all three won state championships. On the '89 highlight video, after his oldest boy, Greg Jr., won the title, Greg Sr. blurts, "This is the greatest thing I've gone through in my life."

Fast forward to '94, after his third son, Ryan, had been part of the Jaguars' third straight championship, Trebil smiles into the camera. "This is what Jefferson is about: you see people putting their arms around each other, a lot of sharing and caring," the proud father and coach gushes. "Any program that does that is going to be successful."

Then Sats fills the screen. "I'm very happy for Greg Trebil—he has coached all these kids, had three boys win titles—what a dad who deserves that for all the time he's put in coaching these kids."

Two years later, the warm fuzzies hardened into cold pricklies. Trebil jumped ship. He took the head coaching job at the Academy of Holy Angels in Richfield, the suburb next door. You couldn't blame him for wanting to coach at the next level, especially with his boys all graduated. But the *way* he left caused his fall from grace.

Four hockey standouts who had come through the Jefferson Booster program with Trebil defected to Holy Angels during Trebil's first year. Sats suspected Trebil lured them away. He couldn't forgive that trespass against his program.

Sats's son Jeff, who played at Jefferson with Greg Jr., summed up the Saterdalen sentiment against Greg Sr.: "He wept tears of joy for this program three times but showed no loyalty."

It had been an ugly parting, yet something about Trebil burned even deeper in Sats's belly. Sats hadn't won a state championship since Trebil left. When someone suggested Sats owed his success to Trebil, Sats seethed. That threw gasoline on his burning desire to win another title before he retired. With both Jefferson and Holy Angels off to a strong start in '01, they looked headed toward another section final showdown, the rubber game of the coaches' grudge match.

On Channel 14's broadcast of last year's section final, Jeff Saterdalen provided the color commentary. Since he graduated from Jefferson in '88, the landscape of high school hockey had shifted. Two of Holy Angels's skaters in the final came from Jefferson's system. "What made high school hockey so much fun was that we went to school together and played together since Squirts," Jeff said on the air. "That's something we're losing in high school hockey because of teams like Holy Angels and Hill-Murray, even USA Hockey, coming in and taking kids away."

High school hockey players have become free agents. Under the state's permissive open enrollment and transfer laws, they can attend the school of their choice, which means a high profile hockey program that will give them a shot at playing in the Tournament and at getting the exposure needed to land a coveted college scholarship. Though outright recruiting is taboo under league rules, some coaches manage to wind up with a strong new crop each season.

Trebil is one of those. He makes no secret of the fact that he relies on transfer students to keep the quality of his hockey program high. But in 2000–2001, the steady stream of talented hockey players—including seniors—transferring to Holy Angels triggered the MSHSL's most ambitious investigation of possible recruiting violations.

Before the '01 season, Rob Rankin was up for grabs. The gifted goal-scorer didn't want to languish away his senior year at Eagan, where boys' hockey was synonymous with losing. He wanted to showcase his skills in a respectable program, like Trebil's at Holy Angels. Rankin had applied to the school but had not yet been accepted. That summer, the center attended the Stars summer hockey camp Trebil conducted.

After watching Rankin strut his stuff in the summer camp along with two other top prospects, Trebil initiated a meeting with the Holy Angels administration—Gary Rufsvold, athletic director; Jesse Foley, admissions director; and Jill Reilly, president/principal—on July 7, 2000, to lobby on behalf of hockey transfers seeking admission to Holy Angels. Two weeks earlier, he had phoned Reilly to remind her that he needed top-notch transfers to maintain a quality AA program. She remembers Trebil told her he hoped those transfers would be granted admission, because he did not want to coach at the A level, which he considered inferior. Everyone at the July 7 meeting except Trebil recalled the coach reiterating this position. The implied threat was that he would quit if the administration didn't comply. The MSHSL investigator concluded his report, "There is no doubt that Mr. Trebil pressured the administration in this matter."

The Holy Angels administration had plenty of reasons to deny Trebil's request to admit Rankin. For starters, the school already had reached capacity at 775 students. There were an additional thirty-plus qualified applicants on a waiting list. What's more, the board had established a policy against senior transfers, recently clarified by the curriculum committee after two senior hockey players had been granted exceptions—one each in the previous two school years. If the administration buckled, Rankin would be the third senior hockey player admitted in three years.

Rufsvold, the athletic director, warned that senior transfers gave the school a bad name among other coaches—like Sats—who viewed Holy Angels as crooks plundering their talent. That image was not the initial intention of the Sisters of St. Joseph who founded the school in 1877.

Maybe Rankin applied to the Academy of Holy Angels because it had been named a Blue Ribbon School of Excellence, which appealed to him as a strong student, but his reputation as a hockey player exceeded his academic strengths, and his interest in Holy Angels would no doubt be perceived as being for its big time hockey program. Admitting him under the circumstances would certainly give the appearance that he was a hockey transfer, not just another incoming student.

That wouldn't sit well within the Holy Angels community. Some parents paid the $6,250 annual tuition to buy their child a spot on the varsity that he wouldn't win otherwise at a larger school like Jefferson or Edina. They didn't want their child's chances eliminated by a last-minute transfer. In April, the admissions department had already admitted two hockey players out of five total students granted admission at the time, including a sophomore heralded as one of the state's finest up-and-coming defensemen. Even without admitting Rankin, the administration had opened itself up to criticism from the parents whose children would be bumped.

The Holy Angels administration had plenty of solid ground upon which it could turn down Trebil's request.

But it didn't. Rankin was in.

Reilly, the president/principal, allowed that the 775 limit could go as high as 780 and agreed to make room for one senior admission. The senior-transfer policy afforded a loophole "for students who bring unique abilities to the Holy Angels community." Foley, the admissions director, claimed Rankin "by virtue of his impeccable academic and behavior record and *his hockey ability* [emphasis added] certainly was a fine candidate for such an exception."

When others learned about the administration's decision, all hell broke loose at Holy Angels.

Ed Cole sent his son to Holy Angels to play hockey for Greg Trebil. Cole, who had coached youth hockey, knew Trebil by his reputation in the Jefferson Booster program and as a Team Minnesota coach. Trebil convinced Cole to forego his son Andrew's second year of Bantams in Eden Prairie to play j.v. at Holy Angels his freshman year. That was the year the Stars made it to State, and Trebil picked Andrew for the twenty-man Tournament team. But over the next two years, Cole saw the influx of transfer hockey players squeeze his son's varsity ice time. Cole felt betrayed. "The mistake we made was that we put our trust in you," he wrote Trebil during Andrew's junior hockey season, when Andrew came home from games in tears and talked of quitting.

"We thought you'd develop our son. We NEVER thought you'd bring in junior and senior transfers."

When Cole, also an assistant football coach at Holy Angels, caught wind of the hockey transfers admitted prior to the '01 season, including two prize defensemen—the position his son played—he went over the edge. The week after the July 7 meeting, he wrote a letter to the MSHSL that accused Trebil of recruiting players.

Four years earlier when Sats had complained about Trebil siphoning Jefferson players, Skip Peltier, MSHSL associate director, had checked into the claim with a call to Trebil but decided there were not sufficient grounds for further inquiry by the league. The widespread school-swapping had been a burr under Peltier's saddle ever since a 1988 state law made open enrollment and transferring legal.

"Recruiting is a concern," he said one morning in a conference room at the MSHSL office in Brooklyn Center. "But transferring for athletic reasons is nearly impossible to detect."

When Cole's letter crossed his desk, however, Peltier seemed to have a bona fide case. This time the MSHSL launched its most extensive investigation to date to discover whether Trebil had violated bylaw 308, which forbids asserting undue influence in soliciting transfers. "We wanted to put all schools on notice that we take these allegations seriously," said Peltier, who had won the '63 title for St. Paul Johnson with kids from his neighborhood.

An attorney argued on Trebil's behalf that the coach shouldn't be reproached for his passion to win. "It would be a shame if a man who has devoted a life (mostly as a volunteer) to coaching and helping young people become very successful hockey players would suffer any material consequences or humiliation if his only shortcoming here was a greater than reasonable influence or pressure relative to achievement in a sport," the attorney wrote to the independent investigator hired by the MSHSL.

The following summer, over a piece of banana cream pie, Trebil maintained his innocence. His wide lips and brooding eyebrows slouched into a frown. "A lot of what you see these days is kids have more choices than they used to, and they're exercising those choices," he said. "I don't in my heart believe I did anything wrong."

He refused to discuss the recruiting issue further.

The Holy Angels administration refused to answer any questions. After president Jill Reilly received three voicemail messages throughout the course of a week requesting her version of events, she turned the matter over to the school's outside legal counsel. The attorney warned the curious caller to back off.

But Ed Cole was eager to talk and fill any ear turned his way. An impulsive and emotional parent, he didn't like the way his son was being treated. He had talked to Rufsvold, the athletic director, and he had talked to Trebil, the coach, but he had gotten nowhere. So he went to the league. Rufsvold, Cole alleges, told him his son would have a hard time making the team senior year if he didn't drop the matter.

Andrew Cole didn't think Trebil was treating him fairly. Andrew thought since he had played football and hadn't skated in the fall captains' practices, his hockey coach had pushed him aside. It hurt Ed Cole to see his son benched.

Andrew didn't play hockey his senior year. After the 6'5", 205-pound defenseman pocketed a football scholarship to the Naval Academy, he decided not to go out for hockey. He joined a small but growing fraternity of frustrated Holy Angels hockey players who had quit during the Trebil years.

Cole could accept his son's decision to cancel another season of misery, but what really boiled his blood was that all this was happening at a Catholic school. Winning hockey games, it seemed to Cole, had superseded the Catholic school's mission to educate and nurture students in a spiritual environment.

It's a given that Catholic schools—like all private schools—must recruit students. Lacking the natural resources of public schools, which fill up *de facto* with the students living in their district, private schools must appeal to students—and their parents—to choose them. Whether they like it or not, they are caught up in a competitive marketplace and must attract customers to stay in business. "People say Holy Angels is recruiting, but so is every other private school," said one suburban Catholic high school's former admissions director. "Coaches tell kids or parents or alumni to talk to kids about transferring all the time. But if you're just bringing in kids to prostitute them for their athletic ability, that's crossing the line."

————

Meanwhile, Holy Angels' Catholic rival across the suburbs, Benilde–St. Margaret's, erected a large cross atop an addition financed by a thirteen million dollar capital campaign. That cross was the lightning rod for the controversy sparked by the BSM boys hockey team. Some of those who had contributed handsomely to the renovation believed the administration had lost sight of what the cross stood for.

Five years previous, BSM president Jim Hamburge convinced the board to commit to athletic excellence and success to stay competitive in the marketplace. "The board approved the philosophy critical in helping the school achieve enrollment stability and growth as well as financial stability and growth," Hamburge explained.

The strategy worked. The school hired a full-time athletic director, and its teams went from embarrassing cellar-dwellers to proud state champions over the next five years, garnering nine titles in several sports and activities, including two in hockey. Enrollment jumped ten percent, and the school ran a waiting list. BSM was able to parlay that success into the ambitious capital campaign.

The commitment to athletic excellence and success boosted the school's sagging image, as evidenced by the hockey program's slick twenty-eight-page yearbook. Transfers played a key role in serving the school's broader purpose of attracting more students. Therein lay the rub.

The '01 varsity hockey team rostered six players who hadn't attended BSM the prior year. Two of those were true freshmen, one was a repeat freshman, two were sophomores, and one was a junior. Not all were Catholic. One of the sophomores came from another state and lived with the team manager's family for half of the season. That sophomore had been on the school's waiting list for two years because his grades hadn't met the admissions criteria. When he was finally admitted—ahead of students with better academic creden-tials—critics claimed his hockey skills earned him preferential treat-ment. "Did he get in because of hockey? Of course he did," said BSM hockey coach Ken Pauly. "But, at the same time, he had brought up his grades."

Parents shelling out the full $6,600 annual tuition themselves were upset when there wasn't room on the team for their sons, who had to compete not just against each other but against stars from around the metro area for a spot. A small but powerful group charged that the ninety-three-year-old Benedictine school of 810 students had become a sports factory at the expense of Catholic education.

In the twenty-one years Hamburge had been at BSM as an administrator and its president, the percent of non-Catholic stu-dents had tripled. Non-Catholic athletes had been admitted ahead of students from Catholic grade schools who had traditionally been given priority. The hockey team had a slightly higher percentage of non-Catholics than the overall student body. Hamburge admitted that athletes were sometimes granted admission primarily because they were athletes, just as minorities were sometimes given preferen-tial consideration to promote diversity. "There will always be excep-tions, and someone has to make those decisions," he said.

But the parents took exception to that where hockey players were concerned. The practice put the high school on the college level, where institutional survival and market position supplanted aca-demic standards and personal formation. "You're hiring a student to perform a function for your own end," said Paul Pattee, M.D., whose son was cut as a junior that season. "The school would say, 'We're giving these kids a chance to turn around,' but I take issue with that. They're brought in as hired guns—they don't have the commitment to academics."

In January of the '01 season, Pattee drafted and presented a peti-tion (signed by a dozen sets of parents) to the school's board. The petition complained about the "large influx of young, skilled role players" on the hockey team and challenged BSM leadership "to prove that recruitment *doesn't* exist."

The board heard them out but didn't budge. It denied any recruiting violations. The MSHSL never investigated.

Hamburge saw the parents' frustration as a natural consequence of the school's commitment to athletic success, which meant not every student who wanted to could play varsity. "In a state where hockey is not only a sport but a religion, it becomes more difficult for parents to accept something as traumatic as getting cut from a team," he said.

———————

Back at Holy Angels, one Catholic parent grieving his son's lost chance to play varsity took matters into his own hands.

Kevin Kranz, whose sons had come up through the Jefferson Booster program, had a history with Greg Trebil. Several years back, when a Grand Rapids boy showed up at Bantam tryouts, Kranz's wife, Kathy, then the Booster registrar, called the District 6 director to see if the boy from out of town was eligible. At a crowded booster club meeting, Trebil, then the Bantam coach, criticized her for doing so. But when the Kranzes enrolled their oldest boy, Kelly, as a freshman at Holy Angels, Coach Trebil assured them bygones would be bygones.

That pleased Kevin and Kathy. Their son Kelly had learning difficulties. They liked that a smaller Catholic school could offer him more personal attention. They also figured his chances of making the varsity were better at Holy Angels than at Jefferson, provided Trebil gave Kelly the chance he deserved. Junior year, he skated with the j.v., but senior year, Kelly got the phone call he dreaded.

Sunday afternoon, November 19, 2000, Trebil, who didn't teach at the school, called the Kranz boy from his office at Minuteman Press, the print shop Trebil owned on Bloomington's East Side. Trebil told Kelly he hadn't made the team. It was a numbers game.

Kelly hung up, dejected. His father Kevin was incensed. A month ago he had seen his younger son displaced from the Jefferson Peewee A team when two kids moved in, one of them uncannily like the Grand Rapids boy whose family had signed a purchase agreement but hadn't yet moved into the area. Now transfers had bumped Kelly. *A numbers game? Kelly had done everything Trebil had asked. He'd played more physical. He'd competed in Canada. He'd grown five inches and put on twenty-five pounds. But now that Trebil had gotten his recruits, Kelly was expendable. That was his numbers game. Trebil hadn't been truthful. He had strung Kelly along. He only cared about what was best for him. Whatever would let him win.*

Fifteen minutes after Kelly hung up, Kevin pounded on the door of Trebil's shop. "Open up! I want to talk to you!"

Trebil was discussing the final cuts with his assistant Guy Olson. "Hang on a minute." He laid the phone down and unlocked the front door.

According to the police report, Kranz pushed his way into the shop and started screaming, "You fucking cocksucker! You destroyed my family, my whole family!"

Over the open phone line, Olson could hear "thumping or hitting sounds."

Trebil explained those sounds thus: the 6'2", 245-pound Kranz tried to kick the coach in the groin but missed. Instead, Kranz's heavy boot connected several times on Trebil's left thigh and knee. Trebil later showed police the bruises. "I tried to defend myself without aggressively fighting back because I did not want to escalate the situation," reported Trebil, who is about six-foot-four-inches, 235 pounds.

Kranz took a wild swing at Trebil's head. "I'm gonna rip your head off and shit in the hole!"

The altercation lasted less than five minutes. Kranz left, and Trebil called the police, who tracked down Kranz at BIG. In Kranz's version, he confronted Trebil, demanding, "Can you quantify what a numbers game is?"

Trebil stared at the floor without answering.

"I guess it means now that you made all of those kids promises and got all the kids you wanted to recruit, that's the numbers game."

Kranz claimed Trebil stuck his forearm into Kranz's chest and pushed him toward the door. Kranz tripped over his boots. He grabbed at Trebil and took the coach down with him. They wrestled. Kranz said Trebil kicked at him, and he kicked back out of self-defense, landing about three blows.

The city attorney charged the fifty-one-year-old Kranz with misdemeanor disorderly conduct and two counts of misdemeanor assault. He pled guilty to "intentionally inflicting or attempting to inflict bodily harm upon another." Meanwhile, Trebil filed for a mutual restraining order. The judge barred the two men from contacting each other in any way for two years.

———

Gossip about the fight quickly spread through the Jefferson hallways and around Billabong's barroom. Some suggested Kranz had a reputation for running off half-cocked, but others believed Trebil may have brought it upon himself this time. Sympathies ran divided.

In Bloomington, where Trebil still lived and worked, there were those who held him up as the cornerstone of Jefferson's success; others cursed him as a turncoat. Sats, for one, still nursed a grudge. When he lost those four players to Holy Angels during Trebil's rookie year, Sats feared an exodus of his custom-groomed talent. He made an impassioned speech to the Jefferson booster club about loyalty. "I talked about sticking together, the fact that if they stayed here they would know they'd always be trying out against Jefferson kids," Sats recalled after the '01 season. "If you go over there, you don't know. You could be a starter one year and a non-starter the next year because a new kid comes in, which is exactly what's happened every single year."

Sats delivered that speech the year before Timm Lorenz moved in and nudged Brett Shelanski out of the running for a varsity spot. The irony did not escape Sats's critics. "A coach's desire to win will usually take precedence over the loyalty speech," observed another coach who had also won a state title. "Tom Saterdalen has a singular purpose: Bloomington Jefferson hockey. Anything he proposes or pushes, that's first and foremost in his mind."

Sats had reason to be concerned. Holy Angels had targeted several of the up-and-coming players in his ranks. Three sophomores on his '01 varsity roster—Justin Wild, Ryan Van Bockel, and Brad Peterson—all received invitations from the Holy Angels captains to attend a Stars game and hang out with the players afterward at a pizza party when they were Bantams and such solicitation was legal. Peterson had also been invited to Trebil's summer hockey school, which he skated in before his first year of Bantams. After the pizza party, a Holy Angels player who had been Brad's buddy in Peewees stepped up his efforts to lure Peterson to his school. He had good reason: Peterson was the Jefferson Bantam A leading scorer, with 53 goals and 89 points.

Brad was flattered to be courted as an eighth- and ninth-grader for his hockey talents. So, too, were his parents. "It was heady to be wanted, to have people interested in you," his father Randy admitted. But, in the end, Brad indulged his dream to wear the Jaguars sweater.

Not so for his Bantam linemates. One jumped to Holy Angels. The other, Tyler Hirsch, a certain Division-I prospect, ended up at Shattuck–St. Mary's, a boarding school in southern Minnesota that played a lengthy junior season. All told, kids who had come of age in the Jefferson Booster program were playing at five other schools during the '01 season, including three at Holy Angels. Some defected knowing they wouldn't make the Jefferson varsity, but others, like Hirsch and Shattuck teammate Zach Parisé, could've played anywhere. Had Hirsch and Parisé, one of the nation's top college prospects, stayed at Jefferson, they would have made the '01 Jags invincible.

––––––––––

In 1988, Minnesota was the first state to pass an open enrollment law. Under the law—initially opposed by the MSHSL—student-athletes are free to choose the school they want to attend, private or public, regardless of whether or not they live within the school's boundaries; their host district must release them. By 2001, eighteen states and the District of Columbia had mandatory open enrollment laws similar to Minnesota's, and another fourteen states had voluntary open enrollment.

Although the NCAA requires transfers to sit out a year of athletic competition, the MSHSL grants transfers immediate eligibility at their new school provided they were eligible and in good standing at their old school. (Under growing pressure, the MSHSL did pass a rule in 2002 that requires athletes switching schools a second time to sit out half of the varsity season.) There are seventeen different ways for kids to transfer schools, with open enrollment and interdistrict transfer the most popular. In the mid-1990s, two legislators tried to stem the flow of athletes by requiring transfers to sit out two years, but their bill was killed in committee.

Although Minnesota's open enrollment law was originally intended to raise academic standards and grant parents choices for their children's education, athletes in all sports were quick to exploit the law's possibilities. The most prominent transfers occurred in hockey, where kids struck out for the public or private school program most likely to advance their careers. "We've created an environment like Texas football or Indiana basketball where there is the hope that if you play in the right program, you can get a scholarship," Peltier said. "Read *Let's Play Hockey* and you see a list of players from Minnesota who are playing Division I. Parents read that and say, 'Okay, if we're going to get there, we have to find the right program.'"

Some parents obviously thought Elk River the right program in '01. When Jefferson played Elk River in early December, the Elks' starting goalie was one of three players from Buffalo, a nearby outlying community, to open enroll at Elk River that season. The Elks also had attracted Darin Ciavarella from North Dakota. The joke among coaches was that anything north of Maple Grove and south of Brainerd—basically, a one hundred–mile territory—belonged to Elk River. But the Elks' coach, Tony Sarsland, claimed to have affidavits signed by the three Buffalo transfers stating they weren't recruited.

Sarsland's claims didn't assuage one jilted parent's anger. Sats came into the dressing room after warmups and told his Jaguars to shoot high. He said the father of the senior goalie cut a month earlier had tipped him off that the Buffalo transfer goalie went down easily and often, leaving him vulnerable up high.

Across the metro area, Eastview became a sort of hockey hostel for players willing to abandon their families elsewhere and live with host families. Eastview was a spinoff of Apple Valley High, less than five miles away on the West Side. This year's Eastview seniors would be the first graduating class to have gone the whole way through the four-year-old technology showcase where students gave Power Point presentations on topics ranging from Jack London to strep throat. Too young yet to have forged an identity for itself in hockey or otherwise, Eastview was best known as the location where *Sugar & Spice*, the teen flick about cheerleaders turned bank robbers, was filmed. For the '01 season, Orlando Alamano and Darin Olver called Eastview home. The next year, three more hockey carpetbaggers—a pair of brothers who had played with Alamano in Fresno and one of Olver's buddies from Oregon—would show up, ready to step into the expansion team's varsity lineup.

Parents of displaced players grumbled there must be some sort of pipeline leading to Eastview with the coach at the switch. Other residents didn't want to be funding varsity programs for outsiders, especially when they took away the spots of local kids whose families paid taxes. Together, they urged an investigation.

In the fall of 2001, Independent School District 196 completed an internal inquiry that found Alamano and Olver hadn't established sufficient legal guardianship in Eastview. That rendered them ineligible for varsity competition for the first ninety days of the school year. The Lightning forfeited its first seven wins and a tie for the '01 season. The ruling didn't change its post-season results. The inquiry—prompted by the MSHSL—found the Eastview coach in violation for helping the players find housing but didn't turn up any evidence of explicit recruiting.

The district also set forth a new rule that extended the MSHSL's ninety-day waiting period to a full year that out-of-district transfers must sit out if they didn't meet the full eligibility requirements. That sent the second wave of carpetbaggers packing.

Eastview coach Mike Gibbons blamed the MSHSL. A college recruiter for fourteen years at Colorado College and University of Denver, Gibbons wanted the MSHSL to spell out the transfer rules as clearly as the NCAA. "The high school league has to get its act together and make it very black and white what can and can't be done," he said. "The high school league makes it so easy for kids to transfer, but then they try to clamp down—it doesn't make sense."

Affidavits and protests of innocence notwithstanding, it's hard to believe that the transfers aren't getting some encouragement from the coaches who stand to prosper from their interest. "If coaches ever say, 'Hey, [transfers] just show up'; they're lying," said one private school hockey coach. "When the kid calls, you can either encourage or discourage that."

Despite the frequency and openness with which athletes transferred schools, the MSHSL pleaded it was powerless to sanction the free-agency lunacy. "If done for sports, we don't want it happening," said MSHSL executive director Dave Stead during the '01 season. "But there's no way to stop it because state law allows kids to transfer. We could deny eligibility and the student would go to court. The court would issue a temporary restraining order (allowing the athlete to continue to play). Then it would be moot when it was all over because the kid achieved what he wanted to."

At least one Lake Conference athletic director, who claimed kids cheated and lied all the time to transfer from one school to another, was more cynical about the league's position. "The unofficial line from the high school league is, 'If you can't find a way for a kid to be eligible at your school, you're not trying hard enough.' They're afraid of parents fighting it and overturning a decision."

Although Peltier said the league trusted the integrity of individual schools claiming their internal investigations did not turn up any violations, he did not expect individual athletes or their parents to incriminate themselves. "There are kids I'm sure who are recruited, but how do we discover that?" he said. "If a kid tells what really happened, he won't be eligible. We could ask, but how much do you want to make them lie?"

So it was that the league had set out to investigate whether Greg Trebil had violated bylaw 308, "Undue Solicitation of a Student": "When a student has participated in an A squad, B squad, junior varsity, or sophomore game, any verbal or written contact initiated by a representative of another school soliciting the student's transfer to participate in that sport will be considered as asserting undue influence, for which the school may be publicly censured, removed from tournament competition, or suspended from the league."

Ed Cole alleged that parents of Holy Angels players solicited parents of top players at other schools to transfer to the Catholic school. His letter and later testimony detailed a conversation he overheard between two Holy Angels fathers selling Trebil's team to the father of a varsity hockey player at another school. The boy transferred to Holy Angels before the next year. The boy's father remembered the conversation differently.

In September 2000, shortly after the MSHSL began looking into Cole's charges, the investigation changed course. Holy Angels board member Rick Solum, a high-powered partner at Dorsey and Whitney, the state's largest law firm, proposed a plea bargain, whereby Trebil would confess to lesser violations if the more serious recruiting charges were dropped. The independent investigator continued to question almost twenty witnesses outside Holy Angels while Solum negotiated a "consent agreement" with the league. In the confidential arrangement, Trebil acknowledged he reserved ice time for captains' practices, checked up on kids in captains' practice, and failed to encourage hockey players to go out for football. The coach paid a five hundred dollar fine and submitted to a year's probation. Case closed.

Solum praised Trebil's willingness to "fall on the sword" for the good of the school. But, basically, the coach walked away a free man. After the MSHSL's $10,625 investigation failed to produce hard evidence of recruiting, Trebil didn't miss a practice, didn't miss a game, and didn't get removed from tournaments. The consent agreement was reached prior to the start of the season, but by the time the investigator's report was made public in February, Trebil's team was ranked fifth in the state and Rob Rankin hovered among the state's leading scorers.

When Sats's assistant, Mike Thomas, heard that the MSHSL had dropped the recruiting charge, he snorted, "They didn't have the balls to nail him."

Indeed, in the era of open enrollment and easy transfer, the MSHSL had nailed only one school for recruiting violations, when a girl in a Northern Minnesota school district was lured to the rival school's basketball team. "Frankly, it's pretty hard to prove," Stead said after the Trebil investigation ended.

Had Trebil recruited players? Peltier sighed and looked away. "We spent a lot of money to do a thorough investigation, but we didn't find evidence of recruiting."

Cole accused the league of conducting a sloppy investigation. He requested the case be reopened. Peltier denied his request.

The Holy Angels administration fired the whistleblower from his assistant football coach position. It refused his offer to work as a volunteer. It barred Cole from coming onto the campus other than to pick up his younger son, attend his activities, or participate in parent/teacher conferences. Saying Cole's behavior had raised safety fears, the principal stipulated Cole's younger son could return to Holy Angels for his sophomore year on the condition that the father would refrain from intimidations, threats, and outbursts. He also must agree not to cause public humiliation to others.

"Because I did step up, I have been damaged," Cole protested to Peltier. "My reputation has been destroyed."

Ed Cole's fate gave pause to others poised to complain about transfers at their schools.

Coaches, meanwhile, breathed a collective sigh of relief heard round the state.

Fans and former players like Jeff Saterdalen were left to lament the state of hockey. Their cynicism and despair was understandable seeing high schools, once considered the last bastion of innocence in athletics, succumb to the practices that contaminate college and pro sports. After the proliferation of transfers had tainted the '01 Tournament, *Let's Play Hockey* would print a letter to the editor from Bloomington resident Erik Vetsch: "This [open enrollment] is a virus and is ruining everything I once held as the most sacred thing in the world—the state title!...Nowadays, the state title can be bought."

CHAPTER NINE

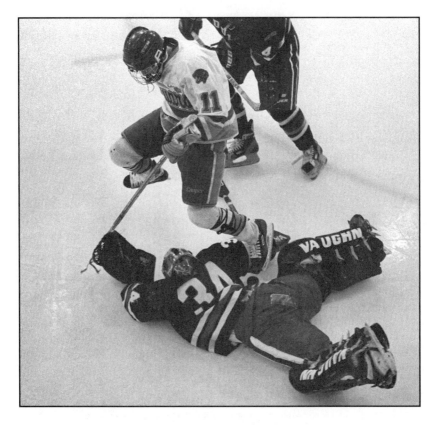

RISE AND DEMISE
OF A DYNASTY

Grand Rapids came to town December 23. On a sunny and cold Saturday afternoon, Sats reminded his boys that pride was on the line. That was true whenever a metro team played a team from the Iron Range, but the pride factor intensified when these two traditions faced off.

Twenty years earlier, when the Indians and Jaguars met in the opening round of the 1981 Tournament, the course of Minnesota high school hockey history turned on one play. With time running out in the third period at the St. Paul Civic Center, Jefferson trailed the defending champions 2–3. The Grand Rapids blueliner, trying to keep the puck in the Jefferson end, stumbled and fell. Steve Bianchi scooped up the puck with a clear path to the Indian net. He raced the other Grand Rapids defenseman the length of the ice....

———————

Grand Rapids lies on the edge of Northern Minnesota's Mesabi Range, a stretch of rolling hills where the earth is the color of a rare T-bone. The area is steeped in iron ore and hockey lore. In 1890, Leonidas Merritt and his six brothers discovered a rich vein of high-grade ore about sixty miles north of Duluth that triggered the red gold rush. Within two years, more than 120 mines had opened on the Range, creating an employment boom. Italians, Croatians, Serbians, Slovenians, Irish, Finns, Swedes, and Greeks streamed to the area to work the mines and settle the towns that sprang up around them. They excavated the building blocks for the nation's rapidly expanding infrastructure.

Those same European immigrants pioneered ice hockey in the New World. Shortly before the turn of the century, they traded the ball of ice polo for a round disc, lengthened their sticks, and endured the long, cold winters by skating up and down natural sheets of ice. By 1922, there were five indoor ice rinks on the Range (more than twice the number in the Cities), including Eveleth's three thousand–seat Hippodrome, the "Madison Square Garden of the Northland." Teams from Eveleth, Hibbing, Virginia, and Chisholm starred on the Minnesota hockey scene prior to World War II and stocked pro and amateur teams across the nation. Postwar, their sons and grandsons monopolized the high school hockey scene: from 1945 to 1980, Range teams won half of the first thirty-six Tournaments.

Eveleth—home of the Leonidas Mine, which at 650 feet was the world's deepest underground mine when it opened in 1908—was the Range's hockey talent mother lode. The town produced a tenth of the United States Hockey Hall of Fame's inductees, including three Eveleth High alumni goaltenders who had become NHL legends: Frank Brimsek, Mike Karakas, and Sam LoPresti. When a Finn named Willard Ikola boarded the bus with his Eveleth Golden Bears teammates in February 1948 bound for St. Paul, 175 miles directly south, the sophomore goaltender knew full well that he traveled to the fourth state high school hockey tournament in the footsteps of giants. The year before, Ike's team had endured a long bus ride home after losing in the semifinal game to Roseau.

Ike, the squat kid with brown bangs that fell across his forehead, was a goalie because his older brother was a goalie. He had the equipment. That included a pair of homemade leg pads fashioned from mattresses, basketball knee guards to protect his arms, and an old inflatable baseball chest protector with a slow leak. During games, Ike had to call timeout to blow it up. "I never did find that damn leak," he laughed more than fifty years later.

Ike and his teammates were as awed by the Cities as they were by the legends who had played before them. Everything was bigger than life. At thirty-two stories, Minneapolis's Foshay Tower soared more than ten times taller than Eveleth's Park Hotel. The teams stayed at the St. Paul Hotel, where they were amazed they could order anything off the menu in the restaurant. Ike cheated his lucky pregame meal of soup and bread—the boys binged on sundaes and milkshakes. They even snuck in their buddies. "Our bill was probably three times bigger than anybody else's in the tournament," Ike said.

Over seven thousand fans, more than the entire population of Eveleth, filled the St. Paul Auditorium Saturday night, February 21, 1948, to watch the Golden Bears trounce Warroad in the championship game. That weekend, Eveleth overpowered its opponents 23–5, and Ike made fifty-four stops in three games. They finished the season undefeated and returned home champions. (After the loss to Roseau Ike's freshman year, he didn't lose another game in high school.) Ike stood tall in those footsteps, along with another Eveleth legend in the making.

That year, the world beyond the Range got its first glimpse of John Mayasich, a Joe DiMaggio in skates. As a ninth-grader, he was already a smooth skater with the instincts and hands to score three goals and assist on two more. Over the next three years, Mayasich scored hat tricks in seven of the nine Tournament games he played. His senior year, 1951, he racked up a record fifteen goals. Many of the ten Tournament scoring records he holds, such as Most All-Time

Goals (thirty-six) and Most Goals One Period (four), seem as untouchable as DiMaggio's fifty-six–game hitting streak.

During Mayasich's varsity years, Eveleth won seventy-nine straight games and four straight titles—a feat no other team has repeated. Its seventy-nine–game winning streak over that stretch is another mark unlikely ever to be surpassed. Behind those amazing accomplishments stood the dapper Cliff Thompson, who coached the Golden Bears from 1926 through 1958 and compiled a record of 534–26–9 for an astounding .938 winning percentage.

Fifty miles down Highway 169, ore gives way to lumber as the primary industry in Grand Rapids, where Range hockey pride reached its apex in 1980. Three weeks after a young American Olympic team—over half of its players Minnesotans—pulled off the Miracle on Ice, the Grand Rapids Indians won the state title. The Indians had already won two championships in the '70s. Neighboring Range schools Hibbing and International Falls each won a title that decade as well. A younger Grand Rapids team returned to face Jefferson in the opening round of the '81 Tournament.

————

Steve Bianchi raced Grand Rapids defenseman Glenn Palso the length of the ice. Palso had the angle to beat him. Hurling through the neutral zone, Bianchi looked for a teammate breaking with him but found he was alone. *My god, I've got to do this myself.* As Palso bore down on him across the Indians' blue line, Bianchi cut sharply to his forehand and slid the puck between the defenseman's skate and stick. Knowing the Indians goalie liked to go down, Bianchi dropped his shoulder—and the goalie dropped with it. Bianchi reached around to his backhand and flipped the puck into the net to tie the game with 3:11 left in regulation.

The Jaguars won in overtime and, feeling invincible after Bianchi's goal, they won their next two games to take home their first title. These days, Steve Bianchi shows that clip to his six-year-old son, a first-year Mite. The classic play might just as well be a complete training video for the Jefferson program. The summer before that season, Bianchi had had surgery on his knee to repair a congenital condition—*osteo chrondritas de sencans*—that cut off the blood flow to the end of his femur. He'd had to quit football and baseball, but there was no way he would quit hockey. He worked hard to rehabilitate the knee, and it carried him when the Grand Rapids defenseman fell and the rink suddenly opened up before him.

That moment, when Bianchi seized upon a lucky break, embodied Jefferson hockey. "Luck is when preparation meets opportunity." Sats had drilled that motto into his team and driven them to overachieve. The gritty bunch had worked hard to prepare, and when the opportunity arose, they grabbed it. Thus a dynasty was born of hard work.

Simultaneously, when that Grand Rapids defenseman fell to the ice, the Range tradition crumbled. With Steve Bianchi streaking by, the state's hockey power shifted. Northern dominance gave way to suburban numbers. Over the next twenty years, no Range team would win the state title outright. Once the Tournament split into two divisions to give smaller schools the chance to compete among themselves, four Range teams would win the lesser title. Smaller schools could opt up to play AA, but no Range team that did so would bring back another championship. Eveleth, combined with nearby Gilbert, had won the 1998 Class A title, but the luster was gone from the titles won by the undisputed champions who preceded them by fifty years.

The barstool wisdom that circulated through Eveleth's watering holes theorized that love had robbed the Range of its glory. Eveleth teams used to throttle teams from Virginia, twelve miles up Highway 53. Virginia turned out the likes of Jeff, Steve, and Jack Carlson, inspiration for the Hanson brothers in the '77 cult classic "Slap Shot." But then the Eveleth boys started to marry Virginia girls. "That's what screwed up Eveleth hockey—all the mixed marriages with Virginia," Willard Ikola explained.

More likely, the reason for the Range's reversal of fortune lay in the mines. The year Grand Rapids won its final title, the Leonidas Mine closed. A variety of factors—increased transportation costs, economic downturn, foreign competition, and depletion of the high-grade variety—strangled the iron ore market. More mines

closed. By 1989—the year Jefferson won its second championship—
St. Louis County mines employed only 5,664 workers, down from
11,441 at the start of the decade. Other jobs in the mining-
dependent economy evaporated. People left to find work elsewhere.
Over that period, the county's population fell by nearly 10 percent.

The trend continued in the '90s, though not as severely. Birth
rates on the Range ran below the state average, and death rates ran
higher. The student-aged population declined, meaning fewer kids
to stock the varsity. In January 2001, the LTV Steel Corporation
shut down its iron mine and taconite pellet production plant in
Hoyt Lakes. At Parents' Night for the Mesabi East High Giants, nine
of the sixteen boys on the varsity greeted parents who were unem-
ployed. The team's future—like its community's—stood in jeopardy.
Meanwhile, the metro suburbs saw a rise in overall population and
student enrollment over two decades.

So, too, St. Paul and Minneapolis schools, long the counter force
to the Northern powers, saw their numbers drop with the suburban
boom. By the mid-1970s, the coup was complete. When
Minneapolis Southwest was runner-up to Grand Rapids in 1975, it
marked the last time a city school from either Minneapolis or St.
Paul would reach the championship game. The power shifted with
the population.

Hockey rinks had sprouted among the rows of new suburban
houses. Edina opened Braemar Arena in 1965; Bloomington followed with BIG in 1970. The indoor ice laid the foundation for
youth feeder programs.

The game changed with the demographics. When Mayasich
played in the late '40s and even for a generation after him, hockey
players relied on their stickhandling, passing, and playmaking abilities. But power replaced skills. Size and speed are the hallmarks of
today's game. That game favors larger schools with deeper rosters
of bigger kids. The smaller Northern schools were more likely to
rely heavily on a top line. When they faced suburban schools that
could skate three or four lines, that top line, despite dazzling skills,
was often worn down by bigger kids who could knock them off
the puck.

Willard Ikola realized the tide had turned already in 1977 when his Edina East Hornets played the Roseau Rams in the opening round of the Tournament. The tiny northern town of Roseau had turned out one of the state's greatest lines of all-time—Neal Broten, Aaron Broten, and Butsy Erickson—but by the second period they were running out of gas, overmatched by Edina's depth. In two trips to the Tournament, Neal Broten—who would go on to win an NCAA title at the University of Minnesota, a gold medal at Lake Placid, and a Stanley Cup with the New Jersey Devils—failed to capture the state championship. "I was bawling in the locker room after the game when we lost," Broten said the night he was inducted into the United States Hockey Hall of Fame. "It's something you always look back on and wish you could go back and play again; it's that special."

Ike had been chipping away at the Northern school dominance for a decade. He had returned from the service to coach the young suburb Edina's high school team in 1958–59. His first season, the team went 4–9–3, but over the next thirty-two years, Ike never had another losing season. In 1969, when his Hornets defeated Warroad in overtime, they became the first suburban team to win the state championship. Jefferson was the second in '81. By then, Edina— bordered by Bloomington to the south and Minneapolis to the east—had won five titles.

Ikola established Edina as a powerhouse the likes of his native Eveleth. Wearing his signature houndstooth hat, Ike became a regular fixture at the Tournament, where he took his Hornets a record nineteen times.

As a player, Ike observed the *de rigueur* goaltender superstitions. As a coach, he traded his lucky T-shirt for a hat. When he started in 1958, all the coaches wore hats, in part because the rinks were so cold. Ike bought a five-dollar brownish-red tweed houndstooth hat labeled "The Champ." He wore it religiously for every game.

But his luck almost ran out one day. Eating lunch in a Duluth restaurant, he saw a man outside walk by sporting "The Champ." Ike tore out after him, "mad as hell." Under the influence of a few beers, the man had inadvertently grabbed the wrong hat.

Confronted by the irate Ike, he promptly returned it. "I didn't have to fight him for it, but I probably would've," Ike laughed.

By the time Ikola retired in 1991, "The Champ" was stained by sweat on the inside and fingerprints on the brim, but there had been plenty of magic in that old houndstooth hat. Wearing it, Ike had coached 616 victories, more than any other Minnesota high school hockey coach, and won a record eight titles. He retired the winningest coach in the history of Minnesota high school sports.

––––––

The rise of the Jefferson hockey empire had been simultaneous with the demise of the Range rule, but some scribblings on the wall foreshadowed Bloomington-Jefferson headed toward a similar fall. Following its three consecutive championships, Jefferson entered the '95 Tournament ranked No. 1 and heavily favored. Duluth East crushed the Jaguars 5–0 in the quarterfinal game. "When an era ends, it usually crashes like that," John Bianchi said. "You seldom play an overtime thriller decided by a beautiful goal; you just crash, and that's exactly what we did."

That was Bianchi's last season. Since he had retired and Trebil had left, the Jaguars had been to the Tournament three times but only once, in 1998, advanced beyond the first round, where they promptly lost again to Duluth East. This year's team had the talent to reverse the trend and win another championship that would return Jefferson to its former glory. Could they?

Tommy Gilbert and friends were the first senior class not to benefit from Trebil's tutelage. They were talented but not as disciplined as Trebil's teams. Individuals sometimes tried to win a game single-handedly rather than play as a team. They were prone to take selfish penalties. They also lacked the fire that Bianchi had instilled in teams past. On the ice and in the dressing room, this group lacked an intensity Sats failed to kindle. And losing did not seem to disturb them as deeply.

If they didn't go all the way this year, the prospects for next year's team—minus Tommy, Duncs, Nick, Timm, B.J., Jimmy, and Shacks—seemed remote. After that, Sats was finished, and the future was uncertain. He had not named an heir, but whoever it was would have large skates to fill. They would also be working against another shift in demographics. Changes in the community suggested yesterday's glory wouldn't be repeated tomorrow. With Bloomington built out and its population aging, school enrollment was dropping. Jefferson, a midsize high school with 1,800 students grades nine to twelve, struggled to keep pace with the growing suburbs' megaschools like Eden Prairie (enrollment 2,254) and Elk River (2,068).

Peering down the pipeline, the outlook wasn't promising. The Bantam A team, depleted by the loss of its three best players (one to Holy Angels, two to Jefferson's j.v.), finished a mediocre .500. Short on the characteristic Jefferson strengths, this year's Bantams were slow skaters and inept passers. Despite the Peewee A team's championship, stars like Peter Mueller couldn't be counted on to wear the Jefferson Blue. He might follow his older brother to Breck, the private Episcopalian school that won the 2000 Class A title, or open enroll at another school if the Jaguars looked to be weak. Tony Bianchi, the Squirt A coach, worried that parents of the better players coming up through the Booster program might choose other schools. He predicted "a gap of goodness" following this season.

Fans of the glass-is-half-empty persuasion saw Jefferson's program soon to be fueled only by the fumes of tradition, but tradition alone wouldn't win championships—ask Grand Rapids. These days, it took talent, and talent in numbers, to win titles. This year seemed the Jaguars' last chance—if it wasn't already too late.

———

Two days before the Grand Rapids game, on the shortest day of the year and one of the coldest, the Jefferson varsity hockey players knocked on neighbors' doors, soliciting canned goods and cash donations for the student council's annual food drive to benefit homeless shelters. The sun had shone that day, but not for long— less than nine hours. It had been dark when they arrived at school and dark again when they left after practice. Stiff winds from the North Pole gathered speed over the Canadian plains and blasted the Cities, sending windchills down to -45°F.

Bundled in multiple layers under their letter jackets, Duncs and Nick teamed with Ryan Briese to work the tony South Bay neighborhood. They rang half a dozen doorbells, thawed out in Duncs's dad's Dodge Durango, then hit another six houses. If people weren't home, they rearranged their lighted lawn reindeer decorations in Kama Sutra positions. The three friends collected 283 items, better than Tommy, Jeremy, and Van B., who succumbed to the cold after bagging fifty items and hit the mall to buy Christmas presents.

———————

The Grand Rapids Thunderhawks—the Indians in less sensitive times—showed up at BIG the night before Christmas Eve 2000 cloaked in the Range's venerable one hundred–year-old hockey tradition, but a mere shadow of their former selves. They had won only a third of their games the previous season and struggled this year to a 2–4 record. They played for pride, no longer for glory.

The puck dropped Saturday afternoon at 3:15 P.M. but eluded both nets the first period. In the second, Jefferson had a good opportunity with a powerplay, but thirteen seconds into it, Bernie took a tripping penalty to wash out the advantage. The teams remained scoreless past the eleven-minute mark, when Jeremy misplayed the puck behind the net. As he scrambled back into position, a Thunderhawk banked the puck off his skate into the deserted net. For the first time this season, an opponent had beaten the Jaguars to the scoreboard—and this time it was the lowly Thunderhawks.

With just ten seconds left in the second period, Nick buried a rebound to tie the game. He hugged Duncs and Jimmy happily. He had scored his first big goal of the season. Beforehand, when Sats had passed out gum, Nick had gone with a new color, looking to change his luck. Red worked.

In the dressing room between periods, Sats lit into his players. "You've got to get hungrier. It all depends on how bad you want it. You've got to work harder. There's not a guy in here who's worked hard enough."

Bernie, taking a drink of water behind Sats's back, lowered the green water bottle and made an incredulous face. *Not working hard enough? You kidding?*

When Sats left, Nick, Jimmy, and B.J. all complained how tired they were. Tommy, in one of his lengthiest motivational speeches of the season, said, "It's all in the mind."

In the third period, Grand Rapids's pride kept Jefferson from scoring but couldn't will the puck past Jeremy. Sats shortened his bench, alternating Bernie's and Duncs's lines. When the BIG announcer declared, "One minute remaining," the score was still tied 1–1.

The fans poised to start the ten-second countdown. Jimmy fired a shot from the point. The Thunderhawks's goalie butterflied to make the save. Duncs, parked in front of the net, gathered in the rebound, swiveled to the open side, and deposited the puck in the goal. The clock showed 9.9 seconds remaining.

Jubilant in the dressing room, Duncs spit out his mouthguard, pulled off his helmet, and announced, "That was better than any pot high." He looked around playfully. "Well, almost."

Against Eastview, Duncs had scored what turned out to be the game-winning goal, but against Grand Rapids, he had delivered his first clutch goal. The tough forward already led the team in takeouts, but his dramatic gamewinner may have been the necessary confidence-boost headed into the Holiday Classic, where he had burned up the tournament last season.

Bernie's six goals and thirteen assists through the first seven games had put him on pace to score seventy-six points by Tournament time, which would leave him only one point behind Mike Crowley's record season total. But Grand Rapids had shut out Bernie and Tommy for the first time that season. Duncs's line had stepped up to carry the team, but the two goals Duncs, Jimmy, and Nick managed were the fewest the Jags had scored in a game so far.

After the closely contested game, the Thunderhawks boarded the bus back to Grand Rapids with their pride still intact, but the Jaguars entered the Holiday Classic with theirs in question.

CHAPTER TEN

HOLIDAY CLASSIC

Christmas morning, Minnesota was the coldest place in the nation. By the time Apollo's chariot chased Santa's sleigh back to the North Pole, the town of Cambridge, just north of the Twin Cities metro area, reported temperatures of -33°F *before windchill*. Bloomington thermometers registered a balmy -17°F at 8 A.M., where some Jefferson players still nestled snug in their beds and those with younger siblings groggily peeled the wrapping off presents.

Tommy hadn't set an alarm to find out what Santa had left him under the tree. Along with his younger brother Cory, a sophomore on the j.v., and his older brother home from college, Tommy counted sleep among his favorite gifts. Duncs, however, was up early with his two younger half-brothers, Sam and Jake, after attending Midnight Mass with his mom and stepdad. He would see his dad Steve later in the day. Nick and his younger brother, Ben, spent Christmas morning with their mom and her new husband, whose two younger sons looked up to Nick.

That afternoon, Nick went over to his dad's nearby apartment. His mom had given him a green-and-white Abercrombie jacket and some other clothes. Mike Coffman scored with his gift of an Easton shaft that Nick planned to use the next night in the Holiday Classic.

Bernie spent the day with his older sister, a sophomore at a St. Paul Baptist college, his mother, Nancy, and her new husband, Ron. Bernie planned to make the three-hour drive to Hayward, Wisconsin, over New Year's to see the man he called "Dad," Kevin Bernhagen. Kevin had come along when Bernie was three, earning the Dad title. Bernie's birthfather had walked out on his mother when she was four months pregnant with Bernie. Bernie had met the man but had no further plans for him. Kevin's abrupt departure seven years later deepened the father void.

Nancy had struggled to make ends meet from what she earned cleaning houses. A religious woman, she thanked God that her son, Michael, had hockey. The sport became his surrogate father. From hockey, he won attention, affection, and praise.

Yet Bernie's elementary school teachers had reported all was not well. At conferences, they told Nancy that Bernie, whose IQ placed him in the 98th percentile, was not achieving up to his full potential. And there were occasional outbursts of anger he didn't seem able to control.

Bernie was not a troublemaker in the traditional sense. He was well mannered, and he didn't interrupt class or bully other kids. By high school, he wasn't prone to partying or delinquency. But a smoldering anger occasionally erupted when an adult denied him what he wanted, an opponent cheap-shotted him, or a classmate kicked his hand when they were going for the same ball in phys ed class. A month of anger counseling with their pastor, a family friend, had helped provide Bernie some insight into what triggered his temper, but their sessions hadn't tamed it.

Life had slashed him in a way he couldn't forget. A genius on ice, he was the classic troubled artist, expressing himself on skates but fighting the circumstances that set him apart. Intelligent and articulate, he had more self-awareness than the average teenager, even if he sometimes had trouble keeping that in perspective. "Personally, I do think I know more than most people because of my life experiences," he said one day after school in the Jefferson cafeteria.

Bernie valued his ideas over others'. Admitting he was stubborn, he knew that put him on a collision course with certain teammates and his coach. He shrugged, "I won't do certain things." Bernie answered to his own high standards, not theirs.

He respected someone like his grandfather, his mother's dad, who retired early from General Electric and built a house on a golf course in Arizona. Bernie wanted that sort of independent success for himself. He saw himself in ten years established in a career and happily married. Hockey might or might not be part of his future beyond high school. "Mainly, I want to be happy," Bernie said. "The only way is if I'm successful."

———

Christmas meant the Holiday Classic, an elite tournament among four of Minnesota's top teams: Duluth East, Hill-Murray, Edina, and Jefferson. The round robin tournament gave fans a mid-season measure, and the three games played in three days with periods extended to twenty minutes gave the players a test. Come March, they would have to win three games in three nights to finish the season as state champions.

The Holiday Classic tradition dated back twenty years to when teams played at the Met Center. It moved to St. Paul's Civic Center, then again three years ago to Edina's Braemar Arena on Ikola Way. Some of the state's best players had starred in this tournament. Last year, Duncs had written himself into its history with a seven-goal, five-assist performance and experienced the highlight of his career to date. That had been something good for his dad to remember.

Playing in front of the crowds and reading his name in the papers had pumped Duncs. By the third game, he was hot and flying. When the refs awarded Jefferson a penalty shot after an Edina player shoved the net out of place, Sats wanted Joey Wineberg, the team's leading scorer, to take it, but Joey was too nervous. Enter Duncs. The crowd blared into his helmet at center ice, where he waited for the ref's whistle to challenge the Edina goaltender one-on-one. Duncs's team was down by a goal. "I was shitting my pants," he said the week before this year's Classic. Duncs faked to the goalie's glove side, then pulled the puck to his backhand and shoved it in low. An intense rush surged through his body. With the crowd roaring for him, he felt on top of the world. "I would take scoring a big goal over getting stoned or drinking beer any time," he said earnestly.

Duncs was excited to repeat at the Classic, which Jefferson had won last year. The team was on a five-game winning streak, and he was coming off his game-winning goal against Grand Rapids. Before the school year started, Duncs had broken up with Gianna Gambucci, a cute defender on the girls' team. Duncs said he wanted to focus on hockey. By Christmas, the couple had gotten back together. Reminded of his earlier resolve to swear off girls for the season, Duncs smiled. "That's a long time."

Shortly after last year's Classic, Duncs had crashed. He found out his mother's sister Diane—whom he counted as one of his good friends—had lung cancer. The news drained him. He couldn't talk to his friends. He didn't want to get wasted. So he headed to B202. Confiding in Sats, all of his sadness and fears spilled out. His coach sat with him and respected his tears. Sats said what he could to comfort and reassure Duncs. "Keep your head straight," Sats told him. Duncs left feeling better. A year later, Duncs's Aunt Diane was still very sick, but he had found some peace with his God over her illness.

———————

Sats's wife padded his sweater collection with two more as Christmas presents. Most of the time, Sats bought his own sweaters. In his characteristic deliberateness, he waited until a sweater he had his eye on at Marshall Field's department store went on sale, then purchased it, deducting his wife's employee discount. With some thirty-five sweaters in his closet, Sats could wear a different one each game, which is exactly what he did. If the houndstooth hat was Ike's trademark, the sweater was Sats's. In the Holiday Classic opener against Duluth East, he wore a woolen, earthtone-checked pullover.

The Duluth East Greyhounds had graduated only four seniors from last year's state tournament runner-up team. Goalie Dan Hoehne, the team's best player, returned with three veteran defensemen and seven forwards, including Nick Licari, who as an eighth-grader had played on the Greyhounds' championship team that knocked off Jefferson in 1998. The Jaguars had beaten Duluth East in a 10–8 shootout at last year's Classic when Duncs scored four goals, but the strong-skating, physical Greyhounds had manhandled the Jaguars in the preseason scrimmage.

With a loss to Elk River and Osseo, the Greyhounds had since dropped from their preseason top ranking to fourth in the state and ninth in the nation, but they remained a favorite to return to the Tournament final. Duluth East had emerged in the '90s as a perennial powerhouse under the leadership of Mike Randolph, Sats's likely successor as Minnesota's premier high school hockey coach.

Before the game, Sats had one word for his players: mindset. They would get tired playing the equivalent of an extra period, but he wanted them to go top speed every single shift. They could if they willed themselves to do so. They could with the right mindset.

Bernie was saying something to the player seated next to him, but Sats's word found its mark in Nick. He came out inspired, skating hard and laying hits. The program listed him at 6'2", 170 pounds, but that may have been padded a bit. Without his jersey and shoulder pads, you could count the ribs on Nick's washboard chest. Earlier in the season, he had let others push him off the puck, but he started hitting Greyhounds that night right off, playing much bigger than his size.

Nick's linemates, Jimmy and Duncs, also came out inspired. On the Senior Line's second shift, Duncs pulled the puck off the boards and broke in with Jimmy on a two-on-one. The defenseman went down to block the pass, but Duncs managed to slip the puck underneath him to Jimmy, who one-timed it home from the far post.

Two shifts later, Nick fed Duncs high in the right circle. He waited patiently to pull the trigger. Before the game, Sats had told them to shoot at Hoehne's feet, where they would find his Achilles' heel. Duncs fired a wrist shot low to the stick side that beat Hoehne cleanly.

With less than a minute remaining in the period, Nick nailed an East player off the puck and set up Duncs in the slot. Duncs beat Hoehne low again. After one period: Senior Line, three; East, zero. In the past two games, seniors Duncs, Nick, and Jimmy had combined for all five of the Jags' goals over three periods.

The Duluth East radio broadcast pair, seated alongside the lighted Christmas tree in the press box, groaned over the Hounds's missed chances. Jeremy repeatedly denied them. Fans tuned in to the action back in the port city took heart that their boys didn't let up in the second period. The game remained tight.

From inside his zone, Bernie hit B.J. with a pass in the neutral zone, then beat him to the East blue line with his hustle, but nothing came of their rush. Bernie was used to success coming easily. He also passed on the high expectations for himself to others. He came back to the bench complaining, "What kind of shift is that?" By the end of the first period, when he missed a steal and the Hounds's defender grabbed at him, Bernie cross-checked him behind the play and out of sight of the refs. His mindset: frustration.

Early in the second, Bernie found Tommy slipping behind the East D with a long, bouncing pass. Tommy broke in alone, but Hoehne came out to challenge him and deftly poked the puck off his stick. When an East forward antagonized him at the end of the period, Tommy slugged him in the chest. More frustration.

Duluth East outshot Jefferson in the period and Licari scored on a bad angle to pull within two, 3–1. With twenty minutes left to play, it was still anybody's game. The Jaguars animated the dressing room with war stories from the first two periods. Sats came in to pace among the orange peels. "Mindset, guys," he shouted. "MIND-SET!"

Duncs's heartburn was acting up. Manager Dave Daly tossed him a roll of Tums. Duncs peeled off a couple of tablets. He had already gobbled four from the container he kept in his locker back at school. Traditionally a slow starter, Duncs doubted at every level whether he could handle the challenge. His confidence had taken some time to catch up. This year, as an alternate captain and the team's go-to guy, he had renewed his doubts.

Now, with Bernie and Tommy struggling, there was extra pressure to pick up the slack. Duncs had been there before. In the Bantam playoffs versus Eden Prairie, Mike Erickson's line had shut down Bernie and Tommy's Magic Line. Duncs picked up his play and scored a hat trick to carry the team. "It was the first time I saw Matt will himself to take over a game," Steve Duncan said with obvious pride. When Duncs found his confidence, he could do just about whatever he wanted with the puck.

Sats returned. He diagrammed a forecheck strategy on the board and warned his forwards not to get caught too deep inside the East zone. "It's all in your mind, you guys, who wants to go the hardest," he said, his voice rising. "Every shift, bust your ass." He rose to a crescendo. "Focus, focus. Good focus."

Jeremy made a big stop on an East breakaway, then Duncs stole the puck at his blue line and lumbered toward the East end with only a defender and Hoehne to beat. His patented move—the one he per-formed over and over in practice—was to dangle the puck in front of the defender, then pull it back when the D swiped at the puck and go wide around his off-balance opponent. This time, Duncs went outside-in on the defender, threading the puck between his skates and slipping past him untouched. He juked right to left on Hoehne, who lunged for the pokecheck. Duncs swerved around him but at that high speed the puck squirted off his stick, and he couldn't get off the shot. Still, he had attempted and executed two absolutely beautiful moves. The confidence was back.

East was checking Bernie's line closely, same as Grand Rapids had, and it was working to slow them down. Try as he might, Tommy couldn't fight through the East defenders. Even the rink seemed to be against them. When Bernie lofted one of his favorite flip passes to Tommy streaking deep across the middle, the puck hit the low aluminum foil-wrapped ceiling and was whistled dead. Just past the halfway mark, Bernie slashed Licari in front of the Jefferson net. Licari went down, and Bernie went to the box for two minutes.

With the fans on their feet, Jefferson killed the penalty, then came up empty on its own powerplay. At 16:19—past the point when a regular game would've been over—East pulled within one goal. The Greyhounds poured on the intensity, pounding any Jag within sight of the puck and scrapping with newfound vigor in the corners. Randolph pulled Hoehne for an extra attacker. Black-and-red jerseys swarmed the Jefferson net.

Duluth pressed hard. With a minute left, Duncs finally dumped the puck out of his zone. The puck rolled the length of the ice into the empty Hounds net, seeming to ice the game. The Jefferson fans cheered, but it was premature. Duncs's shot had come after a whistle. Sats switched lines, and East continued to pour on its attack. Thirty seconds later, Bernie hit the Hounds' net. The Hounds fought until the final buzzer, but Jeremy withstood the challenge. He finished the game with thirty-five saves, fourteen of those in the final period.

After the game, half-a-dozen reporters wanted to talk to Duncs and Nick. They ignored Tommy and Bernie. Even though Bernie had scored late, his empty net goal wasn't enough to pull his line out of its funk.

Duncs was elated. They had just beaten the preseason favorite behind his two goals, and he was off to another great start at the Holiday Classic. He and Jimmy and Nick were clicking, playing like a first line. In the past two games, they had scored five goals and hadn't given up a single one.

Duncs had come on strong, and Jimmy hustled hard, but Nick's play had proven pivotal in the line's surge. In keeping with his goal to play hard offensively and defensively, Nick had dived to keep the puck in the zone on the powerplay, thrown himself in front of East's shooters, and banged bodies at both ends of the ice. When he felt the fatigue closing in during the final period, he reminded himself of Sats's invocation. *Mindset* echoed in his ears the way it had off the dressing-room walls. His side ached. His legs weighed heavy. *Mindset,* he repeated to himself on the bench. *You're not tired. Skate your ass off.*

Each shift, he started over, focused on what he had to do. He ended the game with four takeouts and two blocked shots. His new Easton stick had set up three goals. In the Classic opener, Nick had played a breakout game.

That got him noticed. A coach from the Tri-City Storm, which played in the junior United States Hockey League, caught up with him walking out of the rink. He told Nick they planned to protect him and Duncs in the high school draft, guaranteeing Nick a tryout with the team that summer.

Nick was so jazzed he couldn't sleep. At 3 A.M., he flipped on the computer to read the Varsity Online account of the game, which praised his line's play. So far, only Division-III schools had expressed interest. He didn't even know where the tri-cities were—Nebraska, maybe?—but he would play in Thailand if it could get him onto a Division-I team. The juniors route had worked for his dad, who had landed a scholarship with Michigan after a year with the Junior Stars. Nick's future suddenly dawned bright.

Nick slept well past noon. Karen grilled him a pregame steak outside, standing over the backyard grill partially buried in the snow. "The neighbors think I'm crazy," she laughed.

Jaguar parents cut out of work early to catch the 5 P.M. game against Hill-Murray. When the Jags' bus pulled up to the Braemar Arena, the late afternoon sun glinted off the twin rinks that looked like a pair of pole buildings in a barnyard rather than the premier rink in a posh suburb. The boys passed through the lobby, shuffled down the bleacher steps, and turned left toward the dressing room. Sats stopped at the concessions stand for his pregame coffee with Thomas, who sipped hot chocolate from a Styrofoam cup.

Sats worried that his boys weren't ready for this rematch with Hill-Murray. Even though the Pioneers were off to a slow start, he still considered them a threat. After Jefferson thumped the Pioneers 5–2 in the season opener, the revenge factor gave Hill-Murray more to play for this time around. Sats feared his team was tired from last night's battle with Duluth East and overconfident about this game. Their mindset was whacked.

Back at school, when the team gathered around the green chalkboard, Sats had asked Tommy if he had anything to say about the Pioneers' goalie after beating him four times. Tommy shrugged. "I didn't really notice him."

"Didn't notice him? This is the goalie I'm talking about."

"No, because the puck was in the back of the net."

His teammates laughed. Sats persisted. "But how did you score?"

"Low, rebounds."

Sats shook his head. "If you guys get satisfied, you're going to get your socks blown off. You have to be ready to play every game. That'll prepare you for life."

Downstairs in the Braemar dressing room, the players were talking about last year's Tournament. Watching a game in the Target Center's upper level, Tommy had picked out of the air a paper airplane launched from six rows back without turning his head. Sats interrupted them when he walked in. "Guys, we've got to focus. You're not focused like you were last night."

When the door closed behind him, Nick said, "Okay, Tom, tell me how you did it."

Tommy just smiled.

Out in the hallway, Sats whispered, "We're going to get our ears pinned back."

Once they gathered around Timm for their pregame huddle, the Jaguars got down to business. "This is a big tournament," Bernie said. "There are lots of people watching."

"Play the body," Duncs said.

Midway through the first period, Duncs dished a saucer pass to Jimmy, who put Jefferson on the board first—same as he had done last night.

Five minutes later, Timm sprawled to pokecheck the puck from a Pioneer attacker, but Nick failed to stick with his man, who swooped in and fired the loose puck over Timm. One all.

That brought the Hill-Murray cheerleaders to life. "We want another one, just like the other one."

It wasn't to be. Jimmy fed Duncs at the Pioneers' blue line. Duncs busted through the defense, the goalie dropped, and Duncs snapped a wrist shot over his shoulder.

With less than a minute left in the period, Duncs found Nick on the right side, and Nick popped in the feed to redeem himself for his earlier mistake. After the first twenty minutes, it was Senior Line 3, Hill-Murray 1.

Brad Peterson scored in the second after Sats benched him a couple of shifts for not playing aggressively. Hill-Murray countered in the third. But Jefferson escaped with a 4–2 win.

Bernie and Tommy took nine shots each—B.J. fired another five—but the first line failed to score. Had the Senior Line not converted three of seventeen shots, the Jaguars would've lost 2–1.

Tommy had played hard but was shut out for the third game in a row. Teams had started checking his line more closely. When Tommy got the puck, he was often double-teamed. A recurring image was of one or two opponents draped over No. 15. He sometimes muscled his way through these maulings and got off a pass or shot, but the coaches complained he didn't pass quickly enough. Too often, Tommy tried to win games by himself. Sats saw him respond to his slump by trying to force the play instead of letting it happen.

The other rap against the team captain was that he didn't hit. Tommy was strong, but not tough the way Duncs was. He went into the corners cautiously. Even though Tommy entered the Classic with the team's third-highest takeout total—after the bruiser Duncs and team enforcer Adam Dirlam—the coaches wanted him to use his size to create more opportunities.

Three games without a legitimate goal left both Tommy and Bernie frustrated. Bernie quickly peeled off his gear and slumped onto the bus waiting outside. His face was glum. "Winning is gay when you don't have any part in it," he said.

———

More snow fell the next day before Jefferson's third and final Classic game against Edina. Channel 11's Belinda Jensen, the belle of weather broadcasters, called for eight inches and sounded the National

Weather Service's winter storm warning. With road conditions quickly worsening, Mall of America retailers shut down and sent employees home early. A local radio station played "Ditch Bingo," where listeners phoned in reports of cars that had spun off the road throughout the metro area's highway matrix. When Timm arrived at school with Duncs and Nick aboard his red Dakota Sport pickup, he whipped a few donuts in the parking lot's fresh snow for laughs.

Bernie and Tommy passed the puck in the hallway, following their regular pregame routine, but Tommy was in a sour mood. He had gone over to his girlfriend's house after the Hill-Murray game, but she hadn't been able to soothe his frustration. Bernie had just gone home. He hadn't wanted to see anyone.

In the gym, the players shot baskets, tossed a football, and talked about Holy Angels handing top-ranked Eden Prairie its first loss earlier that afternoon in a lesser holiday tournament. "If we win, that will make us number one," Bernie said.

First, they had to get by Edina.

About half the size of Bloomington, Edina is an affluent suburb populated by physicians, attorneys, CEOs, entrepreneurs, and professional athletes. Its "Country Club Neighborhood," with million-dollar brick and stucco houses lining streets shaded by majestic elm trees, is one of the metro area's most desirable places to live. Edina's concentration of wealth made green a fitting school color. High irony would strike later that season when several Edina varsity and j.v. hockey players were arrested for counterfeiting money. The local barber shops buzzed with the story of federal agents busting the players at a school dance.

But there was nothing fake about Edina's rich tradition of success on the playing fields. Since opening in 1949, Edina High had garnered over one hundred state titles in nineteen boys' and girls' sports. Even taking into account a nine-year stint that included East and West high schools, that total was still more than twice the number any other high school had collected. The most titles had come in hockey—nine, a state record. Willard Ikola had hung eight of the championship banners in Braemar, including three from his years at Edina East. The road out front was named after him, and a plaque in the lobby commemorated his record number of wins, but Edina had not proven a one-coach wonder. Six years after Ike's retirement, the Hornets won the 1997 Tournament. The photo gallery in the concourse overlooking the main rink framed more than one hundred heroes from Edina's illustrious hockey past, players who had graduated to college and professional hockey, the likes of Jim Knutson, Dave Maley, Wally Chapman, Paul Ranheim, et al.

The Hornets had made it to State last year under rookie coach Curt Giles, a former North Stars defenseman. Edina upset Eden Prairie in the 6AA section final by banging in the tying goal off a faceoff with only four seconds left to play in regulation. While the Jaguars watched, waiting for their section final to follow at Mariucci Arena, Edina battled Eden Prairie through three overtimes before putting the game away in the fourth. This year's team returned last year's leading scorer plus five other forwards. Ranked low by Edina standards—twelfth in the state—the Hornets were still dangerous. As the Holiday Classic hosts, they had perhaps more to play for than any other school in the tournament. Ike's legacy lived on in this year's team through his grandson Willie Ikola, a junior forward.

Edina was also known as the home of the babes. The Hornets's student section looked like a reunion of *Seventeen* cover girls with their makeup meticulously applied and their hair expensively styled. Later, Bernie would tell his teammates how, getting checked in front of Edina's student section, he had scoped tomorrow's trophy wives through the Plexiglas and thought, "You're hot, you're hot, you're hot."

The way Edina flaunted its success made the Hornets not only the team to beat, but the team to hate. At one Tournament, television cameras picked up Edina fans, long derided as cake-eaters, touting a banner: "Cake is the breakfast of champions." During rare losses, they taunted, "That's all right, that's okay, you're going to work for us one day."

Gathered around the green chalkboard, Sats said, "Of all the teams, I just hate to get beat by Edina—they suck. Nick, how do you like Edina?"

"I hate 'em," Nick said. At last year's Classic, Nick had dumped the puck and turned to head for his bench when one of Edina's stars blind-sided him and knocked him out. After Joey Wineberg scored and raised his stick in the air, another Hornet cross-checked him from behind, sending Joey head-first into the boards. He had been lucky to escape with only a separated shoulder. Sats's first item on the board was "Will run all the time after whistle—be ready."

Duncs had worked with the Edina captains at Gemini Sports over the summer and played with them on all-star teams, but he still hated to lose to Edina. Just thirty-seven seconds into the game, skating in on a two-on-two, he pulled his signature now-you-see-it, now-you-don't move on the strong-side D, skirted him, then cut across the goal mouth and squeezed the puck into a sliver of daylight between the goalie's skate and the far post. That highlight goal would show up the next night on the Wild's television broadcast in the Wells Fargo Prep Report, high school hockey's Sportscenter.

On the next shift, Bernie tried a move nearly identical to Duncs's but got stood up by the goaltender. Later that shift, Tommy banged home a loose puck in the slot to put Jefferson up 2–0 a minute into the game.

But Tommy's first goal in five games didn't prove to be the team's panacea. On a two-on-one, Bernie fumbled Tommy's pass. Later Tommy shoved a pesky Hornet after the whistle. Another Hornet dropped Duncs with a cheap shot to the ribs behind the play. Willie Ikola scored to pare Jefferson's lead to 2–1.

Between periods Sats was not happy with his skaters. He berated them for taking two stupid penalties. He replaced Brad Peterson with Jeff Rysavy on the third line. Even though Peterson had scored against Hill-Murray, Sats had been upset by Peterson's foul-mouthed complaining and reluctance to play the body. "You've got to prove yourself," Sats told him during the Duluth East game. "This is where we find out who the men are." With the benching, Sats had just filed a statement on the sophomore's budding manhood.

Bernie was not happy with his skates. He sent Kelly, the team manager, to get them sharpened. "Got any money?" Kelly asked.

"My mom does."

Kelly left with Bernie's skates in hand to find Nancy.

The Zamboni had finished its run and Edina was back out on the new ice before Kelly returned with Bernie's freshly-sharpened blades.

"Hey, you guys, go real slow for me," Bernie said.

"Why don't you go real fast for us?" Tommy said.

When the second period started, Jefferson would have a minute remaining in a powerplay. Sats gave specific instructions to Bernie, Duncs, Adam, Nick, and Tommy on the play he wanted them to set up. "Get it to Tommy at the top of the umbrella. Take the shot, and go for the rebound."

Fifteen seconds into the second period, Tommy dribbled the puck behind the Edina net—exactly opposite of how Sats had told him to work the powerplay. The Jaguars failed to score on their man advantage.

Five minutes into the period, an Edina player stripped Bernie of the puck. The Jags' star center hooked the Hornet and took back the puck, but got whistled for hooking. A minute later, Edina scored to tie the game.

On his next shift, Bernie slashed a Hornet so viciously that he broke his own carbon shaft into two pieces. Another penalty. Edina capitalized on the opportunity and went up 3–2.

Sats benched Bernie. "You can't do stupid things," he told him, but the unspoken message was stronger: "My way, or you don't play."

Kelly ran another errand to find Nancy in the stands. Bernie had a second stick in the trunk of her car. Ron ran out to fetch it. He would have to buy another shaft to replace the one Bernie had broken. That had been a $110 slash.

"Is Sats angry at Michael?" Nancy asked.

Kelly nodded.

"Well, maybe he can learn from his mistakes," she said wistfully.

Between periods, Sats ripped his team a new exhaust pipe. He reminded them that they hadn't worked the powerplay like he had instructed them. They had taken selfish penalties. "You're trying to do it your own way, and that doesn't get shit," he shouted. The veins strained against his neck. "If you trust us, we'll get there." He glared at his captain and added a sarcastic parting shot, "Tommy, helluva effort. Best period you played all year."

Tommy and the rest of the players slouched. Peterson, who hadn't played a minute that period, sat with his chin on his chest and eyes downcast.

During the third period, unaware of Sats's tirade in the dressing room, Mary Gilbert said, "Tommy's fine until Sats starts yelling at him. We don't agree with that." She did admit she wished Tommy, whom success had befriended, would show more desire. "He could have a little more fire, if you ask me."

Elsewhere in the Jefferson section, Nancy hoped to see Bernie get back into the game. Mike Coffman, pleasantly surprised with Nick's inspired play, wondered if the Senior Line could pull the Jaguars back into the game. Karen flinched at Nick's every check. Duncs's younger brothers by his mother's second marriage batted about a Skoal tin with miniature sticks, trying to score past their father Dave's feet. Steve Duncan waited for his son to will the Jags to victory and give him something more to remember. Merrelyn Lorenz bounced her knees even though Timm watched from the bench. Randy Peterson wondered why his son wasn't playing. If Sats would just give Brad the opportunities, say, put him on the powerplay, Brad would shine the way he had in Bantams, his father reasoned.

Six-and-a-half minutes into the period—the first time that season Jefferson had been down entering the third—Tommy, frustrated in his effort to even up the game, slashed an Edina player and sat two minutes. Killing the penalty, Nick forechecked deep in the Hornets's end. He forced the puck loose, picked it up, twirled in front of the net, and tied the game single-handedly. He had put his new Easton stick to good use. Thank you, Dad. Merry Christmas.

Just past the midway mark of the period, a Hornet speared Duncs and knocked him down. Duncs finally snapped. He scrambled to his feet and rapped the offender across the wrist. The refs assessed him a minor penalty for slashing. The Jags fought off the Hornets's charge to keep the score even. Bernie still chilled on the bench.

With 5:35 remaining, Jefferson got its chance to win the game when an Edina defender was penalized for holding. Sats called time-out and gathered his team around him. He decided to put Bernie back into the game. The penalties his two captains had taken in the third undermined his point with Bernie. No. 11 wasn't surprised. On Sats's powerplay, he was the field general, the one who handled the puck along the side boards. And even though he had taken more penalties than anyone on the team except Adam, Bernie remained the team's leading scorer. Sats needed him.

Sats gave explicit instructions to his top unit. Get the puck to Tommy at the top. Take the shot. Put in the rebound. This time, do what you're told.

They did. They got the puck to Tommy, he let fly a shot, but the Hornets cleared the rebound.

Bernie brought the puck back up high. He slipped it to Tommy, but the middle lane was cut off, so Tommy slid the puck back to Bernie, who uncorked a slapshot. The goalie blocked his shot, but Duncs slammed home the rebound. Tommy, Bernie, Adam, Nick, and Duncs embraced as one. Their fans went nuts.

The goal stood up. When the final buzzer sounded, the Jefferson parents and fans were on their feet whooping out hearty applause for their boys' effort. The Jaguars had swept the Classic with their 4–3–come-from-behind victory. They ruled as the midseason champs. Sats smiled and shook his players' hands on the ice. Randy Peterson stood with his arms folded. His son hadn't gotten off the bench. Randy wasn't smiling.

After his exceptional tournament, capped by his shorthanded, game-tying goal, Nick once again found himself surrounded by reporters. "Up until the penalties, we had a bunch of momentum," he said. "I wanted to help get it back."

Nick had become the contributor he had set out to be. With two goals and five assists in the Classic, he had raised his on-ice value to +11 for the season. In the tournament's three games, he averaged almost four takeouts per game and put two-thirds of his shots on the net, highest on the team. His confidence soared.

All this from a guy Sats had expected to move down to the third line a few games into the season. "Nick is a great unsung hero," the coach told the reporters. "He is not the prettiest player, but he works so hard. His goal was the big one."

Duncs had scored his third game-winner in four games. He had shone once again in the Classic, further padding his father's rapidly bulging emotional scrapbook. A reporter told Steve that his son's five-goal and eight total point-performance this year made him the Classic's all-time leading scorer.

The players stuffed their equipment back into their bags, collected their sticks, and headed upstairs to the lobby, where parents and friends waited to slap them on their backs and congratulate them. Nick enjoyed a moment with his father. "Good job," Mike told his son.

A small boy waited outside the Jaguars' dressing room in a scene familiar with one played out the night before in Pittsburgh, where four-year-old Austin Lemieux had stuck his head into the Penguins's dressing room after his father's first game back and said, "I saw you." In Edina, Duncs's three-year-old brother Jake waited in his new cowboy hat, bursting with similar pride in his big brother. When Duncs finally emerged, Jake said, "Good game." Duncs smiled and escorted him up the stairs.

CHAPTER ELEVEN

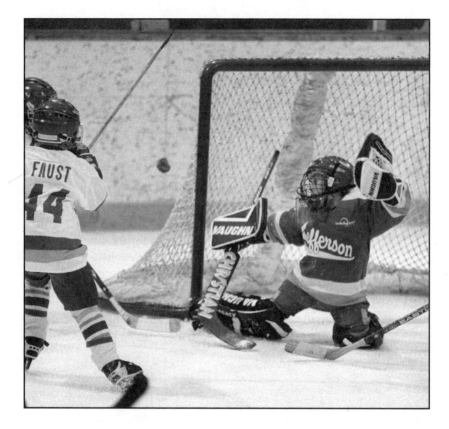

LORDS OF THE RINK

Make a wish, John Heckt. What's the farthest your nine-year-old mind can stretch? To share the ice with the Jefferson Jaguars, whose greatness you've heard your father extol? Be paired with alternate captain Nick Coffman in the annual Mite Game on New Year's day? Done. Happy New Year.

The White Mites made their wish come true by outselling the other Jefferson Mite teams in a fund-raiser. The prize of skating with their heroes motivated John Heckt and his eight- and nine-year-old team-mates to sell. With a little help from their parents, they took orders for a record five thousand dollars–worth of nuts, candy, and pizzas.

They had talked about this game for weeks. Their parents encountered no struggles getting the boys out the door for the 11 A.M. game. The boys even volunteered to go to bed early on New Year's Eve to ensure they were well rested. They didn't want to admit it, but they were a little nervous to go up against the varsity. One boy worried aloud whether the older, bigger players would be able to check. His mother didn't help matters on the van ride to BIG when she said, "I heard they were talking about having Mite munchies for breakfast." In the dressing room, the boys warned their goalie about Duncs's slapshot.

While the varsity players led the Mites through a series of preliminary drills, the younger boys' parents crowded the players' bench, armed with their video cameras and Nikons. Most would go through at least two rolls of film that morning.

To the varsity parents standing along the railing, it seemed like just yesterday that their boys had been the pint-sized bodies under large helmets looking like bobbleheads on skates. Tommy had been to heaven himself as a nine-year-old paired with his neighbor and idol Joey Bianchi.

Last summer, Duncs had relived the fantasy when agent Brian Lawton invited him as one of only two high school players to skate at the conditioning camp for his NHL clients and prospective clients. As a little tyke playing pond hockey, Duncs had pretended to be Mike Crowley, Mark Parrish, or Dan Trebil—the very guys he was invited to skate with on BIG's Rink 2, along with Phil Housley, Shjon Podein, Ben Clymer, and other assorted professional and college players. Duncs still had one of his Squirt jerseys that Trebil, '92, had autographed. "Growing up in Bloomington, you look up to these guys as the greatest people in the world," Duncs said. "They're everything you want to be."

The children saw the older players pictured in the newspaper, watched them play on television, and relived the excitement in the highlight videos. No one else in the community received that sort of adulation and attention, save the professional athletes who lived among them, but they were untouchable. Varsity hockey players would actually say hello when they saw the younger boys ride by on their bicycles. That won a personal affection. The lords of the rink enjoyed celebrity status nonpareil in Bloomington.

So it was that when Chris Tucker, wearing his Jaguars jersey with the *C* embroidered on his chest, walked into a Bloomington grade school cafeteria the autumn after scoring the game-winning, overtime goal in the '89 championship, adoring children mobbed him. Fifth- and sixth-graders thrust napkins, notebooks, and milk cartons in front of him to autograph. The children's honest and uninhibited hero worship reflected the community's love affair with its varsity hockey players.

Everybody wanted a piece of the champions, whether it was '81, '89, or the early '90s. The players were in such high demand for team banquets, classroom visits, Booster practices, and other public appearances that even though Sats divvied up the duties, they had to turn some down. "It was almost run like you were on a professional team; you were that much in demand," Mike Parrish said.

At Jefferson High, the hockey players occupied the top link on the social chain usually reserved for football players. In the popularity contest that crowned the homecoming king, senior defenseman Bryan Shackle reigned among his peers. Jimmy Humbert's girlfriend was elected queen. Teachers treated the hockey players like royalty. Other kids admired them.

Tucker had shown up at the grade school as part of the district's A Positive Peer Leadership program to speak on a panel of captains about his decision to be chemical-free. In addition to being drug-free role models—in itself a tall order for a teenager—the hockey players were held to a standard of exemplary behavior. Yet just as the gods of Greek mythology frequently misbehaved whenever they ventured off Mount Olympus, so, too, were Jefferson's mythical heroes prone to falling short of the moral codes prescribed them. On this year's team alone, Bernie had done time for his fight and Duncs had served two suspensions for chemical violations. They weren't gods; they were human. Boys, at that. It was a long fall off the hockey player's pedestal—with no soft landing. A kid who lost his footing could easily get hurt.

But at the Mite game that ushered in 2001, the players all turned in a positive public relations performance. After the game, they posed with their younger partners, who didn't yet reach to the varsity players' height, even with the older boys on one knee. The parents slipped out on the ice to take closeups. The Mites beamed so brightly no flash was necessary. John Heckt leaned slightly into Nick, his smile showing all mouthguard.

In a playful writeup that ran in *Let's Play Hockey*, John's father, Paul Heckt, quoted Sats before the game saying of the Mites, "They will be our toughest opponents this year. We won the Holiday Classic, but this is bigger. We've never beaten these guys. I still remember our 1993 team that was undefeated going into this game. The Mites were the only blemish on our record that year. I'm nervous, to say the least."

In the spirit of the Washington Generals—the long-time dependable losers to the Harlem Globetrotters—this year's varsity played along with tradition. Even though Nick scored four goals, the varsity couldn't put away the Mites. Late in the game, with the score tied 8–8, the Mite coach emptied his bench. Small white jerseys swarmed the varsity net. Make another wish, John. The young Heckt grabbed a rebound, wobbled to his left, and tapped in his first goal of the season to clinch the game with only eight seconds left on the clock. As the running time ran out, the Mites buried him in the hog pile celebration.

Paul Heckt ended his article on a serious note: "Instead of sleeping in late and watching football on their day off, these fine young men decided to give something back to a very appreciative group of eight- and nine-year-olds."

The father of the boy paired with Duncs called Steve Duncan later in the week to tell him, "If that's the kind of kid who is going to lead our country one day, it gives me great confidence." That call was something to remember.

Yet, the game was bittersweet for Charlie Pickerign, whose younger brother Will scored two goals. Five years earlier, Charlie had faced the varsity as a Mite. Now a Peewee, Charlie watched his younger brother celebrate with the disillusionment brought on by his advanced years. "You find out later they let you win," the older Pickerign said. "It's a little devastating, sort of like finding out there's no Santa."

Two days before entertaining Jefferson's future in the Mite game, the varsity confronted Jefferson's past. The twenty-eighth annual Alumni game brought the '01 team face to face with players representing more than a decade of Jefferson tradition. Coming home reminded the old-timers that they were part of something bigger than themselves. Those who had skated in the Jaguars jersey shared a special bond.

Years later, guys who had played together remained tight. Players from the dynasty years got together every summer in Vegas, where they spent half the weekend watching highlight videos and talking about old times. This past summer when his buddies asked about room assignments, Mike Crowley told them to check the BIG windows. He had taped the assignments where the Booster A and B rosters had been posted when they were kids.

Ironically, for all their success, the alumni gathered for the '01 Alumni game looked up to the current varsity. The younger players were fit and virile, emboldened by testosterone and illusions of immortality. They had yet to taste the aches of age, and their tomorrows still held endless promise. Jim Broz, '89, poised to hurdle thirty, admitted to pregame nerves. He had been working out to prepare for this game. He worried how his rusty skills would measure up against today's younger, more energetic players.

Past met present casually. The atmosphere was loose, the checking light. Only a handful of alumni and varsity parents watched in the stands. The varsity wore its mesh practice jerseys. The old-timers wore Jefferson Alumni jerseys with their names and year of graduation printed on the back. In the spirit of all-star games, offense outweighed defense.

With limited reserves, the older players returned to the bench gasping for air. The varsity had a longer bench and younger legs, yet failed to live up to the past greatness. Sats didn't keep score, but the players did. Yesterday's heroes won 10–6.

Afterward, the players, past and present, munched homemade bars and swilled Gatorade in the Rink 3 lobby. They glanced at the Rams-Saints playoff game on the TV suspended in the corner and debated which team would be the more favorable opponent for the Vikings to face next weekend. With the food and football in familiar surroundings, the gathering had the feel of a family reunion—which, of course, it was.

Sats mingled with the alumni, asking about college and careers, girlfriends and wives. His former players were cordial but cautious. Even though they had staked their independence as adults in the years since graduation, they found themselves feeling like they were back in high school in their former coach's presence. Their relationship with Sats was layered with father-figure issues. They regarded him with a mixture of respect and resentment.

Those who went on to play college hockey recognized that Sats had prepared them to succeed. Their coaches told them, "You come from Jefferson; you already know how to play." For that they were indebted.

Sats knew the game, ran efficient practices, and pushed his players, but it was the lessons he taught them about life that stayed with many alumni. Mark Parrish's mental soundtrack includes a speech Sats gave at the Tournament his junior year. "You never know if you'll get back," Sats told the boys in the bowels of the Civic Center. "Live for the now and not for tomorrow. Do it now." Making his living precariously in the NHL, where an injury can suddenly take away all of one's tomorrows, Parrish shakes his head. "That's something I live by today. I try to take each day as best I can."

Sats taught them to respect authority. When he found out one of his players had lipped off to the school librarian, Sats saw to it that the miscreant greeted Ms. Van Blarcum the next morning with a letter of apology. Jefferson Dean of Students Pete Helberg, thirty years Sats's junior, admitted he was intimidated to meet the man he had held in awe while growing up a Jaguars fan. After working with him six years, Helberg had seen Sats connect with troubled kids no one else could reach, and not just hockey players. "He is the kind of guy who will listen and help," said Helberg, whose own sense of humor made him popular with students despite his role as disciplinarian. "I hope they say that about me when I leave."

Not all of the alumni said nice things. Sats could be moody—jovial one day, aggravated or withdrawn the next. His players found him hard to read. They weren't always sure what lay beneath his jokes and his tirades. Try as they might, some felt they could never quite please him. At times, he made awkward or inappropriate comments they weren't sure how to take.

Sats's players sometimes questioned his motives. One player who had been through chemical-dependency treatment worried Sats would blackball him, so he enlisted Bianchi as his advocate. Sats gave him a second chance. Others didn't feel they got that from him, especially after Bianchi left. They accused Sats of playing mind games. One alumnus, upset about the way Sats had treated a friend of his, spurned Sats's invitation to the alumni game. "Most of the guys can take the mental and emotional abuse that Saterdalen dishes out, but he couldn't," the absent alumnus said after his friend quit the team.

So the alumni traded small talk with Sats warily, like walking on a pond the first day the ice reaches across the surface. They knew the ice might not be safe, but they were drawn to test it. Oddly, all these years later, they found themselves still thirsty for their coach's approval.

———

On a frigid day in December, one alumnus returned to BIG unbidden but drawn by something he couldn't quite name. He walked down the Hall of Fame—past his younger face immortalized twice on the walls—to Rink 1 where he knew the varsity was practicing after school. He did not enter the rink. He hung back in the concessions lobby and watched through the windows. The faint reflection of his image in the viewing glass was transposed over the players drilling on the ice.

The nine years since graduation had filled out his face, now stronger and even more handsome underneath his dark, curly hair. He pitched his hands in the pockets of an expensive leather jacket.

A high school hockey star with a college degree, he was young and virile.

He was adrift.

He had dumped a promising career. Abandoned his home. There had to be something more. Something else. He wasn't sure where it was. He could go up North to ski for a few days. Maybe travel in Europe. He wasn't sure.

Nine years. Nothing had been the same since he had stepped off of the Civic Center ice. The second time—the last time—he had raised the state trophy that capped the undefeated season and won All-Tournament honors. The cheers still rang in his ears. So long ago. Just yesterday. They had razed that building to put up the Xcel.

He couldn't get that feeling back. Not as captain of the college team. Not trading bond futures. Not even thinking about marrying his high school sweetheart.

He watched the varsity run through the Paynesville drill, shooting one-two-three from queues starting at the center, blue, and goal lines while Sats kept score. He had run that drill hundreds of times out there. He could feel the ice gliding beneath his blades, whiff the warm sweat issuing from his equipment, see the line of his shot on the net. He opened his eyes. This ice belonged to this team now, to Gilbert and Duncan and Coffman and Bernhagen and the other names he read in the paper that went with the colored jerseys on the ice.

He stayed until the Zamboni chased the players off the ice and then turned and walked quietly out of the arena.

CHAPTER TWELVE

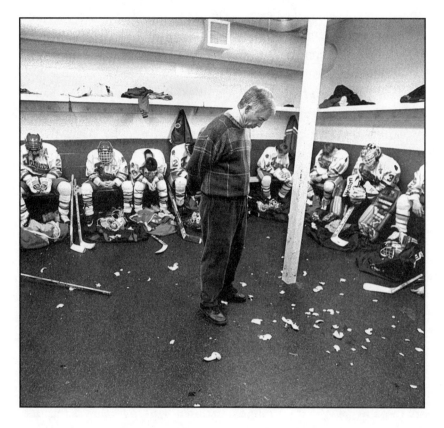

CURSED TO BE NO. 1

I would like to be the jaguar of your mountains
and take you to my dark cave.
Open your chest there
and see if you have a heart.
—ancient Mayan song

The jaguar inspired mystical reverence in ancient cultures. The Aztecs called a band of elite warriors the Jaguar Knights. The Mayas believed the nocturnal carnivore embodied the night sun. Guarani Indians marveled at the beast's ability to kill with one leap, biting its prey through the skull or neck rather than strangling it the way most large cats did. Even Teddy Roosevelt, who hunted the western hemisphere's largest feline in Brazil, expressed admiration for the "big, lithe, formidable cat."

These days, *panthera onca,* all but extinct in the United States, has become a threatened species. Jaguar habitats have shrunk by two-thirds in Mexico and Central America and by more than a third in South America. Despite local laws against killing jaguars and an international agreement outlawing the trade of their pelts, cattle ranchers freely shoot the predators to protect their livestock, and poachers fetch a lofty price on the black market for the rosette-spotted, Grey Poupon coats.

Bloomington's version of *panthera onca* inspired similar awe and jealousy. 2001 raised the bounty on the Jefferson Jaguars' hides.

———

The New Year dawned bright in West Bloomington. The sun shone low in a clear sky; the snow twinkled Jefferson blue. The Jaguars' Holiday Classic sweep combined with Eden Prairie's two non-conference losses in its holiday tournament catapulted Jefferson to the top of Varsity Online's national ranking over teams like Detroit Catholic Central, Mount Saint Charles Academy (Woonsocket, Rhode Island), Boston Catholic Memorial, and the rest of the Minnesota field. Jefferson's elite ice warriors rang in 2001 as the nation's best team.

On January 2, at the first practice since beating Edina, Tommy tried to downplay his team's top billing. "It's no big deal," he shrugged in the dressing room.

Nick called his bluff. "You brought a printout to school the day the rankings came out. I thought you were pretty excited."

Tommy didn't smile.

"What *do* you get excited about, Tommy?"

"Winning games."

Sats congratulated the boys on their Holiday Classic effort. "Nick single-handedly scored the tying goal. He showed determination— and what it will get you. Bust your ass, and things will go your way."

Nick beamed quietly behind his helmet's plastic shield.

Sats pointed out that at 10–1, the Jaguars had the chance to set a record for most games won by any Jefferson team. That season, the MSHSL approved three extra games on the schedule, which boosted their chances.

Tommy, Duncs, and Bernie wore the weighted twenty-five pound vests as penance for their penalties against Edina.

Sats had benched Bernie to send the message that he must control his temper. But when Bernie missed the net in a drill, he smacked a puck that sailed high along the glass within inches of Coach Thomas's head. After getting stopped in the practice-concluding showdown, Bernie flung his cracked stick high into the empty bleachers. Sats doubted his message had found its mark.

———————

Thursday, January 4, the day of the White Bear Lake game, the mercury reached 39°F, the first time in exactly one month that temps had crept above freezing. Convertibles drove with their tops down. Kids walked outside Jefferson wearing shorts. Icicles drooped from the school's roof. The thaw weakened winter's grip, if only for a day.

The Associated Press released its weekly Minnesota rankings. To nobody's surprise, Jefferson jumped from No. 4 to No. 1. Eden Prairie, the only team to have beaten the Jags, slipped to No. 2. White Bear Lake rated No. 8.

In front of the green board, Sats said, "All you guys read the paper today. They did, too. They're going to want to kick our ass."

That's the way it had been since they first pulled on a Jefferson sweater. The Jaguars skated with a target painted on their chests.

Minnesotans are not self-promoters. Submissive Scandinavian Lutheran mores dictate modesty. The cultural norm punishes those guilty of blatant self-aggrandizement. Watch a car driving up the shoulder on I-494, trying to merge out of turn. Other drivers will deliberately squeeze out the cheat. The state's inferiority complex nurses a blanket resentment against the best. Communities across Minnesota hated Jefferson the way the nation despised the damn Yankees.

Other teams derived a special satisfaction from defeating Jefferson, though for many teams that was a rare and uncommon pleasure. Even when they weren't playing Jefferson, they wanted to see the Jaguars lose. At youth tournaments from here to Canada, fans rooted against the team from prestigious West Bloomington.

Tommy, Duncs, Nick, and the others knew from their early days the fans were against them. Their coaches told them since they were Squirts that they were Jefferson; they were good. They would win. Coaches tossed the torch to their ten-year-old hands.

"Expectations are high, but that's good," said Peewee A coach Denny Connelly after his own team assumed the No. 1 ranking. "The kids learn to play under pressure at a young age."

Tommy's dad concurred. "In a program where the tradition of winning has been there, the expectations are higher," Kelly Gilbert said. "The program has built in a winning tradition which probably has helped [the boys] more than hurt them. Everybody who plays them wants to beat them. I think that's a good thing. It gives them high esteem."

By high school, the pressure mounted along with the stakes. The Jaguars knew they were expected to beat the lower-ranked teams. At No. 1, that meant everybody.

———

White Bear Lake missed being immortalized in American letters when F. Scott Fitzgerald recast the summer playground for St. Paul's elite as Black Bear Lake in his short story "Winter Dreams." (Perhaps the hard-drinking writer satisfied a grudge after his wild parties prompted the White Bear Lake Yacht Club to evict him.) Mark Twain's telling of White Bear Lake's legend in *Life on the Mississippi* fell short of winning the lake or its namesake city any lasting fame. Instead, the city with the fashionable shoreline made a name for itself in hockey. But in fourteen trips to the Tournament, the St. Paul suburb's main high school had never survived the first round, another black smudge against its name.

2001 could be the Bears' year. They were riding a hot streak and ranked No. 8.

Over the years, the Bears had been the Jags' nemesis. As Bantams, they upset Jefferson in the semifinals, ending the Bloomington boys' hopes of a state title. Last year, they "knocked the living snot out of us," Sats reminded his players before the game. Tonight, the Jags would seek their revenge in White Bear Lake's home rink, Aldrich Arena.

Coming off his sensational Holiday Classic performance, Duncs suffered an emotional setback when his Aunt Diane lost her year-long battle with cancer. He traveled from her funeral in northern Minnesota to the game. His realities shifted from the pew he shared with his tearful mother to the dressing-room bench alongside his immortal teammates. Lacing his skates, emotions alternately sad and beautiful swirled through him.

The familiarity of Duncs's affection for hockey soothed his grief. With the Jags short-handed, he took a pass up the right side and ripped a shot through the goalie's legs. That one was for Aunt Diane.

White Bear Lake pounded the Jaguars, but the Bloomington boys didn't let up. They battled evenly through a hard-fought period, until a wrist shot over Timm's shoulder with just 0:48 left in the period erased Jefferson's lead.

The Jaguars slunk into the dressing room.

White Bear Lake played even harder in the second period. When Tommy coughed up the puck, the Bears capitalized to take a 2–1 lead.

A Bear defender pulled Bernie to the ice from behind. Scrambling to his feet, Bernie hesitated for a moment with his stick poised in both hands over the offender's head but then skated away to join the play. Later Sats told him to pass the puck back to Tommy on the point during the powerplay rather than skate it back, and Bernie obeyed.

In the dressing room after the second period, Bernie said, "We've got to play some D. The rankings have gone to our head."

Sats interrupted him when he walked in. "Anybody learned any-thing?"

"We've got to work hard," Bernie said.

"Yeah, you're not competing." Sats paced. "It's embarrassing."

He walked out.

"Come on, guys," Duncs said. "Let's step it up."

The Jefferson fans in Aldrich Arena kept wishing for a comeback, but the players kept losing their edges, losing the puck, and losing the battles in the corners. The powerplay couldn't find the net, Bernie's line couldn't score, and Duncs's line couldn't carry the team. Timm gave up another goal. White Bear Lake's 3–1 lead seemed insurmountable, and it was. Timm made thirty saves, but the offense failed to click. The Wells Fargo Prep Report Highlights the next night would show White Bear dethroning Jefferson.

The White Bear Lake fans crowded into the student section had ridden the Jaguars the entire game, but with two minutes remaining, they taunted: "OVER-RATED, OVER-RATED." Afterward, silenced for heads down, the Jags hung their heads and listened to the Bears hollering and high-fiving next door.

In the hallway between the two dressing rooms, Bears coach Bill Butters told the media, "I never have to get them up for Jefferson. All we had to do was open the paper and see Jefferson was No. 1."

Sats had little to say in the dressing room. Talk of setting records hadn't worked to motivate his boys, nor had telling them after the second period they weren't competing, nor had reminding them about being embarrassed like last year. He knew they couldn't be up for every game, but what would it take for them to win the critical ones?

———

The next day before practice, the dressing room scuttlebutt was that Sats was in a sour mood. On the way into BIG, he stopped to talk to one of the community service crew—a former college hockey player—mopping the floor. The guys walking by smelled booze. "Sats has been drinking," Bernie announced.

Just then, Sats walked in. "Are you drunk?" Tommy jibed.

But Sats quickly sobered the mood with a ten-minute lecture. "My wife gave me shit last night when I got home. 'I thought this was one of your "good teams,"' she said, 'but I never saw your good teams play like that. There was something missing.' Know what that was?"

"Hustle?" Jimmy ventured.

"Focus?" Nick guessed.

"Pride," Sats said. "Only two guys worked hard every shift last night. The rest didn't. You can't look yourselves in the eye in the mirror and say, 'I made a mistake. I'm responsible.'"

He stood in the middle of the dressing room; his tone was even, serious. "I heard you horsing around in the shower after the game. I would've been gone so fast, but you didn't seem disappointed in the way you played. If the '93 team had lost a game like that, I never would've heard them screwing around. Or the '92 team, or the '94 team, or the '81 team—they played seven overtime games, won six, and tied one—they never quit. You guys look at the rankings and think all you have to do is go out and play. Start taking pride in the jersey. Start taking pride in yourselves."

When Sats started talking, the players looked at him dutifully. Gradually, one by one, they lowered their heads. Even Bernie, his mouth open in disbelief, dropped his chin. They couldn't hold his gaze.

After Sats walked out, Duncs turned to Jimmy on his left and said sarcastically, "I'm inspired."

———

On the ice, Sats stopped the Senior Line during a 5-on-2 breakout drill and circled the team. "The puck's in the corner, but not one guy said, 'I got it.' Did you, Duncs? Nick? Jimmy? Adam? Kory? You've got to talk."

"We're too smart," said Tommy, who resented Sats's guilt trips. "We don't need to talk."

"That's a goddamn copout," Sats shot back. "If you're not talking, you're not involved."

———

Sats hated to lose. As a Squirt, his son Jeff worried in the stands during varsity games. If the Jags lost Saturday, his dad would mope around the house all weekend. If they won, Jeff knew he was more likely to get whatever he wanted, from cookies to sleepovers.

"He could be the most competitive man I ever met," Jeff said.

The two used to play racquetball. One day, during Jeff's junior year, Sats—who finished third four times in the state racquetball championships—skunked his son. "I thought you were an athlete," Sats mocked. "I just beat you left-handed."

Jeff dropped him with a right to the gut.

The lowest he ever saw his dad was after the '88 Tournament. The Jaguars took third, but the bronze medals offered meager consolation after a disappointing 6–3 semifinal loss to Hill-Murray. A senior, Jeff had played his last high school game; his father had coached him for the last time.

Back at school, Sats helped his son clean out his locker. Jeff's arm was in a sling; on his first shift of the first Tournament game, he had separated his shoulder. He played the entire Tournament in the worst pain of his life—there was no way he was going to shortchange his dream to win a Tournament—and scored six points. But that pain was a flesh wound compared to what he felt Saturday night cleaning out his locker when he should have been on the Civic Center ice competing for the state championship. His dad felt Jeff's pain doubled by his own. They went home and talked late into the night. "You made the right choices," Sats told Jeff. "But things don't always go your way. You have a bright future." The moment felt bleak as bronze.

———

Tom Saterdalen grew up with something to prove. The internationally acclaimed Mayo Clinic ruled Rochester, ninety miles southeast of the Twin Cities. Tom was a working-class kid, the son of a hard-drinking farmer turned salesman, in a town dominated by doctors. His father worked hard to compensate for his eighth grade education and passed that work ethic on to his son. Tom was driving a tractor at eight, planting crops and cutting hay by ten. But when classmates asked, "What does your dad do?" he couldn't brag like the other kids. His dad hoisted propane tanks two days a week for Rochester Gas and Appliance and sold food plans for freezers the rest of the week.

He was close to his mother, who worked part-time at Mayo as a technician. His father and older brother drank with gusto; Tom abstained throughout high school. He could talk to his mom. She was his ally in the family. A basketball player and runner in high school, she encouraged him to play sports.

That's where Tom sought to close the class gap. Not blessed with abundant natural ability, he discovered that hard work gave him an edge, inspiring the motto he later used with his teams, "Hard work beats talent when talent doesn't work hard." He earned eight varsity letters playing hockey, baseball, and football at Rochester John Marshall High, one-upping his brother Dave, older by four years. "I still remind him of that," Sats said forty years later.

Rochester was progressive—it had indoor ice in the '50s. Tom watched the Mustangs at the Mayo Civic Auditorium with his parents, who held season tickets. By eleven, he had landed a job as the semi-pro team's stick boy. Hanging around those players—many of them NHL-caliber by today's standards—at the rink and on road trips was the best coaching he ever had. Polishing their skates and taping their sticks, he learned how to play the game and how to break it down.

Tom's mom was diagnosed with cancer during hockey season his senior year. The Mayo doctors gave her six months to live. Tom stayed in Rochester to be near her, passing up a partial football scholarship—forty dollars plus books—to Bemidji State. He enrolled in the local junior college and played amateur hockey for the Rochester Colts. His mother died two years later.

During his mother's illness, Tom got serious with Diane Hendricks. They had known each other since grade school when Tom used to throw water balloons at her. Sats left for two years of college at Bemidji State, almost three hundred miles north, but he married Diane the summer before his senior year. He was twenty-one; she was nineteen.

The newlyweds spent a year in the small paper mill town of Cloquet, where Sats coached hockey and taught phys ed. Sats returned to Bemidji State to earn his master's degree in education and served as an assistant coach to the hockey team. From there, they moved to

Superior, Wisconsin. Sats coached four years and won two state titles at Superior, but hockey wasn't to Wisconsin what it was to Minnesota.

Once accepted into the University of Minnesota's doctoral program in education, Sats wrote Glen Sonmor, the Gophers's head coach, and offered to be his assistant at no charge. Sats wanted to get into college coaching and figured Sonmor would be an excellent mentor. He got more than he bargained for. Over three years, Sats had the chance to work under Sonmor, Herb Brooks, and Ken Yackel, three of the state's top hockey minds. Sats completed the coursework for his Ph.D. but put his dissertation on hold when Brooks offered him five grand to coach the Gophers junior varsity. The next year, with two small children to feed, Sats applied for a Division-III college job at University of Wisconsin at River Falls. When River Falls offered the job to International Falls' Larry Ross instead, Sats accepted the Jefferson post and headed unwittingly into his historic tenure.

By the dawn of the third millennium, Sats had compiled the most impressive résumé of any of the state's active hockey coaches. Hard work and preparation had gotten him there. "[The Jaguars] knew more about our powerplay and kill than we did," said Chris Bonvino, who played on the '84 state champion Edina Hornets. "They weren't as talented, but they beat us once that year because they were so well prepared."

In his preparation, Sats paid keen attention to detail. Talking with assistant coach Stan Palmer, '76, between periods of a game, Sats mentioned an opposing defenseman played like one of Stan's teammates. Sats quizzed Stan on who he had paired with at the end of the season more than twenty-five years ago. Stan couldn't recall. "Danny Dryer," Sats said. "He shot right, like you, and wore Bauer skates."

Sats was committed to his teams. When his son Jeff—whom Herb Brooks had recruited to play for St. Cloud State—was poised to break the university's all-time goal-scoring record in 1992, Diane pressed her husband to leave the Jaguars game early to see their son make history. Sats refused. "What sort of message would that send to my seniors?"

Sats was organized, with his stats plugged into a computer program that could show him after each game where his players stood to date in fifteen categories. He constantly jotted himself notes. At Transfiguration Lutheran, which he attended every Sunday morning at 9:30, he scribbled thoughts on the worship leaflet. Off nights, he scouted opposing teams. His wife Diane had to be careful to check his pants pockets for programs stuffed with scouting reports before she put them in the wash.

He had proven himself but still felt he had something to prove.

————

Over the years, Sats had served plenty of satisfied customers. Angie Humbert was one.

Angie raised Jimmy and his younger brother alone. Divorced ten years, she sat with her ex at games, but she knew Jimmy missed having a father around at home. The single mom tried to stay a step ahead of the boys and blocked their Internet access to porn sites. She worried about how to pay for Jimmy's college on her commissions as a technical recruiter. But she was grateful for all Jimmy had learned playing for Sats.

"It's about more than hockey," she said one night at Billabong. She saw high school hockey setting her son up to succeed later in life the way a college education could rescue a kid from the ghetto. "He's gained confidence and seen what hard work will get him."

Nick's mom was another fan. Karen had observed Sats wave to his grandkids in the stands when he walked to the bench. She often saw the coach in her neighborhood strolling with his wife. Karen figured Sats must be a good guy to be married to such a special woman.

But the prophet wasn't always appreciated in his players' homes. Three times during Sats's twenty-eight year reign, Jefferson parents rallied to hurl him from the parapet of his success. There was the petition during his second year to oust him, then Al Horner's ad in the *Sun Current* in '92. In between, a father whose son Sats benched cried favoritism to the superintendent when Sats promoted his assistant John Bianchi's son, Tony, from the j.v. Even though the '86 team won ten games in a row after Tony's promotion, the superintendent surveyed parents back fifteen years, putting Sats's job at the mercy of the school board.

In the end, the team made it to the Tournament and Sats stayed. But winning came at a cost. Success bred expectations. Being ranked No. 1 inspired comparisons to successful teams of the past. Parents had seen what Sats had done for other people's sons; they wanted the same—or better—for their sons. If Sats didn't shepherd their sons to the Promised Land, his walks with Diane weren't going to stifle the complaints.

————

Two days after the White Bear Lake loss, the Jaguars traveled south down I-35 to play Lakeville, the fastest-expanding suburb in the Twin Cities. The young, upper-crust suburb's housing boom had stretched Lakeville High beyond capacity, but the numbers had given the hockey team a boost. The Panthers stood 4–1 in the conference, tied with Jefferson for first.

Saturday evening, Jefferson pounded the Lakeville goal but couldn't penetrate it. Finally, the third line connected at 11:25. Tommy added a powerplay goal with a minute remaining in the first, but six and a half minutes into the second period, Jeremy gave up a soft goal, which trimmed the Jaguars' lead to 2–1.

Suddenly, at the midway mark of the second period, Lakeville coach Randy Schmitz yanked his starting goaltender. No. 30 was fielding warmup shots while the starter plopped onto the bench. Jefferson had outshot Lakeville 28–6; the starting goaltender had stood on his head to keep his team in the game. The move baffled Jefferson fans. *What in the H-E-double hockey sticks is Schmitz thinking?*

Lakeville parents standing along the glass clued them in. That week, the starter—also a team captain—had challenged Schmitz's coaching decisions and sworn at him in the process; the coach disciplined his captain with a half-game suspension.

The move revealed only the tip of the team's troubles. A week earlier, the players mutinied. They decided at a players-only meeting— held at the starting goalie's house—that the coach must go or they would quit. Twenty-seven of the varsity and j.v.'s thirty-three players were ready to turn in their jerseys if the administration didn't meet their demand.

A day later, parents of the team's six seniors talked the players out of quitting, but that didn't right the team's course. The players and parents complained that Schmitz played favorites and didn't communicate. They griped about the way he shuffled players back and forth between varsity and j.v., playing them two periods each in back-to-back games, an unusual practice.

Bottom line: Schmitz had failed. In fourteen years behind the Lakeville bench, he had not led the Panthers to the Tournament. "It raised the level of frustration for players because Coach Schmitz was not positioning them to win games by putting the best players on the ice," explained Kim Kerchner, the starting goalie's father and one of the parents who talked the boys out of quitting. "Looking back, the boys were right. We were wrong. They should've walked. They should've embarrassed the coach and forced him to resign."

Amidst the turmoil, Lakeville lost to Jefferson 4–1.

A month later, the day before the Panthers traveled to BIG for their conference rematch with the Jaguars, the Lakeville parents aired their dirty laundry in the *StarTribune*. The lengthy article ran on the sport section's front page, complete with a four column-wide color photo of Schmitz yelling behind the bench. Lakeville's activities director, Craig DeYoung, put the blame back on the parents. "It's really just part of a huge problem we're seeing more and more," DeYoung said. "It's parental involvement in a negative fashion within high school activities. People aren't used to hearing the word 'no,' particularly at Lakeville. We're seeing more and more instances of parents who disagree with a coach's decisions and who seem to want to take it a step further."

An air traffic controller's job was a stroll in the park compared to coaching high school hockey in Minnesota. A 1998 *StarTribune* survey of sixty-six metro head coaches revealed that twenty-nine of the coaches had been at their schools less than two years, a turnover rate of 44 percent. Many of their predecessors had failed to weather the parental storm. Varsity hockey coaches were as threatened a species as the *panthera onca*.

———

They didn't do it for the money. Considering all of the hours Sats clocked scouting, preparing, checking on players, thinking about hockey, and actually coaching, his $5,501 annual coach's salary came down to about 83¢ an hour. Something deeper drove the Minnesota high school hockey coach.

Remember the 1987 movie *Wall Street*? In a critical scene, corporate raider Gordon Gekko (played by Michael Douglas) takes the microphone at a shareholder meeting and sermonizes: "Greed—for lack of a better word—is good. Greed is right. Greed works."

Those coaching high school hockey may have started with noble intentions, but those who survived possessed the greed to win. "Everyone I know has gotten into coaching because they care about their kids," said one insider, a hockey coach who knows. For a year, his stock topped the charts when his team won the state championship.

But, he explained, something happens to that initial good intention. Winning can alter your perspective without you even knowing it. "Winning is a drug—it does things to you," the coach confessed.

Once you have tasted that sweet high, you want it again. And again. And again. You don't ever want to come down. When you do crash, you're willing to go any length to get up again. Recruit outsiders. Cut seniors. Betray loyalties. Lie to children. Play mind games. "You're walking a fine line—how do you win in this competitive society and not lose your soul?" the insider mused. "Once you're at the top, man, you don't want to go down."

The more you gain, the more you want. "Sats has had a large dose of it for a long time—the attention, recognition—winning is his drug of choice," the insider chorused. "It's like that scene in *Wall Street* when Charlie Sheen's character asks Gekko, 'How many yachts can you waterski behind?' Truth is, it's never enough—they want to go every year."

If you buy this theory, the Tournament becomes a needle in the coach's arm—the big win that will put him back on top. He's just another junkie looking to score. The kids are the coins he can trade for that fix.

CHAPTER THIRTEEN

EAST MEETS WEST

Nowhere were the Jaguars hunted more vehemently than in their own back yard. Ever since Thomas Jefferson High opened in Prestigious West Bloomington thirty years ago, the blue collar East Side's John F. Kennedy High Eagles preyed upon their affluent neighbors. Throughout the '90s, when the rich got richer and the poor got poorer, the crosstown rivalry burned strong, fueled by resentment and arrogance. When the two sides faced off January 9, 2001, in their annual Lake Conference matchup, the game assumed dimensions larger than the rink's 200' x 85' surface. Wherever labor squared off opposite management, poverty railed against privilege, or tenant battled landlord, there Kennedy stalked Jefferson.

A social and economic yin-yang defined Bloomington, with Bloomington Ice Garden the demarcation point. Walk out the arena's front door and a wetland preserve greets you. Beyond the cat-tails poking through the snow, young families in the '80s and '90s settled into the expanding development. Streets named South Bay Drive and Bloomington Ferry wind around lakes and golf courses, ski areas and parks, hiking trails and more wetlands. The residential streets open onto wide driveways that end in three-car garages attached to custom-built houses. On the northern edge, glass and steel office buildings reflect city parks. Slip out of BIG's back door, pass the Zamboni, and the streets straighten into a tight grid, lined by strip malls, industrial parks, and railroad tracks. The houses shrink into postwar ramblers with single-car garages tucked into alleys; apartment complexes overlook freeways. Here dwells the city's aging population, growing old with their houses, and the new wave of immigrants from places like Laos and Somalia. The gap between east and west is the difference between a jumbo mortgage and Section 8 subsidized housing. Urban blight confronts suburban bliss at the ice rink.

The community splits along political lines. In November, the East Side reelected three Democrat state legislators; West Bloomington retained three incumbent Republicans. Al Gore's pres-idential ticket narrowly carried the city, where George W. Bush was heavily favored to the west.

In 1987, five years after a sharp decline in students closed Lincoln High, the school board consolidated students district-wide in grades five through eight. With student enrollment still dropping, the move allowed the district to keep open Kennedy and Jefferson by adding ninth-graders to the high schools and busing fifth- and sixth-graders to Oak Grove Elementary and seventh- and eighth-graders to Olson Middle. But a task force proposed a plan for 2001 to create three middle schools to house grades six through eight, which would reduce school sizes and engender neighborhood schools. The plan carved the city east, west, and central, meaning some students from an affluent pocket just north of Jefferson would be bused to the central school on the East Side. Parents from the neighborhood with homes appraised at over half-a-million dollars campaigned vociferously against the integration, which threatened property values, among other things. One Olson teacher sympathized. "Those paying higher taxes in West Bloomington deserve better schools," he said. "They shouldn't have to go to the East Side."

There was another wave of opposition from the East Side, which feared the proposal would segregate Bloomington into a three-tier community by its middle schools: rich, middle, and poor, running west to east. Parents on the East Side feared their children would get short shrift. At a packed school-board meeting in late January, with the overflow crowd in the hallway watching the proceedings on TV monitors, one mother addressed the decision-makers in a quaking voice, her face flushed, "I want our community to be more whole and less divided." The school board approved the proposal with the concession that students living within a mile of Olson but slated to be bused across town would be given priority for intradistrict transfers.

The city's two high schools embodied Bloomington's economic divide. Kennedy had a vocational-technical school atmosphere; Jefferson supported a college-prep curriculum. Kennedy catered to more students with learning disabilities and behavior problems; Jefferson abolished its internal alternative school. Kennedy housed the district's English as a Second Language program; Jefferson hosted foreign exchange students. Jefferson wore a white face: almost 90 percent of its 1,779 students in the 2000–2001 school year were Caucasian. Over a quarter of Kennedy's 1,704 constituents were students of color. Although only 3.5 miles separated the two schools, they stood worlds apart.

Kennedy's school police officer occasionally took guns off students while Jefferson's liaison officer was more likely to relieve students of twelve-packs. Violence was more common at Kennedy; mental health and recreational drug use were bigger concerns in Jefferson households. Although parents of Jefferson students tended to be more involved in their children's education, Kennedy parents were more likely to take responsibility. "Call a Kennedy parent, and he says, 'What did my kid do?'" observed one teacher who had worked on both sides of town. "Call a Jefferson parent, he says, 'What did you do to my kid?'"

East and west sought to settle the score in athletics whenever the two schools met. In the state's hockey capital, the showdown took place on the ice rink.

"Kennedy and Jefferson is the Sharks and Jets," said *Sports Illustrated* columnist Steve Rushin, who graduated from Kennedy in '84. "I'm sure in 100,000 towns across America where there are only two high schools and you're stuck with each other, that rivalry is going to develop. You've got to hate somebody, so you pick the other school because it's there, especially in high school when you're just a roil of emotions."

Yet, the Kennedy–Jefferson rivalry began well before high school. Before they learned the freezing point of water, Bloomington kids flashed colors to show their loyalty. They wore navy blue hats with Kennedy stitched in gold or powder blue hats with Jefferson stitched in silver. Even kids at the centrally-located Nativity Catholic grade school identified themselves by the high school nearest their neighborhood. Kids spotting a rival school cap in the stands below them spat on it. East Side kids joked about "Jags fags"; West Side kids laughed at "trailer trash." They hated everything about each other.

———————

Rink 1 didn't provide a level playing field. Kids growing up west of BIG attended the top camps and wore the finest equipment; whatever potential they had was likely to be developed. East of the arena, more kids came from single-parent homes where their mothers or fathers worked odd hours and were not available to drive them to games or practices. After school, they baby-sat younger siblings and raised themselves.

There was a time, though, when Kennedy had been a hockey power itself, Jefferson's equal and occasional better. In the mid-1970s and throughout the 1980s, the Eagles and Jaguars battled in the section playoffs to advance to the state tournament. Kennedy made the trip seven times, winning it all in '87 and finishing second in '84. As late as 1991, Kennedy edged Jefferson in the section final, but that was the Eagles's last trip to the Tournament.

Kennedy's venerable coach Jerry Peterson retired in 1992 after twenty-one years, yet that was only a footnote to the East Side's downfall. Shifting demographics clipped the Eagles's hockey wings. The influx of immigrants came from countries where hockey pucks didn't exist. Despite the NHL success of Jarome Iginla, Scott Gomez, Paul Kariya, and a handful of other non-Caucasians, hockey remained a white-bread sport. Korean-born Brian Johnson— adopted by a set of blue-eyed parents—was the only non-white on the Jefferson varsity. (His teammates affectionately dubbed him "the Asian sensation.") Socioeconomic factors rendered membership exclusive. Kennedy's rising minority population thinned its ranks of hockey prospects.

In the end—like most American situations—it came down to money. Success these days comes at a considerable investment, one that the families relegated to the East Side's low rents couldn't always make. Take a price tag tour at Bloomington's Westwood Sports, which outfitted Jefferson and Kennedy kids alike. Bauer 7000 skates: $429. Jofa 6090 shin pads: $99.99. Socks: $12. Louisville TPS breezers: $134. Bike Hockey Joc: $28. Bike Protective cup: $7.50. Bauer Vapor 4 shoulder pads: $99.99. Jofa JDP 6035 elbow pads: $44. Louisville HG1 leather gloves: $170. Bauer 5000 helmet: $80. Jofa 480 cage: $30. Shock Doctor mouthguard: $20. Easton Z bubble graphite shaft: $105. Bauer Lindon heel curve blade: $18. Roll of white tape: $3.50. That'll be $1,280.98, please.

Goalies, try $4,089 to cover special skates, custom leg pads, extra-protection breezers, reinforced cup, chest protector and arm pads, blocking and catching gloves, neck guard, mask, and stick. Super-sizing hockey equipment doesn't come cheap.

Add to the expense of equipment registration fees, tournament travel, summer leagues, camps, clinics, skate sharpening, extra stick blades, etc., and you could pay a private high school's annual tuition. Multiply that cost by the number of kids playing each year. The children of a single mother working the second shift on a software packaging line are more likely to wind up playing basketball.

That said, Jefferson could not be neatly summarized as a luxury campus for rich suburban kids. The school had its share of fringe kids, those whose families didn't have the money for their children to participate in activities, who couldn't afford the private music lessons necessary to make it into the band. The school's population ranged from the boy whose father gave him a thirty-five thousand dollar car to the boy living in an apartment without furniture. The fringe kids didn't qualify for the elite cliques; they considered those kids stuck up. They weren't going to waste three bucks on a ticket to a hockey game. They skipped the pep fests and hung out instead in the lunch room. The school tended to shun them reciprocally— they weren't bringing Jefferson any glory. Those kids made up the forgotten faces of any high school, marginalized in this case by money and talent.

Still, nobody wanted to beat the mighty Jaguars more than the Kennedy Eagles. The East Side kids had suffered a decade of domination at the hands of Jefferson. Coming up through the ranks, the Jefferson kids had pummeled the Kennedy kids on Blade Day. Tommy's teams, from Mites to Bantams, had never lost to Kennedy. Kennedy High hadn't beaten Jefferson since December 17, 1991. Then, the loss inspired the Jaguars' sixty-game unbeaten tear. But in 2000, the unthinkable had happened.

In their first meeting, Jefferson spanked Kennedy 5–0 with Timm earning the shutout. In the conference rematch, Jefferson once again seemed headed for another routine victory, but Robbie Kinsella bucked history. With only 3:30 left to play, the Eagles' All-Conference wing tied the game. Then, in his first shift of overtime, Kinsella collected a pass at center ice and broke in on a two-on-one. His shot from the faceoff dot beat Jeremy on the short side. That shot—off the blade of a working-class kid and past the glove of a boy who had left behind the East Side—was heard round the city.

Kennedy's daily television news show set clips of Kinsella's goals to music. When his overtime shot struck gold, chills ran down the Kennedy hallways from one classroom to another. For the first time in ten years, Kennedy had defeated Jefferson. Later that week, an East Side man spied Sats walking into a store. He parked his car, followed

Sats inside, proclaimed to his face, "Jefferson isn't the only school in this town with a hockey team," and walked out. The night of the Big Upset, one Kennedy boy dialed Bloomington numbers at random and announced excitedly to whomever answered, "Kennedy beat Jefferson." For that one night, the fortunes had reversed.

————

The upset stung Jefferson. Coupled with a subsequent loss to Eden Prairie, it snapped the Jaguars to attention. They turned their season around and won six straight games to land in the Tournament, blasting Kennedy 6–0 along the way in the first round of the section playoffs. Yet, a year later, Nick still smarted from the Kennedy loss. Pulling on his breezers at school Tuesday night, he said, "It was the worst loss of the season."

The boys felt the pressure not to let last year's history repeat itself. "It's a lose–lose situation," Duncs explained, rattling his Tums. "Everybody expects us to win, so if we do, it's no big deal. But if we lose, it's front page news."

The first item Sats had written on the green board was: "Will play very hard; make their season." With his team assembled in front of him, he explained, "This is their state championship. You guys had to pay for it last year."

————

The full moon hovered over BIG. The parking lot filled early. Cars lined nearby residential streets. The largest crowd of the season—some 1,400 people—streamed into BIG, Jefferson to the home side, Kennedy to the visitors'. For the conference rematch next month, they would swap sides.

In the hallway behind the concessions stand, the Kennedy cheerleaders stretched nervously. Their excitement had mounted throughout the week, manifesting itself in the navy "Beat the Jags" bandanas they had fashioned for themselves and the players, the good luck signs they taped to their lockers, and the banners they painted for the game. They knew there would be no television appearances for them at the Tournament; Jefferson was their biggest game of the year. "We beat them in football," said one cheerleader, adjusting her bandana. "This is our year."

Down the hall, Emily Finley and the Jefferson cheerleaders primped in a private room ripe with perfume. The girls' faces sparkled with glitter. "If we lose, it's going to be tears," Emily said. A senior, she had been there last year.

At the other end of the arena, the officials summoned the captains to their cubicle. "Keep it clean," the refs told Tommy and Kinsella. "Have fun."

They returned to their respective teams. Like Tommy, Robbie Kinsella was a talented all-around athlete more comfortable letting his actions speak for him than delivering motivational speeches. Last year's upset had granted Kinsella, a varsity hockey player since ninth grade, instant superstar status, but he had not let the thrill go to his head. There was still this, senior year. Kinsella ducked into dressing-room A, where, unlike Tommy, he had a thin supporting cast waiting for him.

His Kennedy Eagles bounced their knees in anticipation. At the start of the season, they had set three goals: 1) Win the holiday tournament; 2) Finish 18-7; and 3) Beat Jefferson. They lost the holiday tournament final and, going into Tuesday night's game, they stood 6-7. Beating Jefferson remained the only goal they hadn't failed. They could redeem their season in one night. In the Eagles' team program, half of the players listed "beating Jefferson" as their most memorable hockey moment. They had tasted the sweetness; they wanted another bite.

Coach Todd Kennedy paced before them. "We're not in a position where we need to prove anything—we did that last year," he said. In his fourth year as Kennedy's head coach, whispers of Jerry Peterson's success still haunted him. He wanted the win to prove that last year wasn't a fluke. "The key is to keep our emotions in check. Play the game, like it says on the bottom of our practice jerseys; just play the game."

He stepped out, and a temporary vacuum sucked through the room. The Eagles sat fully dressed, visors down on their gold helmets, ready to play. Their stomachs scrambled. They tapped their sticks, punched gloves, jiggled their skates.

An affected redneck accent cracked the silence, "Come on, boys."

"Just another Lake Conference game for these Eagles," Kinsella chipped in. "Play hard, guys."

"I hate these guys," someone said.

Nervous silence followed.

One of the sophomores stood up and performed a quick jig, briefly slicing the tension.

A whoop rose in the corner, echoed and banged off the cinder blocks, and more whoops swarmed the room. The navy blue rose to their feet and crowded the door. "This is it, guys," someone shouted.

"Work hard," another voice shouted. "Let's work harder than these guys, Blue."

"Don't worry about Bernhagen," the student manager offered. "He's just a big pussy."

The band outside their door struck up a song. The drums thundered.

"Hands in!"

"Eagle pride on three."

"One, two, three, EAGLE PRIDE!"

They charged onto the ice between evenly parted the fans, navy blue and gold to the left, Columbia blue and silver to the right. The cheerleaders flailed their pom-poms. The band banged away.

Kennedy came out hard, but Jefferson came out harder. Faster. Stronger. They had the larger talent base, the skills more professionally groomed. The advantage. They pounded the Eagles. Just like old times.

Even luck played favorites with the Jags. Kennedy's Aaron Forsman, a swift and skilled center, fired a shot on net. Timm kicked out his left skate, but the puck ricocheted back across the slot. He dived across the goal mouth just in time to block the rebound with his arm. Seconds later, Kennedy clanked the crossbar. The blessed tin had spared the Jags.

Jimmy pocketed a rebound to spot Jefferson an early lead. Down and dejected, a Kennedy player decked Duncs after the whistle. On the powerplay, Bernie slid the puck back to Nick who dished it off to Tommy on the far post. With his long arms, Tommy looped the puck around the goalie and stuffed it in the net to put Jefferson up 2–0.

Bernie's mom, Nancy, jumped to her feet and waved her "Jag Rag," a white handkerchief with the Bloomington Jefferson logo on it. The band struck up the school song:

Hail to the mighty Jaguars
Hail to our conquering heroes
Hail, hail to Jefferson
Above all the rest. (Fight, fight, fight!)
Hail to the mighty Jaguars
Hail to the blue and silver
Fight, fight for Jefferson
The champions and the best.
J-E-F-F-E-R-S-O-N
Fight, go, fight, go,
Win team!

Early in the second period, Bernie put the Jags up 3–0. The band played again, and Nancy shivered her Jag Rag.

Seconds later, Bernie carried the puck off the faceoff into the Eagle zone, and a Kennedy defenseman rammed him into the boards. Bernie grabbed his stick and wouldn't let go. The ref whistled Bernie for two minutes while the announcer reported over the P.A.: "Scoring for Jefferson, No. 11, Mike Bernhagen."

Before the game, Sats had warned Bernie that the Eagles would go after him and cautioned him against retaliating. "Bet you won't be able to stay out of the box," Nick teased. They knew him too well. So, too, did their opponents. The word was out: bait Bernie, and he'll bite. The way to beat him was to let him sit himself down in the penalty box, where he couldn't hurt you.

Before Bernie served out his time, the Eagles scored. Kennedy had clawed its way back into the game 3–1. The Jefferson band played a courtesy drum roll. It often played the opponent's school song following a goal but sometimes messed up the notes. The navy blue side of the rink stood and applauded. One mother jammed her fingers between her teeth and whistled shrilly. The goal gave the Eagles new life and reeled the fans back into the action. Whenever Kennedy carried the puck into the Jefferson zone, the navy blue crowd rose to their feet.

From the top row of the visitors' side, a woman with hair dyed red and a "Beat the Jags" bandana around her forehead railed against all that did not go Kennedy's way. Diana Hoffman felt a personal stake in the game, as though her life were being played out before her on Rink 1. While Bloomington's upwardly-mobile families moved east to west across town, life's fortunes had taken Diana and her son Jeff the other way. Now a Kennedy defenseman, Jeff had played in Jefferson's Booster program until Bantams, when his mom and dad divorced. Diana and Jeff crossed the tracks going the wrong way, shoved over to the East Side.

Diana knew the difference between east and west. "Jefferson expects to win; it's not a challenge for them," she said after the second period, her Eagles down 4-1. "The East Side fights that mentality continually because they expect not to win. When they get beat up and lose game after game, I don't care how good of a parent or coach you are, it's hard to instill the idea you're a winner."

To beat Jefferson would let them believe, if only for a night, that life is not always unfair. Winning would soften the blows she had absorbed watching her boy, on the ice and off.

While the Zamboni finished its loops before the third period, a Kennedy student stealthily crept over to the Jefferson side and lifted the *Bling, Bling* sign pressed against the Plexiglas. The Jaguar fans had taunted the Eastsiders long enough. When the Kennedy boy returned to his side and jubilantly hoisted his trophy, navy blue fans erupted in a standing ovation. But his hero's welcome was short-lived—Bloomington Athletic Director Joe Dolan collared the boy and escorted him out into the cold night, perhaps for his own safety.

Five years ago or better, a fan would not have dared to cross sides, the Bloomington police officer on duty observed. He might not have returned. Fights frequently broke out between the fans, mostly in the parking lot. Although it had been a while since the last crosstown rumble, feelings remained intense on both sides, and the cops remained vigilant, a visible presence rinkside.

The rivalry may have been mitigated somewhat by combining the student populations district-wide at Oak Grove and Olson thirteen years ago, yet kids still grew up playing hockey for their respective high school program and identified with the high school they would eventually attend, Kennedy or Jefferson. Introducing them to each other in grade school only personalized the rivalry. When Kennedy scored, one of its players grabbed his crotch in front of the Jefferson students. Knowing he had a lazy eye, they shouted back at him, "You one-eyed lazy fuck!"

The consolidation had not made them friends.

Nick had scored late in the second on a powerplay, and Tommy scored in the third to give Jefferson a comfortable 5–1 lead. With less than two minutes to play, Jeff Rysavy—Brad Peterson's replacement—punched in a final goal.

The cheerleaders declared Nancy Bernhagen the Ultimate Fan of the game. Bernie's mom had lots to cheer. Bernie and Tommy had broken the curse against Lakeville with a goal apiece, then combined for three goals in this game. They had found their mojo.

After the final buzzer, the two teams lined up to shake hands under the surveillance of Joe Dolan and Bloomington's finest. They split into their dressing rooms, stripped off their gear, and parted to their schools on either side of town—all without incident. Nothing had changed. Jefferson had outshot Kennedy 43–19 and won 6–1. East was east; west was west.

CHAPTER FOURTEEN

ATTITUDE ADJUSTMENT

Tommy turned eighteen Wednesday, the day after the Kennedy win. Friday night, Tommy's grandparents, regulars at Jaguar hockey games, took him to the Mystic Lake Casino. At eighteen, he was legal. He bellied up to the blackjack table and laid his bets. He plunked his coins into the slots and pulled the handles. The ritual exercised his new-found rights.

He finished the night twenty bucks in the hole, but that didn't matter, he was eighteen. It is the age of entitlement; the age of enlightenment—ask the boy who just turned eighteen. The boy looks ahead to eighteen as the summit where he can plant the flag

of his manhood. The man looks back on eighteen as an embarrass-
ment of bloated ignorance. It's a dangerous age.

"When I was eighteen, I thought my father was pretty dumb,"
Bing Crosby's character says in the movie *Going My Way*. "After a
while when I got to be 21, I was amazed to find out how much he
had learned in three years."

Sats didn't have three more years with Tommy.

————————

That same Friday, after school in the BIG dressing room, the boys
dressed for practice. Bernie teased Tommy about an earlier embar-
rassment. Duncs repeatedly spit flecks of saliva between his teeth
against the wall to his right, an involuntary tic. Nick lashed a skate
lace around his teal socks. Timm released a voluminous and pro-
tracted burp—he was the team's Pavarotti of belching.

Sats turned to junior wing Jeff Rysavy "Shavvy, you know what a
woman says after you've satisfied her?"

"No, what?"

Sats flashed a gotcha grin. "I didn't think so."

————————

The players took a knee at center ice for Sats to explain a drill.
Steam wisped from their practice jerseys. While Sats talked, the boys
nudged one another in the back and traded jokes. Friday afternoon,
their minds were elsewhere.

"Apple Valley may have the best line in the state," Sats cautioned.
"They're the top scoring line in the conference."

Tommy rolled his eyes. *Whatever.*

Sats preyed upon their pride to reclaim their attention. "If you
win the rest of your games, you'll take the conference." The team's
last eleven regular season games were all conference contests, including a rematch against first place Eden Prairie.

"You just jinxed them," said Jeff Saterdalen, standing at his dad's
left elbow. He liked to come to practice the day before games to
shoot on the goalies.

Sats looked at him as though he had spoken out of turn.

"You told them before White Bear Lake if they won the rest of their games, they would set a record; then they got the shit kicked out of them," Jeff said. "Now you just told them if they win the rest of their conference games, they'll win the conference. You jinxed them."

"You think so, Nick?" Sats appealed to his obedient alternate captain.

But Nick wasn't interested in this father-son repartee. He was saying something to Duncs and missed Sats's question. Tommy missed the question, too.

Sats poked his stick toward his son. "He says I jinxed you—did I?"

"No," Bernie said. "They suck."

"Those guys can talk." Sats pointed his glove to the championship banners on the far wall. "You can't yet."

"Hogwash," Bernie said. "They have Achenbach in net? He sucks." Apple Valley junior Colin Achenbach was already making a name for himself as one of the state's top netminders.

"What about your breakaway against the Kennedy goalie?" Sats retorted. Tuesday night, Bernie had returned to the bench upset that Kennedy's goalie had stymied him up high. "Why didn't he go down?" Bernie had complained. "Because he's smarter," Sats had snapped.

Now, Bernie shrugged. "I thought he would go down."

"Thought?" Sats exclaimed. "Guy sucked a feather up his ass, thought he could fly." He chortled. "I haven't used that since Bantams. My coach used to say that all the time."

The players laughed, but not with him. They stood up, dribbled the pucks, and traded wisecracks. Tommy poked Nick with his stick. Sats had to corral them to start the breakout drill.

Later, they worked on the powerplay. Sats wanted them to talk, but they moved the puck around wordlessly. Sats's anger toward Tommy for his comment that they were too good to talk lingered. *How do you coach a kid like that?* Kids had changed during Sats's tenure. They didn't respect adults like they used to. They didn't listen. He blamed the parents. They didn't hold their kids accountable.

"You've got to talk," Sats shouted. He interrupted the drill and gathered the powerplay unit to yell at them. Bernie and Duncs skated away shaking their heads and cursing.

Sats stopped them again and called over the powerplay unit minus Bernie, who skated around and flicked pucks at the net. Sats resumed the drill but banished Bernie to the other end of the rink. Duncs seethed. Sats let Bernie diddle around with the puck too much. They needed to move it more. Then he played these mind games. *Up yours, old man.*

All of that carried over into Saturday night's game. Jefferson barely squeaked by Apple Valley 2–1. "You play like you practice," Sats often told his team. They wouldn't win the conference practicing or playing like that, let alone make it to State.

Bernie scored a pretty goal early but missed on another breakaway. Achenbach—and Sats—got the last laugh on that one. At the end of his shifts, Bernie skated lackadaisically back to the bench. On the penalty kill, he slashed one opponent in the ankle behind the play and upended another with his stick going for the puck. Both times he escaped calls.

After the game, Nancy Bernhagen waited on a bench in the lobby. Tommy walked by. "Why can't your son score when I pass him the puck?" he asked, half-smiling, half-serious.

Bernie pouted. He walked by without looking at his mom. "Honey," Nancy said. She jumped up to run after him. He didn't stop.

————

Friday after practice, Sats had pulled Nick aside and told him to shoot more. Saturday, Nick ripped a wrist shot top shelf and scored the winning goal.

When Apple Valley scored, Nick returned to the bench and apologized, "Sorry, guys, I screwed up. That was my guy." Sats had been impressed that Nick took responsibility. "I respect that," he told him in front of his teammates.

On the bus ride home, several guys congratulated Nick on his goal. Sweet shot. "Thanks," Nick said. "Sometimes I surprise myself."

————

"Fuck!" The cry rang around the boards. Timm had let in a shot during drills that he thought he should have stopped. He worked hard in practice. Each day, he wanted to improve. He could see the progress he had made from last year. After beating Kennedy, he felt he was playing well enough to be the Jaguars' top goalie. He thought he had proven himself with his 1.83 goals against average and .895 save percentage. He asked Sats if the coaches had picked a regular starter.

"Not yet." Timm's work ethic had impressed Sats, but the question troubled him. He considered it selfish, Timm putting his own interests before the team's.

Timm was scheduled to start against Burnsville, but the day before the game his cries ringed the boards more frequently than usual.

The Burnsville Blaze—formerly the Braves—had been a dominant hockey force in the '80s. During the nine-year stretch from 1983 to1991, Burnsville made seven Tournament appearances, winning back-to-back titles in '85 and '86. Burnsville was still a force to reckon with. They had a young, hungry team.

Angie Humbert, Jimmy's mom, noticed that the Jefferson boys had been flat. Before the game, she jokingly suggested she should hire a stripper to infuse them with some energy. "She could put 'Burnsville' on her shirt, and they could tear it off," Angie laughed.

Five minutes into the game, Duncs moved the puck up to Nick, who broke in with Jimmy on a two-on-two. Instead of passing, Nick shot high, and the Jags led 1–0. "Thataway, Nick," Sats called. At least Nick was doing what he was told.

The Burnsville coach called time-out. His Blaze regrouped and tied the game.

Several scouts had turned out to watch the Jefferson boys. Among them, Tri-City's assistant coach was liking what he saw in Nick and Duncs. Jack McCarten was there scouting for the Vancouver Canucks. The St. Paul native had backstopped the United States to Olympic gold in the 1960 Games. McCarten wanted a look at Tommy, Duncs, and Adam, but instead he got an eyeful of two Burnsville stars combining for three goals in the second period.

With a minute to play in the second and down 4–1, Bernie tried to sneak inside the Burnsville D but was up-ended ass over teakettle. He landed hard on his back. The image served as the game's metaphor.

When the second period ended, Sats told Tommy, Nick, and Duncs he had nothing to say to the team. It was up to the captains to turn things around. He had tried this tactic in the past with varied success.

Duncs stormed into the dressing room. He flung his helmet into the corner and slammed his stick to the floor. "What the fuck's happening? We can't lose to these guys. We're the best team in the state. What are we doing out there?"

He looked around at his teammates, slumped over their equipment, some stripped to the waist. They looked to him. "Those fuckers aren't that good. We're losing to the worst fucking team in the conference. We know we're the best, but we have to play like it."

Duncs gestured toward the hallway. "Don't do it for that guy out there. Fuck him. Do it for each of yourselves. You've got to want it."

He paced among his teammates. "I'm not talking to any one individual. I'm talking to myself, too. You've got to want to be the fucking best. We've got to get up for this. Everybody play hard for fifteen full minutes. We can score three goals in a period. That's horseshit to us. Go out there and shoot."

His speech was impassioned but rather than being edged with anger and urgency, his voice pleaded and implored. Ironically, his words reflected Sats's influence.

"Everybody gets a takeout this period," Nick kicked in. "Remember what we did against Edina."

Tommy asked Duncs if he was open down low when Burnsville worked its trap. He didn't say anything to the team.

Timm had stared at the floor, his hands clenched. Now he stood up. "I fucked up last period, guys." His voice trembled. "But I want to win this game. I'll do my part, you do yours."

Sats poked his head in. "Ice is ready, guys."

Tommy tried to muscle his way through the Burnsville defense but lost the puck. Bernie passed to Tommy on a rush, but the puck slithered off of Tommy's stick. When Sats switched lines, Tommy skated to the bench and raised his arms. *Why are you taking us off?*

In the final minutes, with the game seemingly out of reach, they surrendered to their frustration. Tommy lost the puck behind the net to a freshman defenseman and shoved him in the face, knocking him to the ground. The ref called Tommy for roughing. Just as Tommy's penalty expired, Bernie cross-checked a Blaze and got grounded for two minutes.

"One minute remaining."

The Burnsville fans stood and chanted, "OVER-RATED. OVER-RATED."

At the final buzzer, Timm froze. He leaned with his hands on his knees. His teammates patted him on the back, but he didn't move. He had done his part for the third, turning away seven shots, but it had been too little, too late.

He finally straightened to join the line shaking hands, then stomped into the dressing room.

"Heads down," Sats said.

They leaned forward, hung their heads. From the room next door, they heard shouts and cheers. "Jefferson sucks!"

"That goalie was easy!"

Timm cradled his forehead in his hands.

Duncs draped a towel over his face.

They kept their heads down after Sats left.

"That was embarrassing," Jimmy said.

No one else spoke. They stared at the rubber floor mat, the gray and black speckles swimming together.

Bernie ripped off his equipment and left. Tommy sat silently, his helmet still on, the visor up, like a knight who had just lost a battle. Timm peeled off his chest protector and arm pads, leaned back against the wall, and folded his arms. Sweat darkened his gray longsleeved T-shirt. Nick studied the orange peels littered across the floor. Duncs cried into the palm of his glove.

They sat silent and stung. Five minutes. Finally, Duncs stirred and started to tear off his equipment. The rest followed as though at a prayer vigil, waiting for a cue that it's over, time to leave. The peel of Velcro and the zip of bags sounded loud against the cinder blocks.

They left quickly. Sats returned, sat down on a bench, and waited for the sophomores to sweep the dressing room. Hands in his pockets, he didn't speak. He wanted to get home and go to bed. Put this night behind him.

———

The next day at school, Timm was crabby. During a phys ed floor hockey game, he barked at a kid who accidentally hit him in the face with his stick. Timm had lost two of his last three starts. That was no way to win the starting job.

The team had lost two of its last five. Until Burnsville, no one had beaten the Jags in their own building. Jefferson was certain to lose its No. 1 ranking. Duncs had rated this year's team among Jefferson's best. "Then we lose to a shitty team like that, and I think maybe we're just another mediocre team, getting our hopes too high," he said.

What happened?

Tommy slumped in one of the cafeteria's plastic chairs, his Abercrombie shirt untucked and unbuttoned over a T-shirt, and searched for answers. The rankings had gone to their heads—they figured they could beat anyone just by showing up. They lacked intensity and focus in the dressing room, talking about irrelevant things rather than concentrating on the game at hand. Tommy admitted he had gotten caught up in his own scoring and ice time rather than simply playing for the team.

Tommy also blamed Sats. Not for jinxing the team, but for failing it. "Last night, we got outcoached," he said. Burnsville had changed the way it played after calling time-out; Jefferson hadn't. The Blaze had stolen the momentum. Then, in the third, when the Jaguars needed their best players on the ice, Sats skated three lines instead of just the top two. Some doubted Sats knew how to coach them back from a deficit. The rift between Sats and his players was widening; he was losing them. Tommy shook his head. "The guys aren't listening to him."

Tommy knew his teammates would listen to him, but the reticent captain wasn't sure what he could say to rally them.

He was also frustrated by Bernie, who ran hot and cold and didn't seem to care about anyone other than No. 11. His attitude was disruptive on the bench and during practice. His temper and tongue hurt the team. Tommy had thought about saying something to his linemate. Two weeks earlier, they had gone snowmobiling at Kevin Bernhagen's place in Wisconsin. Tommy had the chance but hadn't found the words or the guts. He dug his thumbnail into the edge of the table.

So much hinged on Bernie. Kevin had chewed him out for not hustling. Even his mother told him after last night's game that he stank. Once, before a Squirt game, she had given him a decongestant for a cold, and he had played in a fog. That was how he played last night, Nancy said. He could be a poet, or he could be a poison.

Sats scratched his head himself. After the loss, he complained about the kids' lack of respect. They didn't do what he told them. Nick, yes, Duncs, sometimes, but with Tommy and Bernie, he felt ready to give up.

Bernie. Want to know what happened with Bernie the day of the Burnsville game? He is walking down the hall eating a cinnamon roll. The assistant principal spots him and tells him to finish his roll in the cafeteria. Bernie snipes over his shoulder, "Tough guy." The assistant principal hauls him into Sats's office. Is this the way your hockey players behave? Bernie starts lipping off. Sats has to play peacemaker.

"Just what you want the day of a game, right?" Sats shook his head. "Kids treat him like God in the hallway. He thinks he is."

After the Burnsville loss, Bernie had exchanged words with Jaguars' assistant coach Mike Thomas. "First kid ever who refused to shake my hand after a game," said the twenty-seven–year veteran coach.

What to do with Bernie? Sats knew Bernie's history. He knew Bernie needed patience and understanding, a little more love than the average kid. But his superstar's behavior tapped him out. Sats had discussed with Thomas the possibility of kicking Bernie off the team. Was his attitude a cancer they should remove before it spread?

There were two obvious reasons not to do that. First, lynching Bernie would cause an outrage, maybe even lead to lawsuits. Second, it would be foolish to dismiss the school's most talented player his junior year. Sats took the high road. "We're educators; that would be giving up on him."

Instead, Sats did what he had done in the past when the team slumped midseason. He called a team meeting the afternoon following the Burnsville loss. Let the players lean on Bernie.

Sats had decided after Friday's horrible practice to have the meeting Wednesday. The timing turned out to be ripe, coming between the Burnsville loss and Saturday night's rematch with Eden Prairie. The loss may have convinced the kids they needed to make a change. They might be receptive to hearing what they should do differently. Saturday night's big game provided the incentive.

After practice Wednesday, the Jaguars' varsity returned to school, showered, and squeezed into the desks Sats had circled in B201. Bernie had suited up but participated only in the skating drills. He had woken up in pain, his right elbow hyperextended in the check that had flipped him to the ice.

"I'm not going to say anything until you guys start talking," said Sats, seated at one of the desks in his windowless classroom. "You're a bunch of good guys, but something's getting in the way of playing hockey." He leaned back.

Tommy took the lead. "We lack intensity. No one's working hard. We're not ready to play."

"You've got to ask who you're playing for," Nick Coffman said. "I'm playing for every single guy in this room."

At Sats's urging, everybody said something, even the sophomores and managers. Their comments detailed their troubles; their tone was somber. Sats took notes.

"We need to start worrying about ourselves, not criticizing other guys," Nick Dillon said. "Encourage a guy if he makes a mistake rather than put him down."

Bernie had been the most outspoken critic.

Sats jumped in. "How many feel we do that?"

Only half of the guys raised their hands.

Thomas, seated behind Sats's desk, said, "Those are all good points, but talk is cheap. We gotta go out and do that. Look at yourselves when you hear things being said. Selfishness can kill a team. There are some people who think they're above being coached. When we talk to you on the bench, we're not trying to belittle you. Our goal is to get to the state tournament and win it."

His remarks were obviously aimed at one guy. Bernie had closed his eyes.

"The bottom line is that we're here to make you better people," Sats said. "If you treat people with respect, it's amazing how many good things happen to you."

"Maybe we should listen to the coaches and what they've got to say," Tommy said. "They've been here longer."

Sats invoked the Jefferson tradition. "In 1980 for the region finals, we had everybody healthy for the first time," Sats said. "We had to choose between two guys, one big and strong who went on to try out with the New York Giants, and the other was a little guy, about ninety pounds smaller, but better defensively. We picked him. Before the game, I saw the big guy put his arm around the little guy in the locker room. 'Steve, go out and bust your butt,' he said. That's respect." That was the year, the players knew, that Jefferson won the region finals and made its first trip to the Tournament.

"It's a big role to play for the Jefferson Tradition," Tommy said. "You've heard it before. Every team wants to beat us. Everybody has got to show up to play. This is not an individual sport."

Sats dismissed everyone but the seniors. "How much would you guys like to win the conference title?" he asked the seven.

"I'd love to," Nick said.

"How bad do you want to go to State and play at the Xcel, Duncs?" Sats asked.

"I want to win," Duncs said. "I'm willing to do whatever it takes."

"Last year, the day after a meeting like this, a senior got busted for chewing," Sats reminded them. "Let's see how much you mean it."

Duncs gnawed on his fingernails.

"You guys don't have next year," Sats said. "You might have to make a stand. If somebody's screwing around, you might have to say,

'Knock that off or I'll break every arm you have.'"

"If somebody was standing in my way of having a great senior year, I'd do something about it," Thomas added. "A cancer will spread."

Putting the desks back into rows, Sats stumbled across a backpack. Who would forget their books the night before semester finals? Bernie.

————

At practice the next day, Tommy thought the meeting had gone well. He was optimistic the team would respond. Duncs was more wait and see. Neither had talked to Bernie.

The captains thought something drastic needed to happen to shake up the team. They had discussed various possibilities for line changes, but Sats surprised them with his new combinations. Only the Senior Line remained intact.

During one agility drill, Thomas had them shout as a team: "We are not over-rated." It was ironic. In the AP poll released that day, Jefferson had dropped to No. 2 behind Elk River. In Varsity Online's national rankings, the Jaguars slid all the way to No. 9.

————

Bernie's elbow appeared ready for Saturday's game. But the oft-injured center's physical status was frequently in question.

In early January, Bernie had complained to Amber, the team trainer, about a tender hamstring and sore rotator cuff. Amber iced, taped, and massaged the players' wounds and bruises. She couldn't make diagnoses or dispense meds, but she could make referrals. When Sats found out Bernie wanted to see a doctor—he checked with Amber daily for status reports on his players—he asked her to call Nancy with the names of several sports doctors who wouldn't sit Bernie unnecessarily.

Amber also kept tabs on the players' medical eligibility. When she asked Bernie after his doctor's appointment for a physician's note clearing him to play, Bernie said he forgot it, but the doctor said he was fine. Then, two days later, Bernie told Amber he hadn't gone to the doctor, so he didn't have a note for her.

Following the Apple Valley game—an away game that Amber didn't work—Sats told her that Bernie had played great. "He's fine," Sats declared. Physically, anyway. For the moment.

———

Jefferson and Eden Prairie contested the Lake Conference title. Jefferson was 7–2 in the conference, Eden Prairie 8–1, the difference being their first meeting six weeks earlier when Mike Erickson and his mates strutted away King Shit. Jefferson had eight more regular season games—all within the conference—but those opponents were long shots. As far as the Jaguars were concerned, they played the Eagles Saturday night for the Lake Conference championship.

Beyond the conference title, each team battled itself to resuscitate morale. Both teams sought to rebound from an upset Tuesday night. Eden Prairie had lost 1–8 to Apple Valley. "Our guys quit," the Eden Prairie coach said. If Jefferson and Eden Prairie wanted to keep their state tournament hopes alive, they needed to prove to themselves they could turn around their seasons. The game was a must-win for both teams.

The TV cameras and print reporters showed up again. Fans lined the glass at both ends. Outside BIG, it was 10°F at game time. Inside it was barely warmer, with the ice hard and fast, perfect conditions for two strong-skating teams.

Merrelyn was sick to her stomach. Timm would start again because Jeremy had played Eden Prairie the first time around. Sats liked to throw a different goalie at opponents.

In the dressing room, the mood was different. The intensity Tommy had found lacking showed up. The players chattered animatedly. Nick thumped his teammates' chests with his gloved fist.

Timm rushed through his pregame ritual, kissing his equipment and visualizing his highlights. With a minute remaining in the j.v. game, he stood by the door, ready. Soon as the final buzzer sounded, he flung open the door and led the team onto the ice.

Following the ten-minute warmup, they returned to the dressing room for the Zamboni to surface the ice. Timm tapped his fingers into his catching glove. Shouts from the Eden Prairie dressing room echoed their way. "Don't let them get more fired up than us, guys," Duncs said. "Go out and hit these fuckers."

That's exactly what they did. No sooner had the puck dropped than Duncs laid out an Eden Prairie defenseman with a resounding hit to set the tone. He recorded four takeouts in the first period alone.

Midway through the first, an Eden Prairie forward crossed the blue line and snapped a wrist shot. Timm raised his glove for a routine save. But the puck struck Timm's glove, bounced off his shoulder, and sailed into the net.

Merrelyn clenched her jaw.

Timm stood alone between the pipes. *Fuck!*

He readied himself for the faceoff at center ice. *How'd that get by me?* Several relatives visiting from out of town sat next to his mom in the stands. He had embarrassed himself before them with his awful performance against Burnsville. *Still plenty of time left. We'll get it back.* If his dad had been there, he would have put two fingers to his eyes. *Watch the puck.* Timm was glad Dad hadn't seen that.

Both teams registered big hits. The refs let them play.

Duncs dumped the puck into the EP end. The Eagles' goalie stopped it behind the net and pushed it toward the corner. Duncs won the race there and threw a centering pass out front. The puck skipped off the Eagles' Mike Erickson's skate into the vacant net to tie the game at 11:45.

Duncs hugged his linemates. He skated along the bench to tap his teammates' fists, then back to the crease to punch Timm's glove. The Jefferson band rollicked the school song. Merrelyn and Timm's relatives clapped mightily.

Both teams played hard. Early in the second period, B.J. knocked an Eagle off the puck in the corner. Nick Dillon gathered up the puck, scooted behind the Eden Prairie net, then reversed his direction to stuff the puck home. Jefferson 2, Eden Prairie 1. Sats thumped him and B.J. on the helmets when they came off.

Eden Prairie stormed back. Several shots just missed. One slid ominously along the goal mouth. Merrelyn pressed both hands to her mouth. Even Debbie Earl, sitting next to Merrelyn, brought her hand to her lips. When Timm misplayed the puck on the side of the net with Jefferson short-handed, Merrelyn suffered a Maalox moment, but Timm escaped unharmed.

Both teams came on strong in the third. Jefferson players dropped to block shots. Eden Prairie's Marcus Paulson came up big on several saves. The sophomore had minded the net for the Eagles' earlier victory over the Jaguars.

Timm misplayed a shot off his blocker. The puck fell to his right, but the Eagle swooping in on the net failed to get good wood on the puck. It slithered wide.

Jimmy flattened an Eagle defenseman almost a helmet taller at the Jefferson blue line to separate him from the puck. Duncs picked it up and headed down ice with Nick. He tried to slide a pass underneath a sprawling defender, but the puck banked off of his shin pad and between the goalie's legs. Duncs pumped his right fist three times in the air. With 5:11 to play, Jefferson led 3–1. Timm exhaled.

But it wasn't over. Eden Prairie launched a flurry of shots that Timm turned away. Jefferson cleared the zone, but Eden Prairie came right back. Merrelyn clasped her hands. *Oh, dear God, don't let them score. Not now.* Timm smothered the puck. She clapped her hands against her knee. *Thank you, Jesus.*

Only 1:06 remained. Eden Prairie pulled its goalie. Sats stood on the bench and shouted instructions.

Eden Prairie buzzed the Jefferson net.

Nobody was still sitting when time finally expired. The band played, "Hail to the Mighty Jaguars." The mighty Jaguars jumped over the boards and rubbed their gloves over Timm's mask. "Great fucking game, Timmbo," Duncs said.

In the dressing room after a quick heads down, Sats shouted, "Great job, Blue," and clapped his hands. This time, it was the Eagles down the hall who had to endure echoes of the Jaguars' jubilant shouts. "I'm so fucking happy right now," Jimmy bubbled.

Even Tommy smiled. Beating Eden Prairie was the best birthday present his teammates could have given him. They had responded to the team meeting. "If we play every game like that, no one can beat us," he said.

Duncs and his buddies rode the wave of their high to a party at the house of one of the girls' hockey players. They partied into the early hours of the morning.

Sats wasn't in a hurry to leave BIG Saturday night. His boys had made mistakes, but they had played hard. "There was a lot of intensity in this game, which had a section playoff atmosphere," Sats told the *Bloomington Sun Current*. They had left their hearts out there on the ice. It was a different team from the bunch that had frittered away the game to Burnsville Tuesday. That's what he liked to see.

CHAPTER FIFTEEN

BROTHER'S LITTLE HELPER

Monday afternoon, the boys sauntered through their warmup laps, circled at center ice, and stretched. Tommy, Nick, and Duncs led them through pushups. Sats skated up to address his team, which now owned first place in the Lake Conference after thumping Eden Prairie.

"Can anybody tell me what happened Saturday night in one word?"

The boys gave him the response he was looking for: takeouts.

Before Saturday's game, Sats had listed two columns of numbers on the locker room board: 20, 24, 21 and 37, 38, 39. The column on the left represented the number of takeouts during the team's three losses; the column on the right showed the team's takeouts in the wins against Elk River, Kennedy, and Edina. The last two games, Sats said, "We played harder than any other." The harder they played, the more takeouts—times they physically separated their opponent from the puck—they registered. Sats considered takeouts the most telling statistic of his team's effort. His message: you've got to bang some bodies to win hockey games.

Saturday night, the Jefferson blue had racked up forty-seven take-outs against Eden Prairie, a season high. From Duncs's crunching check the first shift through the end of the game, it was their most inspired performance to date. At practice Monday, Sats reminded the boys of the takeout's importance. He pointed to two plays in particular: B.J.'s hit that freed the puck for Nick Dillon and Jimmy's takedown that sprang Duncs. "Two checks, two goals," Sats summed up. It was that simple. Or was it?

––––––––

When the second period had ended Saturday night, after Dillon put Jefferson ahead 2–1, Sats compared notes with the other coaches outside the dressing room, and the boys filed past. They were pumped. "Way to go, boys," Duncs said, taking off his helmet. "Way to fucking go."

He stripped off his jersey and shoulder pads, gulped from a blue Powerade water bottle, and tossed it across the room to Bernie. "Nice goal, Nick," he said to Dillon. "That rocked."

"No shit, way to go," Nick Coffman added.

Others piped in their congratulations.

Dillon smiled his impish grin. "Thanks."

He was playing the game of his life. Not only had he scored what would turn out to be the game-winner, Dillon was on his way to a team-high seven takeouts. Listed in the program at 5'7" and 135 lbs, the junior wing had averaged only one takeout per game through the first sixteen.

"How much were those?" one of his teammates asked.

"$39.99 for a bottle of two hundred tablets," Dillon said.

"Of what?"

"Ripped Fuel." The bare-chested Dillon, who had a soccer player's build—what little muscle he had shaped his legs—flashed the plastic bottle from his equipment bag. The label showed a torso with bulging abs and pecs. That was how Twin Labs packaged their pills containing ephedrine.

The managers tossed oranges to the players. Tommy peeled his in silence.

"How many did you take?"

"One," Dillon said.

Sats walked in, and the boys stopped talking. With the toe of his stick, Shavvy chopped the orange peels that accumulated on the floor. "That's it," Sats said. "Keep working. Keep working. Nice job, Dillon." He left to join the other coaches.

"How many'd you take, Duncs?"

"Two." It had messed with his hands—made them shake—the first period, but he had adjusted.

"I took one and a half," said Jimmy, who at 5'6", 142 pounds was built more like a jockey than a hockey player.

"I take three because I'm a little guy," said the 5'7" Shavvy.

Sophomore defenseman Ryan Van Bockel gestured to Dillon. "Give me one."

"It won't work," Dillon said. "It takes half an hour."

"I don't care," Van B insisted. "I want one."

After the team meeting challenge to play with more intensity, a handful of the players tested Ripped Fuel in practice. They liked the extra zip it put in their skates. "It totally helps give me more energy—like a Dew buzz," Jimmy said. "You still get winded, but it helps keep you going."

Sats had pushed them to work harder. They had found something that worked for them. High school football players swore by it. They had been gobbling ephedrine for a decade. The stimulant's reputation for giving players that extra edge to play up to expectations spread like stories of a girl willing to put out. Brands like Ripped Fuel gained tremendous popularity. "If I can go out and get three more takeouts and be more intense, then I will take that fucking little pill," Duncs said.

He was so wired after the Eden Prairie game that he didn't go home until 4 A.M. He couldn't sleep, and, even though his stomach was empty, he didn't feel like eating. The ephedrine—which is also marketed in diet pills—took away his appetite. But those side effects were minor nuisances compared to the game's outcome: ephedrine 3, Eden Prairie 1.

––––––––

Derived from a shrub-like evergreen plant that grows in the desert regions of central Asia and the Southwestern U.S., ephedra alkaloids are amphetamine-like compounds with potentially powerful stimulation effects on the central nervous system and heart. One of those alkaloids, ephedrine, is the primary active ingredient in the illicit drug methamphetamine. It is also the primary active ingredient in Ripped Fuel. Ephedrine, also known as ma huang, is packaged under a variety of brand names—Ripped Fuel and Ultimate Orange are the most popular with athletes—and touted for the ability to facilitate weight loss, boost energy, and enhance athletic performance. Ephedra products are among the most lucrative of all dietary supplements in the $4 billion-a-year industry.

But ephedrine and ephedra are far from safe. In addition to insomnia, tremulousness, anxiety, palpitations, chest pain, dizziness, headaches, and personality changes, the use of ephedra alkaloids can result in strokes, heart attacks, psychosis, seizures, and death. An article published the month before the Eden Prairie game in the December 21, 2000, issue of the *New England Journal of Medicine* (*NEJM*) reported the results of a study involving 140 adverse events occurring from the use of dietary supplements containing ephedra alkaloids, including thirteen cases of permanent disability and ten deaths. The authors concluded, "The use of dietary supplements that contain ephedra alkaloids poses a serious health risk to some persons."

Since 1993, the Food and Drug Administration (FDA) has received spontaneous reports of more than twelve hundred adverse events—including seventy deaths—associated with the use of ephedra alkaloids, though the actual number is likely much higher. "The reporting rate, at best, is no more than about 10 percent," wrote G. Alexander Fleming, M.D., in the December issue of *NEJM*. "Thus, the series of cases reported to the FDA suggests that the annual number of deaths and cases of permanent disability associated with the use of supplements containing ephedra alkaloids in the United States may be substantial."

Particularly alarming was the FDA's finding that most adverse events "occurred in young to middle-aged otherwise healthy adults using the products for weight control and increased energy." They were young adults whose physicians would not have identified as being at risk for heart attacks and strokes. Many reported that the side effects showed up on the first use or within the first two weeks, some even at relatively low doses (12 to 36 milligrams per day). The *NEJM* article described a fifteen-year-old girl with no previous health conditions or concurrent risks killed by a heart attack after using Ripped Fuel for less than three weeks. (Two years later, in the wake of several highly-publicized deaths attributed to ephedra products, Ripped Fuel is now available without ephedrine.)

Dr. Alexander Fleming attacked Congress in his commentary for creating a loophole in the Dietary Supplement and Education Act that obscured ephedrine's dangers and let the stimulant fall into the hands of children: "This act allows inadequately tested drugs to be marketed as 'dietary supplements'—an innocuous and even holistic-sounding term. A compound containing ephedra alkaloids should not be called a dietary supplement; it is a drug."

Indeed the FDA had lobbied unsuccessfully since 1997 to impose tighter controls on products containing ephedra alkaloids. The agency wanted to limit the legal dose to eight milligrams and restrict the twenty-four–hour maximum to twenty-four mg. Twin Labs, which manufactures Ripped Fuel, recommends taking two capsules containing a total of about twenty milligrams of ephedrine three times daily. The label directions state, "Do not exceed six capsules daily," which would be 120 mg of ephedrine, but then later warns, "The maximum recommended dosage of ephedrine for a healthy adult human is no more than one hundred mg in a twenty-four–hour period." Either way, Ripped Fuel's recommended dose far exceeds what the FDA considers safe.

214 • Blades of Glory

The labeling on dietary supplements cannot always be trusted. The *NEJM* study reported that more than half of twenty supplements tested either failed to list the ephedra alkaloid content on the label or had more than a 20 percent difference between the amount listed and the actual amount. The FDA also wanted products claiming to offer energy enhancement to state on their labels: "Taking more than the recommended serving may result in heart attack, stroke, seizure, or death." Through the 2000–2001 hockey season, the FDA remained unsuccessful in its efforts to regulate ephedrine more strictly.

Twin Labs listed ephedrine as an ingredient under its Chinese alias "ma huang"—implying ancient Eastern wisdom—and similarly disguised caffeine as "guana seed extract." Only in the label's fine print is ma huang identified as ephedrine and guana seed extract as caffeine. Yet studies show that the combination of ephedrine and caffeine increases the incidence of adverse reactions associated with ephedrine. The FDA wants to prohibit the mix, which it considers dangerous.

When Nick Dillon mentioned Ripped Fuel to his dad, Pat Dillon consulted a doctor. The family physician told him not to worry about ephedrine, that it wasn't going to hurt Nick. Although their conversation was not a formal consultation, it's easy to see how a parent would take a physician's casual comment as sound medical advice, just as someone might take as a market tip a stock broker's endorsement of a certain stock during a soccer sideline conversation. The physician said the jury was still out on ephedrine, that it was too early to tell whether the supplement was dangerous. He was apparently not aware of the fatalities associated with ephedra alkaloids.

As the team physician for a neighboring suburb's high school football team and an MSHSL tournament physician, he was aware of ephedrine's popularity. Kids can buy the dietary supplement—which is also sold as an over-the-counter nasal decongestant and asthma treatment—at gas stations, convenience stores, health food shops, and grocery stores. Some packaging appeals specifically to adolescents with "active lifestyles." Other varieties are marketed as "natural alternatives" to the street drug ecstasy, a hallucinogenic methamphetamine. An NCAA survey released in the summer of 2001 would reveal that ephedrine use by college athletes was on the rise and that almost 60 percent had used nutritional supplements other than a multi-vitamin in the previous year. Sixty-three percent of those NCAA athletes said they began consuming nutritional supplements in high school. Another study by the Blue Cross and Blue Shield Association released two weeks later estimates that about one million American children ages twelve through seventeen have taken performance-enhancing sports supplements. The publication of the survey results followed news of the deaths of three football players who had allegedly used ephedrine. "I think all of these kids are using this stuff," the MSHSL Tournament physician said. "It's not a question of whether they're using it, but a question of whether it is good for them."

In Nick Dillon's case, ephedrine might have been more dangerous than for other kids. An asthmatic, he used an inhaler loaded with the stimulant albuterol. The effects of albuterol and ephedrine are additive in much the same way alcohol and tranquilizers are. Several drinks may not be enough to make a person pass out, but consumed along with a prescribed dose of Valium, the additive effect could kill a person. Using his inhaler as prescribed and popping Ripped Fuel could put Dillon over safe levels and increase his risk of adverse events. The *NEJM* article reported that a twenty-two-year-old man who used albuterol to treat his asthma had collapsed at a gym while lifting weights. He had also been using Ripped Force, a supplement containing ephedrine. The treating cardiologist believed that the combination of ephedrine and caffeine in Ripped Force along with the man's asthma medication (which included theophylline) caused a heart attack that shortchanged the brain's oxygen supply and left the man neurologically impaired.

One of the three football players to die the summer of 2001 would be Rashidi Wheeler. The Northwestern University strong safety, who used albuterol to treat his asthma, collapsed and died at a team practice. The medical examiner found ephedrine in his system, though he determined it was not at toxic levels. He ruled the twenty-two year old's death a "classic case of exercise-induced bronchial asthma." Suspicions remained, however, that ephedrine contributed to the young man's death.

Even at the levels found in Wheeler's system, the ephedrine could have reacted with the albuterol in a lethal fashion. "The medical examiner couldn't refute the possibility of the asthma medication having some sort of reaction with the ephedrine," explains Jay Smith, M.D., a staff physician at the Mayo Clinic Sports Medicine Center. "Just because it was found at a non-toxic level doesn't mean it was not a contributing factor [in Wheeler's death]."

The family physician wasn't looking at Nick's chart during their conversation about Nick's use of ephedrine. Pat hadn't reminded him that Nick also used albuterol under prescription. But his casual endorsement of ephedrine could have carried fatal consequences.

––––––––––

Nick Dillon's teammates had experienced a variety of ephedrine's side effects, including dizziness, tremulousness, insomnia, and anxiety. Nick Coffman said the drug made it hard for him to think on the ice. Bryan Shackle said it made his brain whir so fast that everything else slowed down. "But then when you don't take it, things go too fast on the ice," Shacks said. "So you almost need to take it to keep up."

The team's drug-induced intensity translated into more takeouts but also more penalty minutes. Ephedrine shortened their tempers. Guys like Jimmy and Shavvy, who hadn't taken a penalty pre-Ripped Fuel, wound up sitting in the sin bin for their transgressions. But all of the players taking Ripped Fuel increased their takeouts. Shavvy doubled his game average from 1.5 to 3; Jimmy nearly doubled his. So what if they took a few extra penalties?

Nick Dillon, the diminutive forward who suddenly started playing like power forward Keith Tkachuk, served as Ripped Fuel's poster child. His seven takeouts and goal against Eden Prairie made for a winning endorsement. And he didn't let up. He more than tripled his average takeouts per game. Madison Avenue couldn't have written a more convincing advertisement. Soon almost half the team had tried ephedrine.

Yet Dillon would pay a price. The rough physical game was not natural for someone his size. He was quick, creative, capable of scoring the pretty goal. With ephedrine, his scoring picked up slightly—he would score four goals in nine games after having scored three in sixteen—but his body would suffer from the increased collisions. Three weeks after Eden Prairie, he separated his shoulder going into the boards.

Tommy Gilbert hadn't tried Ripped Fuel himself—he admitted to being scared of the drug's possible side effects—but the Jaguars' captain gave ephedrine his blessing. If it provided the pick-me-up guys needed to fight the midseason doldrums and stave off burnout, then he approved. He had seen what it could do for them. "If kids are playing good [with Ripped Fuel], I want them to use it," Tommy said.

Leaning against the boards one afternoon at practice, Jimmy praised what swallowing two Ripped Fuel capsules a half hour before the opening faceoff had done to improve his game. He surveyed his teammates running through a skating drill and said, "I think a lot of guys on our team should be using it. We don't play with enough intensity."

———

Right under the list of ingredients, the Ripped Fuel label spells out in bold caps: **KEEP OUT OF REACH OF CHILDREN**. Farther down, "Warning: Not for use by individuals under the age of 18." That covered the majority of the '01 Jaguars.

The NCAA bans ephedrine. So, too, the United States Olympic Committee and the International Olympic Committee ban the use of ephedrine in competition. After ephedrine was implicated in the heatstroke death of Minnesota Viking Korey Stringer in 2001, the NFL banned ephedrine. Those governing bodies believe the stimulant gives athletes an unfair competitive edge and endangers their health. They have outlawed the supplement to keep the competition fair and the athletes safe.*

---

*After a medical examiner determined that ephedra had contributed to the February 16, 2003, death of twenty-three-year-old Baltimore Orioles pitcher Steve Bechler, who collapsed from heatstroke, the U.S. Department of Health and Human Services commissioned a review of ephedra and ephedrine. The results, published in the *Journal of the American Medical Association* (March 10, 2003), concluded

Yet, the Minnesota State High School League, whose governing values include "equity, fairness, and justice" and "activities which support healthy lifestyles" for more than two hundred thousand participants mainly under the age of eighteen, tacitly condones the use of ephedrine, largely out of admitted ignorance. Despite published reports such as the NCAA survey, the football player deaths, and tournament physicians' knowledge of widespread use, the MSHSL had not received one complaint about ephedrine from parents, coaches, school chemical awareness counselors, or its own sports advisory committee. "It's way below our radar," MSHSL associate director Skip Peltier said after the 2001 hockey season had ended. "Dave [Stead, executive director] and I and the staff aren't real knowledgeable about what students are using."

The league has issued a broad statement recommending student-athletes not use certain substances, such as creatine and steroids, but does not mention ephedrine by name. The league does not test for ephedrine nor penalize individuals for its use. Upon first being questioned about Ripped Fuel and similar products, Peltier, who is in charge of chemical use policies, responded, "If an individual is using it in line with the manufacturer's recommendation, that's not a problem."

Given the prevalence of ephedrine use by high school athletes and the preponderance of information suggesting it's not safe, one would expect the league to take the approach physicians have taken with alcohol and pregnancy. Since it's known that drinking can cause birth defects but not known what level of consumption is safe, the medical community recommends no alcohol intake during pregnancy to protect the child in the womb. Why not take a similar approach with ephedrine? It's known that ephedrine can cause seri-

---

that "ephedra and ephedrine are associated with two to three times the risk of psychiatric symptoms, autonomic symptoms, upper gastrointestinal symptoms, and heart palpitations." An accompanying editorial stated, "the public, aware of recent reports of deaths in young athletes reportedly taking ephedra or ephedrine, is right to be alarmed that the regulation Congress has in place does so little to protect them from the hazards posed by these potentially dangerous compounds."

Another study published that month in the *Annals of Internal Medicine* concluded that "ephedra use is associated with a greatly increased risk for adverse reactions compared with other herbs, and its use should be restricted."

In the final days of 2003, the FDA announced its intention to outlaw ephedra products in the coming year. In 2004, the MSHSL Sports Medicine Advisory Committee issued a statement discouraging the use of creatine, androstenedione, ephedrine, or other performance enhancing nutritional supplements, though the league stopped short of banning these substances.

ous problems, even death, but unknown what level of use might be safe, so why not ban ephedrine outright to protect youth?

The league and its doctors maintain that since they can't back up a ban with testing—which would be impractical and likely face legal challenges—they won't ban ephedrine or other potentially harmful performance-enhancing dietary supplements. Yet, back in the '80s, the MSHSL pioneered efforts against alcohol and other chemical abuse. Bloomington schools, led by its hockey coaches Sats and Bianchi, raised awareness and developed the APPL model of intervention, treatment, and prevention using team captains to promote chemically free lifestyles. The program has been highly effective in reducing chemical abuse among high school athletes. Like other high school leagues around the country, the MSHSL bans alcohol and imposes penalties for confirmed use without having to rely on testing. That practice has led to plenty of suspensions and proven a healthy deterrent, even if it is not 100 percent effective. Given the opportunity to make similar inroads in discouraging use of performance-enhancers, the MSHSL passed.

"We can't ever replace the responsibility parents have for their own kids," Peltier said. "Whose responsibility are they legally, morally, socially? I think moms and dads should be watching over them."

———

Two weeks after the Eden Prairie game, with his team having turned things around and won its last five games, Duncs talked about Ripped Fuel. "I haven't found anything bad with it," he said. "All I know is that it has enhanced my game."

In those five wins, Duncs had scored six goals and recorded four assists. He had passed Tommy as the team leader in goals and Bernie in total points. He had also taken three penalties but averaged five takeouts per game. Sats awarded him the "Hit Man" T-shirt for leading the team in takeouts during January.

"It gets my blood rushing, gets me pumped, gets me talking. That's helpful to my teammates. When I'm up and talking, it helps me get the other guys going. That's what this team needs. Seeing other guys get excited excites me so much; it makes me feel like being a kid again, being a Peewee excited to step onto the ice. It wouldn't hurt if more guys were taking Ripped Fuel."

Posted in the window of the coaches' office where Duncs lounged during phys ed class was a 10" x 18" poster that outlined in thirty-six–point blue type the Lake Conference policy regarding performance-enhancement nutritional supplements: "Students should not use creatine, andostenedione, or other performance-enhancing nutritional supplements or chemicals as defined by the NCAA except under the care and direction of a licensed medical professional and only then in the manner prescribed by the medical professional's and manufacturer's recommendations."

The NCAA defined ephedrine as a performance-enhancing supplement; Duncs had not consulted a doctor about using Ripped Fuel, and until a week after the Eden Prairie game, he had been seventeen, which, according to the manufacturer's recommendations, was too young to use Ripped Fuel. "I thought [Ripped Fuel] was illegal," Duncs said. "But it's not."

His confusion was understandable. Even though the use of ephedrine technically was not legal by the Lake Conference policy, Duncs and his teammates thought it was. Who told them it wasn't? Who helped them interpret the rules? The league didn't. The conference didn't. Doctors didn't. Coaches didn't. Parents didn't. Left to their own judgment, the kids concluded their use of ephedrine was legal. In the absence of restrictions, they assumed tacit approval. That was not illogical, not unreasonable. Peltier acknowledged as much: "If you're not telling them no, you're telling them yes."

The MSHSL requires head coaches be trained in first aid, methods, and theory, but does not train them to talk to their players about performance-enhancing supplements. The league could have hired a guy like Sats, who had taught health since 1973 and coached thirty-six seasons, to train other coaches. During his tenure at Jefferson, he had intervened regarding countless students' and hockey players' chemical abuse, shepherded them into treatment, and supported their sobriety. Yet throughout the season, Sats did not speak to his team about the use of illegal performance-enhancers. Before the '01 hockey campaign got underway, he scoffed at the idea that his players might use performance-enhancing substances. "I'm pretty sharp at diagnosing what kids do," he said.

Sats missed the signs of Dillon's ephedrine use. When the flyweight started plastering opponents fifty pounds heavier, Sats figured Dillon had finally tired of bigger guys beating up on him. "A lot of that is maturity," Sats said about Dillon's change in play. "If somebody keeps punching you in the face, you've got two choices: you can either let him keep punching you, or you can punch him back, right? Well, don't you finally get sick of it?"

Seated at his office desk after the season had ended, Sats credited Nick Dillon's competitive spirit for his game-winning goal and team-high seven takeouts against Eden Prairie. "I think Nick is one of these guys the bigger the game, the better he plays," Sats said. Yet Nick did not score a game-winning goal nor set one up in any other game that season. In the final contest of the season—the biggest game of the year—he was all but invisible.

Among the anti-drug posters that papered the walls of Sats's health classroom, one stood out: "Methamphetamine Abuse Patterns." It detailed changes in behavior that might indicate methamphetamine use. Sats had to look no further than the locker room to spot his players' telltale patterns. One boy kept his Ripped Fuel bottle on the top shelf of his locker. Another toted a bottle in his equipment bag. Another laid out on his wool cap atop his locker the two green-gray pills he planned to take. At the ice rink a half-hour before the game started, one player walked around the dressing room and distributed Ripped Fuel capsules to teammates. Between periods another player washed down an extra capsule at the drinking fountain. And on the ice, their play changed.

Sats kept close tabs on his players. He knew their mid-quarter grades, which girls they planned to ask to the upcoming dance, where they had spent the weekend, whether they had seen the trainer after school, whose parents were out of town. He had known them on a first-name basis since they started skating. But he had not confronted any of his players that season about their ephedrine use.

When told later that Dillon had used Ripped Fuel during the season, Sats said, "I suppose it's self-imposed pressure. If I would've known, I certainly would have told him not to. I don't think I'm a coach who wants to win at all costs."

He shook his head. He had heard of ephedrine, was aware Nick used an inhaler, and knew that the combination could be deadly. "I don't know; I always thought Nick played hard all the time—I really did. That [ephedrine] might have had something to do with it, I don't know, I'm not a doctor. I really don't know." Maybe he didn't. The players hadn't flaunted their use, but they had flashed the signs for him to read.

Sats flipped through the stat sheets on his desk and noted that Dillon had finished with forty-five takeouts, a relatively high number for the slight forward. "Maybe we should give some to Bernhagen," he said and laughed.

————

Sats worked them hard in practice the Monday after Eden Prairie. He paced the ice during drills and shouted, "Talk! Talk!" They had three soft opponents coming up, and he didn't want his boys to lose their intensity.

Frustrated with their pace, he interrupted a five-on-one breakout drill and whistled the team to center ice. "We're only asking for an hour of your time," he chided the boys. "If you want to get where you want to be, you've got to be mentally ready. You can't just step on the ice and be ready to play."

No, but they knew what would get them ready. For several players at least, the message Sats preached fell on deaf ears. They had placed their faith elsewhere.

CHAPTER SIXTEEN

PLAYING TO THE
NEXT LEVEL

Before the Jaguars' first win over Rosemount in December, Sats held up Mike Crowley to motivate his team. The night before, the Anaheim Mighty Ducks had called up the Jefferson alum to play against the Minnesota Wild, making Crowley the fifth Jaguar to skate that season in the NHL. "Play so that when you leave here you can go on to the next level," Sats admonished his players.

Tuesday night, three days after beating Eden Prairie, Tommy, Nick, and Duncs sat in the back of the bus on the long ride home from a routine 4–1 win in Rosemount and talked about their hockey futures. Before the game, Sats had circled on the green board the number seven—the number of games left for the seniors. Only a month remained in the regular season. Come June, they would graduate. While classmates applied to colleges—or slit open acceptance letters—Tommy, Nick, and Duncs wondered where they would lace their Bauers next year. As they had since Mites, they contemplated their chances at the next level.

The bus bumped along darkened back roads.

Duncs occupied the rear-most seat. "He said you couldn't go?"

"I had my tickets and everything." Tommy sprawled one leg over his seat opposite Duncs.

"Why not?"

Tommy mimicked Sats's voice: "*Our focus right now is to win the rest of our games.*" Sats had said the same thing to B.J. and Jimmy when he denied their request to skip a day of practice to tour the University of Wisconsin at Eau Claire, a Division-III school.

"*You know what I'm saying?*" Duncs echoed Sats's common punctuation to his instructions.

"Go where?" Nick asked from the seat in front of Duncs.

"Air Force." Tommy had talked to a number of schools, but at the moment, Michigan Tech, Minnesota–Duluth, and the Air Force Academy showed the keenest interest. He and his dad had intended to make an official visit.

"You want to go there?" Nick asked.

"I'd rather go there than play juniors." Tommy had always made the first cut. Central Scouting, a scouting service for the NHL, had just rated him Minnesota's top high school prospect. He didn't want to toil a year on what he saw as a B team just to earn a college scholarship.

"I want to take the year off; see how I do on my own," Nick said, much to his mother's dismay. He had scored 25 on the ACT; she wanted him to go to college. But he had trouble focusing on his studies during hockey season. He'd just found out he failed physics second quarter. First quarter, he had earned an A. He could still ace the tests; he just didn't do the homework. Ultimately, he had missed class too many times—often because he was tired from hockey—to receive credit.

Back in November, Nick wasn't talking about playing big time college hockey, but his recent success had attracted attention that boosted his confidence and inflated his dreams. In the month starting with the Grand Rapids game, he had scored eight goals and seventeen points, second only to Duncs over those eleven games. That night against Rosemount, he netted two goals. The Tri-City coach told Nick the United States Hockey League team had protected him in the high school player draft. Nick was willing to go the juniors route to land a Division-I scholarship. It had worked for his dad. "Juniors isn't bad. It's faster hockey."

"Than *D-I?*"

"Than high school."

"I want to go to college," Tommy said. Last summer he had gotten a taste of USHL when he played a pair of games for the Chicago Steel, which still owned his junior rights. "The USHL is a bar league."

"It's goon hockey, but they're skilled guys," Duncs said. He had the street smarts and playground toughness to survive that. "You bang some bodies."

"Not many guys go straight to college," Nick added.

Opponents already mauled Tommy. With Chicago, that would be magnified. But no colleges had proposed. Despite the phone calls and letters and conversations with scouts after games, he had heard only whispers of desire, no commitment. The Yale coach had come closest to a promise, but then he left the school.

"Martin did," Tommy said.

Last year's Mr. Hockey was the exception, and Tommy knew it. Elk River's Paul Martin had struggled as a true freshman with the Gophers, at times seeming a Peewee among Bantams. Contrast him with another former high school standout, Troy Riddle, who had stepped into the Gophers lineup that season after playing a year of juniors and become an instant contributor.

Even though Gophers coach Don Lucia had told Duncs to finish high school rather than leave to play juniors, Lucia had told the papers that the best players are coming out of juniors. Duncs took note that of the nine incoming Gophers, only Erickson and one other had come straight out of high school. Another, also a '01 graduate, would play USHL hockey that spring. Four had played juniors before cracking the D-I roster; two came from the U.S. National Development Team.

Duncs understood. College coaches wanted kids to develop a year or two in juniors, where they would play over sixty games against tougher competition. "Would you rather take an eighteen-year-old pup out of high school or an older kid who's a year or two bigger, maybe by twenty pounds, and more experienced?" he asked. Should a guy play all four years of college, the coach would have a twenty-four-year-old senior, another plus on the other end.

A pair of headlights flashed across the bus's back windows, the light diffused by a film of condensation.

————

In his usual seat behind the cheerleaders and statisticians, Timm sat by himself and peered across cornfields buried in snow. He had set his sights on college hockey years ago while watching the Denver Pioneers. "Hockey is my life," Timm had said on Jefferson's Career Day, when lawyers and sales reps visited classes. "My ultimate goal is to play college, D-I."

The move to Bloomington had been the first critical step. He would be happy just to play D-I somewhere, anywhere. He knew the odds were long. Teams carried twelve forwards and six defensemen but only two goalies. For every goalie who made it, there were hundreds of guys who shelved their masks after senior year. A couple of D-III schools had expressed interest, but Timm wasn't willing to accept that yet. He would play juniors to get a shot at D-I. But even that was tough. At the season-ending awards banquet, White Bear Lake's Eric Aarnio, the state's top netminder, would be without any offers from D-I or junior teams. By then, Timm still would not have applied to any colleges. Instead, he would mail his hockey résumé to all of the USHL teams, petitioning them for a tryout.

A few rows back, Bernie opined that West Bloomington subsidized the East Side. "They should be cut off." Even though schools could not talk to him officially until the end of his junior year, his mailbox had already started to swell with letters from interested colleges. Tri-City had protected him along with Nick and Duncs, hoping he would forgo his senior year to play in the USHL. But Bernie wasn't sure he would play hockey beyond high school. He had already wearied of the commitment and envied his friends with free time. If he did play college, he wanted his genius to be indulged immediately. Knowing that colleges rarely put freshmen on the powerplay and penalty kill, he might not play. "I don't want to spend the first two years treated just as a regular player," he said.

Bernie had played USA Hockey Select 15 and 16, but hadn't made the Select 17 team because of his attitude, the coach told him. Despite Bernie's abundant skill, Sats doubted that a D-I team would take a chance on Bernie's attitude. NHL scouts considered him too small at 5'9"—that season, only three percent of NHL players stood 5'9" or shorter. He might very well play his last hockey game in the Jaguars sweater his mother had hemmed to fit him.

While Duncs, Tommy, Nick, and Timm pursued D-I scholarships, and B.J. and Jimmy headed for D-III, the Jags' seventh senior, Bryan Shackle, was ready to hang up his skates and his cleats. When the hockey season began less than two weeks after the state soccer championship, Shacks figured he would accept one of several offers to play D-III soccer. His fifteen goals had been tops for the runner-up Jaguars soccer team. But the hockey season had taken its toll—physically and emotionally. On the bus ride home from Rosemount, his ankle throbbed. He had suffered a high ankle sprain in the game. Shacks doubted he would play any sports in college. The homecoming king was burnt out.

————

July 1, 2000, the first day that NCAA rules permitted coaches to recruit high school seniors-to-be, Duncs's phone started ringing at 7:15 A.M. At the USA Hockey Select Festival, Duncs was one of only five Minnesota kids to make the national team the past three years. Last year, talent scouts ranked him one of the top three forwards in the country.

The letters had started arriving junior year, at least one a week. Glowing praise from college and USHL coaches on team letterheads.

Glossy, full-color media guides. *This could be you on the cover.* Steve Duncan kept them bunched together in a messy packet. Duncs checked the mailbox every day.

The Omaha Lancers wanted him to make the Ak-Sar-Ben Arena his home senior year. They promised the USHL competition against bigger, stronger, older players would accelerate his development in ways high school hockey couldn't. Upon graduation, he would be irresistible to D-I schools.

The USA Hockey National Team Development Program wanted Duncs in Ann Arbor. He would play alongside the nation's elite and represent the United States in international competition. The top pro and college scouts would scrutinize his success. Ann Arbor could rocket him to college and pro glory. Check out Rick DiPietro. Ann Arbor launched him to Boston University, where after a year, the eighteen-year-old goalie became the first pick in the 2000 NHL entry draft.

Tempting…but Duncs decided to stay. Sats believed that leaving high school to play juniors would be a mistake. At Omaha, Duncs wouldn't be on the penalty kill and power play, wouldn't have guys gunning for him every shift. "That's what makes him a better hockey player," Sats said. Not the extra games and additional ice time.

But Duncs had a more immediate reason to stay. Playing in the state tournament his junior year had been a terrific high that ended too soon. He wanted another hit. He was willing to pay his dues playing a year or two in juniors for the chance to get back to the Tournament. He could think of no better way to close out his senior year than to win it all. "I would do anything to get that feeling again," he said.

If he could have a big Tournament like he'd had at the Holiday Classic, his stock would soar with Minnesota schools. The spotlight that shined on Tournament stars deepened their luster. "There is a presence the media has that takes you out of the real situation and creates a persona around you," observed Steve Duncan one afternoon, shuffling through the sheaf of recruiting letters his son had received.

That persona could pay off for the college willing to invest in Duncs. Many of the top high school recruits could contribute at the college level—perhaps with a year or two of seasoning in juniors—but name recognition among fans floated the personas up the coaches' short list. "This is still a business of putting people in the seats," Steve Duncan said. "If you get names, these kids draw a following."

————

Tommy stayed, too. He wanted to wear the *C* senior year. He wanted to hear Dick Stanford's trademark Tournament voice announce, "No. 15, Jaguars captain, senior Tom Gilbert." He wanted to play on the Xcel ice. He wanted to skate forward to accept the champions' trophy, then thrust it high above his head. These dreams came first.

Other kids willingly traded high school glory for future prospects. Like basketball players skipping their junior and senior seasons of college to join the NBA draft, a score of Minnesota hockey players each season abandoned their high schools and families to play in the USHL or with the U.S. National Development Team as early as sophomore year.

Jake Fleming was high school hockey's equivalent of Kwame Brown, the 2001 NBA draft's top pick straight out of high school. After a remarkable freshman year playing varsity hockey at Osseo, an unremarkable hockey program, Fleming jumped to the U.S. National Development Team in tenth grade and graduated to the USHL by '01, his senior year. He earned a coveted Gophers scholarship to play the next year alongside Mike Erickson, his peer who had stayed at Eden Prairie.

But Fleming's flight cost him. "If Jake Fleming was playing in high school right now, just think of all you'd be hearing about him," Eden Prairie coach Lee Smith told the *StarTribune*. "Now, if you follow the USHL online, you know who he is, but he's not a household name. Mike Erickson is a household name now."

USA Hockey, the official governing body of amateur hockey, started its development program in Ann Arbor, Michigan, between 1996 and 1997, "to improve the overall level of play in American hockey"—in other words, to groom Olympic talent—under the direction of Mike Eaves, a former Minnesota North Star. The program put the nation's top sixteen-, seventeen-, and eighteen-year-old players on two national teams playing in domestic and international competitions.

Ann Arbor attracted elite players like Jake what's-his-name, particularly out of Minnesota. Others skipped school to play juniors, handicapping the teams they abandoned and shrinking the overall talent pool. The state's high school coaches lobbied that they needed more games to stem the exodus. Even with the MSHSL's concession to add three regular season games to the schedule in '01, Herb Brooks, Olympic men's hockey coach in 1980 and 2002, charged that Minnesota high school hockey failed to develop players adequately.

"The onus falls on the Minnesota State High School League," Brooks said. "Historically it has not promoted the game of hockey the way it should. The high school season could be expanded through March without a doubt. They have the coaches, infrastructure, and venues. With a little extra work and support, it could be done. They should play a minimum of thirty games, especially over the holidays, Thanksgiving, and Christmas, with twenty-minute periods. But the Minnesota State High School League is too much of a forced mediocrity. It is an anchor holding things back. Kids are getting frustrated and leaving."

No other high school sport took kids away from home the way hockey did. In response, Dave Stead, the MSHSL executive director, admitted that Minnesota high school hockey may not serve its best players, but pointed out that playing elsewhere was not always in the students' best interests. "There are some kids who will probably do better not playing at the high school level, just like anyone who gets a promotion for a job. But there are people promoting kids for their own purposes, misrepresenting their skill level."

"The principal purpose of this development program is to prepare the athlete for career advancement either in a collegiate or professional opportunity," states the USA Hockey Official Rules, Junior Hockey

Edition, in its description of junior hockey leagues in the United States. USHL commissioner Gino Gasparini takes that purpose a step further for his Junior A league of thirteen teams spread throughout the Midwest. "Our goal is to be the primary developmental league for all Division-I college hockey teams," Gasparini explains.

The USHL appeals to kids looking for a stepping stone that will give them a leg up in the same way the Ann Arbor program does. While most of the 325 USHL players have graduated high school, they go as young as sixteen, giving rise to the same complaint levied against the USA Hockey development program of robbing the prep cradle. Despite their similarities, however, the two programs have distinctly different agendas. The USHL, with privately owned teams, is a profit venture. Its website asserts, "The USHL prides itself on the professional presentation of an amateur sport."

In Green Bay, Omaha, and Sioux City, team owners are investing millions in shiny new arenas sporting luxury boxes and jumbotrons with an eye toward the return on their investment. Ticket sales and advertising are their two main revenue streams. Recognizing the rich resource of younger talent, they are vigorously wooing minors. In the '01 season, the USHL accepted more high school players than ever onto its teams.

USHL coaches sell the league with the pitch that the play's "as good as D-I" and the promise that players will "come out a step faster." They talk up the team's half-hour television show on the local ESPN cable channel. But it's the glitzy arenas—and dreams of glory they inspire—that seal the deal. In Kearney, Nebraska, the Tri-City Storm played in a flashy new nine-million-dollar rink that held 4,500 fans, about twice the size of BIG. "All we have to do is get them into the building," said Chris Imes, the Tri-City coach wooing Duncs, Nick, and Bernie.

The USHL might be able to seduce kids with its rinks, but high school coaches resented the league's rapacious pursuit of their talent. Watching the Omaha Lancers court his star senior, T.J. Jindra, and drool over sophomore Mike Franks, the pair that had beaten Jefferson, infuriated Burnsville coach John Barger. In the BIG concourse following that upset, Barger told Imes, "We work with these kids since they're this big"—he held his hand palm down at his belt—"then a junior team steals them from us. It's like getting your nuts ripped out."

Not all kids took the bait, of course. Duncs and Tommy didn't. Nor did Ryan Hawkins, a freshman sensation who broke Mike Erickson's Bantam scoring record on the Eden Prairie Bantam A team that won the 2000 state title. Hawkins had scouts chasing him before he had even suited up for a high school game. "I was sitting at home, and this guy from Chicago [Steel] called," Hawkins told the *StarTribune.* "He was describing the team, telling me I'd be playing with twenty-one-year-olds. These are guys that drink and don't wear facemasks. I'm just starting to grow facial hair. I don't think I was ready to go and try out."

Minors playing in the USHL live with host families and take classes at local high schools, though academics obviously take a back seat. Hockey becomes their vocation. Teams pay the families a $186 monthly stipend and outfit players with equipment. The kids don't receive a cent because that would erase their amateur status and render them ineligible to play college hockey. The league maintains it pays them handsomely by offering the opportunity to advance their careers. In the meantime, the players are the product people pay to see, indentured servants to the league.

For those kids who hadn't received scholarships by graduation but wanted to keep their D-I dreams alive, the league's hard sell made the juniors easier to swallow. College hockey wasn't a pipe dream for Minnesota kids. In the 2001–2002 season, what would be Duncs's and Tommy's natural freshman year, 225 of all D-I players, almost 14 percent, hailed from Minnesota. But the odds remained long— little better than one in ten high school hockey players advanced to the college level.

The USHL might provide better odds, but it proffered no guarantees. Of those playing in the USHL in '01, 109 received Division-I offers. About 30 percent advance to the college ranks. The others? They get hurt—or never make it past juniors.

Of twenty-one players who had left high school early in 1999, nearly a third no longer played hockey two years later. Duluth East coach Mike Randolph cited six players who had skipped out of his school early to play juniors, pursuing what they believed the better opportunity to land a D-I scholarship. "That's six failures," Randolph said. "They wanted to take the fast track, but not one succeeded."

———

Guess who's coming to dinner.

Before the '01 Jaguars played their first game, Norm Bazin, a Colorado College assistant coach, called Duncs. He was headed to Minnesota, did Duncs mind if he dropped in? Hell, no. Colorado had been Duncs's first choice. A C student, he worried—even though his mom told him not to—that his grades and ACT scores would disqualify him.

Steve Duncan showed up for the tail end of practice the next day to meet Bazin, a guarded young man slow to laugh. Bazin had arrived early for the November practice to check out Duncs's work ethic. The plan was to eat supper at Steve's bachelor pad, where Duncs crashed every other week. While Bazin chatted with Duncs after he came off the ice, Steve waited in the lobby. He had encountered a lot of situations during his son's hockey career, but entertaining scouts courting his son was new. He shrugged, "I don't know what to do."

For Duncs, the audition had begun after sophomore year with Model Camp, a summer showcase hosted by the University of Minnesota, and at the U.S. National Development Team Evaluation Camp in Ann Arbor. Scouts and professional agents packed the stands. "It felt like we were being watched by ambulance chasers," Steve said.

Rules forbade agents from contracting with high school students, but that didn't stop them from calling. *Anyone helping you yet?* they wanted to know. *Here's my number, and if I can be of help, please, don't hesitate to contact me.*

Junior year the letters invited Duncs to make an "unofficial visit," wink, wink. The NCAA capped the number of all-expenses paid official visits to five but set no limit on unofficial visits. The letters provided specific dates for the "unofficial visits," with a detailed itinerary for a three-hour stop. They offered tickets to an upcoming game. Colleges couldn't call juniors, but coaches could talk to them if the players initiated the contact. "We highly encourage you to contact our office," they urged. Any interested player would be a fool not to.

The letters sprinkled promises that sowed false hope. "Our coaching staff feels that you have the ability and desire to play Division-I hockey in the 2001–2002 season." Read, "You won't have to play juniors, you can step right into our lineup as a freshman." And, from Harvard, "You've been highly recommended to us as a person who could excel academically." Duncs scored 21 on the ACT; the average high school valedictorian matriculating to Harvard scored 28 or higher.

Duncs had made unofficial visits to the University of Minnesota, the University of Wisconsin, St. Cloud, and Mankato. He had met with the Minnesota–Duluth coaching staff. Senior year, Colorado College, Notre Dame, and Union College would offer to pay for official visits, but Sats wouldn't let Duncs leave during the season.

During that first meeting with Norm Bazin, back at Steve's place, Bazin laid out CC's virtues over a meal of steak and potatoes. The coach praised the father's culinary skills and the son's hockey talents.

Bazin left for Iowa but returned later in the season to watch Duncs play a game. By then he was talking to Tommy, too. *We're still interested, very interested in both of you; it's just that we're not able to make a commitment yet.*

Letters kept arriving from other schools. The phone kept ringing.

The coaches wanted to know who else Duncs was talking to, what he was thinking. *Has anyone made an offer? Here's what to watch out for* …which tipped him off to the tricks they might try. *We want a strong, right-handed shot like you. We're losing three right-handers to graduation. We've got a spot for you. Forget juniors, you could play D-I next season.*

But whenever Steve Duncan asked about the money, they got funny. The coaches could offer a percentage, then Duncs would apply for financial aid, which would be processed independently.

The scholarship percentage might be increased each year, but it was always on an annual basis. The days of the guaranteed full ride were a relic of the past; these were renewable one-year deals. Even Mike Erickson hadn't won an all-expenses paid trip to college. But the dollar amounts were always verbal, hazy estimates or ballpark figures. Nothing firm until the kid signed a letter of intent.

Even then, the commitment was one-way. The college didn't have to pay the kid anything until he actually played for them. He could agree to play a year or two or more in juniors without the college having to shell out a cent. Meanwhile, if he had signed a letter of intent, the player couldn't talk to other schools. "Kids get warehoused into never-never land," Steve explained.

The coaches teased Duncs like a fickle flirt, stringing him along while they looked over his shoulder to see if any brighter prospects approached. When Duncs stepped onto the ice, he could feel their eyes all over him. The audition may have begun sophomore year, but senior year was callbacks, when scouts shortened their lists. That season could determine his future. Even the meaningless games, like those against the hapless Rosemount Irish or Eagan Wildcats, meant something. If a coach wasn't there in the stands watching, he would be checking Duncs's stats. It felt like his future could be won or lost in a shift. Small wonder then that the team's emotional leader, top scorer, and most valuable player would feel he needed a little help from his friend, Ripped Fuel, to gain that extra edge.

––––––––

The day after the Rosemount game, Tommy stopped into B202 to check out the game stats. Seated on the corner of Sats's desk, studying the spreadsheet, he said, "There should be a stat for good passes."

"That's for pride," Coach Thomas said.

"I want others to see my pride."

Watching game tapes or in the dressing room between periods, Tommy wanted to be sure the statisticians had recorded his takeout or blocked shot. Those stats were the Cliffs Notes for coaches who couldn't see the games. His goal count mattered much more than his ACT score. Duncs's dad agreed. "To say how a kid played in any one game determines his future is bullshit." He took a drag off of his Old Gold. "They've got stats collected over a long period of time."

It gnawed at Tommy that since his hat trick against Chaska in mid-December he had scored only four goals over twelve games. Other than his four-goal performance against Hill-Murray in the opener and a singleton against Edina, he hadn't scored against any top ten team. *Big players play big in big games*, Sats goaded him.

Bernie admitted he felt "tons of pressure"—from his mom, from Sats, from colleges, and in large part from classmates. "They don't say, 'Why don't you score three goals?' but having four hundred class-mates at a game, that's pressure," Bernie said. "They pay money to see you perform. They go to see Duncan, Gilbert, and Bernhagen."

That led to an internal horse race. Bernie, Tommy, Nick, Duncs, and Timm jockeyed for the team's top billing. The preoccupation with personal stats tugged at the team unity. Duncs knew he played his best hockey when he wasn't worried about his own output, but he admitted after the Burnsville loss that playing for individual glory and the chance to further his own future had taken away from his focus on the team in the moment. "I think it happens any time a team is doing this well; you want to be known as the kid running the team," he said. "It's almost a competition."

———

Sats could help. With the number of players he had sent on to D-I and professional hockey, coaches respected his eye for talent. All Sats had to do was make a phone call or two, it seemed, and he could land an offer for his standouts. But he hadn't, and that bummed out Duncs and Tommy. Pushing as hard as they were for a D-I spot, they wished he would lend a hand. Sats maintained that if they played well enough, they would get noticed. "Sats is convinced we have it made, but he's not exposing us," Duncs said. "That's hard for me, Tommy, and Bernie to swallow."

Timm also wished Sats would make a call on his behalf. He figured Sats held such sway that he could easily influence a scout's decision—

for or against Timm. "It's scary to think he has my future with hockey in his hands," Timm said, still frustrated in his search for a team post-graduation. "I have to kiss his ass but I don't want to."

———————

In his pregame talks, Sats built up Jefferson's opponents with typical coachspeak: "They've got the (pick one):

a) fastest forward in the conference,

b) best line in the state,

c) toughest goalie you've faced."

He had called Rosemount the "most improved team in the conference." But not even Sats could find anything motivating about Eagan, 0–17–1. The best player to come out of the burgeoning burb was a girl.

To be sure, Natalie Darwitz was John Mayasich with a ponytail. By her sophomore year, she held six of the girls' state tournament's eleven scoring records. From seventh to tenth grade, she had scored 312 goals overall. Granted, she had racked those up against some girls still learning to skate backwards, but she proved herself the real thing when she left Eagan High her junior year to join the women's national team. In the '01 season, the national team's youngest player and eventual Olympian recorded 35 points in 32 games.

Given that the Eagan boys couldn't carry Darwitz's pelvic protector, Sats said in front of the green board, "These guys aren't very good. I'm not going to BS you."

The Jaguars weren't exactly a bundle of nerves Saturday night on the long bus ride to Dakota County. Some of them slouched in their seats and napped. Duncs doodled in the condensation on the back window.

Team manager Dave Daly slipped Duncs a tin. He took a dip and passed the tin to Nick, who pinched the Skoal under his lower lip and flipped the tin back to Daly. They had taken up this routine on the Rosemount bus ride to pass the time and catch a little pregame buzz. It was another time-honored Jaguar tradition. As sophomores, they had watched the seniors in the back of the bus do the same thing.

Sitting a dozen seats up from Duncs and Nick, Sats hated when kids chewed. Last year, one of his top players was busted for chewing two days after he had told his teammates he would do anything to get to the Tournament. "Right then, I knew we weren't going to win State," Sats said. He figured they would get there—which they did—but not win—which they didn't.

In reviewing the season Duncs's junior year, Sats asked Duncs if he knew his friend had been chewing. Duncs sank in the padded chair across from Sats. "Mm hmm."

"How could you trust him?" Sats asked.

Duncs didn't say anything.

"The point I want to make is when a guy's chewing, there has to be a bit of doubt about him." Sats believed guys wouldn't see a teammate who was breaking the rules as someone they could count on come crunch time. Even though players argued that spit tobacco didn't hurt their play, Sats countered that when one chewed, he exacted a mental toll on the team.

"I guess there was doubt there."

"Where are you at with chewing?" Sats asked Duncs point-blank.

"I quit the day I got caught. That scared the pants off me."

That day sophomore year in phys ed, Duncs thought they were going outside for class, so he took a dip. Instead, they marched into the gym, and his mouth swelled with spit he couldn't release. His teacher couldn't help but notice. Busted.

On the ride to Eagan, Duncs spit into an empty Powerade bottle. If Sats or Thomas decided for any reason to stroll to the back of the bus, it would be Duncs's third MSHSL violation, carrying a mandatory twelve-game suspension. Through the Tournament final, there were exactly twelve games left. The pinch between Duncs's cheek and gum might not only abruptly terminate his high school career, it could shitcan his hockey future. Coaches would question his commitment and reliability. He gambled that Sats and Thomas wouldn't leave their seats. They rarely—if ever—even looked toward the back of the bus. Duncs figured a dip was a safe bet.

The other guys on the bus knew. Duncs could bring them all down. Without their most valuable player, their chances to make it to State, let alone win it, shrank considerably. If Nick got busted, he would serve only two weeks for his first violation, but without Duncs, *au revoir*, Jaguars.

Across the aisle, Tommy was willing to look the other way. He had asked Duncs how he was doing with chewing but hadn't asked him to quit. He knew Duncs had made the sacrifice of not drinking during the season, so Tommy cut him some slack for not being able to kick his tobacco addiction. He trusted Duncs wouldn't let himself get caught.

Duncs and Nick added a little danger to the long bus ride, like racing a car down side roads at night without the headlights. At least that provided some amusement. Eagan wasted their time. In the dressing room beforehand, Duncs, Nick, and B.J. firmed up plans to hit the casino later that night. Duncs turned eighteen at midnight.

The Jaguars played a sloppy game, pocketed a 5–3 win, and split. Duncs netted two tallies. He wouldn't be as lucky at the casino. After showering at school, he would drop twenty dollars; B.J. would lose forty dollars; and Nick would squander forty-five dollars. But they didn't know that yet. On the bus ride home, Bernie leaned out an open window and tossed pop cans at road signs. Duncs and Nick had a chew.

CHAPTER SEVENTEEN

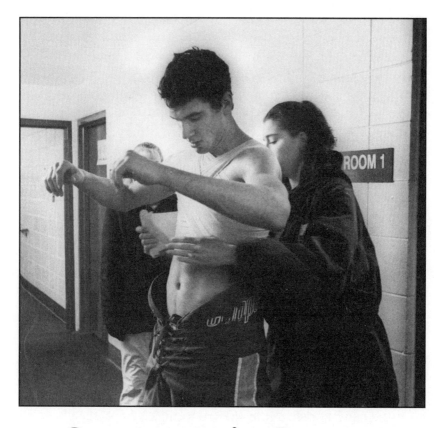

SOMEBODY'S GONNA
GET HURT

Even though Kevin Bernhagen had moved to Wisconsin, he still made the two-plus hour drive to his stepson's hockey games. He had missed only three that year. On an unseasonably warm evening, Tuesday, January 30, he drove an extra twenty minutes through the slop of melting snow to the far side of the metro area for the Jaguars' rematch with the Chaska Hawks.

The drive gave him time to think about his stepson, whom he had turned on to hockey more than a dozen years ago. Bernie's play of late troubled Kevin. Some games, Bernie skated like he didn't care. That sporadic laziness, which dated back to Peewees, proved a sore spot with Kevin. Those days on the drive home, he lectured Bernie on the need to hustle. "If I had to work Saturdays to pay for your training, kid, you got to hustle," he would admonish the boy in the passenger seat whose feet didn't reach the floor.

While his snow tires slogged through the miles, Kevin replayed images of Bernie on skates. He knew when he saw Bernie smiling inside his wire cage face mask, Bernie would light up the ice, but Kevin hadn't seen that smile for a couple of weeks. Worse, he hadn't liked Bernie's cheap play, the stick-swinging and behind-the-scenes retaliatory hits. On the other hand, the former high school football player who still hulked larger than most parents in the stands had seen the bigger defensemen time and again go after his small stepson, and he believed it was necessary for Bernie to stick up for himself. He felt a certain pride that Bernie didn't back down. "It's hockey," Kevin rationalized.

Kevin tromped through the slush in the parking lot of the Chaska Community Center, a multipurpose recreation complex without a designated hockey identity. Although Chaska called itself "A Quality Small Town" and celebrated its sesquicentennial anniversary that year, the 17,500 residents hadn't yet figured out over 150 years how to play quality hockey. From Peewee to high school, they brawled better than they skated.

Sure enough, the Hawks came out hacking, and when the refs didn't call their clutching, high-sticking, and late hits, they intensified their attack. The Jaguars retaliated. Throughout the first period, the two teams pummeled each other.

A Hawks forward, No. 9, wrestled Duncs to the ice, then smacked Timm's glove with his stick after the whistle. A Chaska student cheered. One of the Jefferson adults seated above the Chaska students shouted, "Somebody's got to go after No. 9!"

Tommy rubbed out No. 9 along the Jefferson bench with his elbow.

A Jefferson student raved, "That's it, Gilbert. Draw blood!"

When the period ended, the Jaguars slumped into the dressing room. They had pumped twenty-five shots on the Hawks's net— compared to Chaska's measly five shots on Timm—but only one had gone in. What did they have to do to put these guys away?

"Don't pass up a hit. Finish every check."

"When you hit a guy, put him through the boards."

"We have so many pro scouts in the stands at our games because we're so physical."

"Go to the net—be a mean sucker in there."

Sats's words coursed through their subconscious. Before the season began, the coach had implored the parents, "Will you please tell your sons to be a bit meaner? They're too nice." That message, first sown by Peewee coaches who exhorted their "warriors" to "battle," had rooted itself in their psyche.

They answered the bell for the second period mean. The Jaguar warriors blasted the Hawks through the boards. They stormed the net. Within two minutes, B.J. and Nick netted a pair of goals. The third line added another to put the Jags up 4–0.

The puck refused to bounce Bernie's way. Cruising through the slot, Bernie threaded a rebound between the goalie's legs, but the puck clanked off the pipe and flirted along the goal line. The Hawks's goalie smothered it. Exasperated, Bernie threw back his head. Kevin knew he wasn't smiling.

The brawling resumed. The refs whistled Nick, then Duncs for interference but let another dozen infractions slide. A Jefferson student yelled, "C'mon, Dirlam, kill!" When a guy grabbed Dirlam's stick in the corner, one of the Jefferson dads shouted, "Punch him!" Between shifts, the players complained about the cheap play. They hit the ice intent upon retaliation.

The ugliness on the ice spilled into the stands. Usually opposing fans sat on opposite sides or at least opposite ends, but the overflow crowd had pushed the Chaska students below the Jefferson adults and produced several vulgar repartees shouted through rolled-up programs printed with the "I'm a good sport" code. When the students cheered a cheap shot, one Jefferson parent yelled, "That's why you suck, Chaska. You don't know how to play hockey; you only know how to play cheap!" Several Chaska students responded with obscene gestures.

Shorthanded, Bernie suddenly flashed brilliant. The poet penned one of his masterpieces. He rushed the length of the rink, weaved his way through the Chaska powerplay, and, with a final flourish of his wrist, flicked the puck through the goalie's pads. The six Hawks he had beaten could only chomp their mouthguards. Bernie smiled. Briefly.

With 4.3 seconds remaining in the period, Tommy performed his own highlight reel contribution. He plucked a knee-high pass out of the air with his blade and rifled a slapshot bullseye through the five-hole. That was one for the Colorado College scout in the stands to remember.

Between periods, Sats chastised the refs. "You've got to get this thing under control. Somebody's gonna get hurt." Later, he would snap sardonically, "Lot of good it did, huh?"

Early in the third, the refs looked the other way on several infractions. When a Chaska defender bound Jimmy's foot in a full Nelson, a Jefferson adult shouted, "Pick a penalty and call it!"

"Break his shin," a Chaska student retorted.

On the bench, Jimmy—who had popped a pair of Ripped Fuel tablets a half hour before the game started—vowed revenge. His next shift, the 5'6" forward toppled the Chaska player. The refs whistled him for high-sticking.

As the clock clicked under six minutes to play, the Jaguars leading 6–1, Bernie carried the puck around the corner in the Hawks' end looking to pass. A larger Chaska player crumpled him into the side boards with a clean, hard check. Pain seared through Bernie's shoulder and ignited his fists. He dropped the Hawk with a right cross to the face mask.

Fight! The fans scampered to the glass for a better view.

Bernie burned incandescent with righteous rage. *Nobody does that to me.* The moment magnified and tightened his past into a glowing point at his feet. He gripped his stick with both hands, leaned over, and smashed his foe's helmet against the ice.

The stands erupted in a barrage of shouts.

Jefferson parents criticized the students below them.

"Asshole!" one Chaska kid shouted.

"Scoreboard!" one Jefferson man shouted back.

A bell-bottomed Chaska girl climbed the steps to the Jefferson adult section and told the visitors they should sit somewhere else.

One man said, "I'm a teacher and don't need to be called 'asshole' by some punk kid."

"Asshole," the girl tossed over her shoulder.

"You're showing your class—none!" the teacher shouted after her. "Asshole."

The refs assessed Bernie a five-minute major penalty for cross-checking and kicked him out of the game. They called a rash of penalties in the waning minutes with a uniformed police officer stationed near the opposing fans.

Kevin Bernhagen felt embarrassed. Once again, Bernie's temper had flared out of control. Another suspension. But Kevin couldn't blame him for wanting to pop the guy who'd hurt him. "I don't know if that was the right reaction, but it must've felt good," he said.

Hockey's a violent sport. Strap sharp blades on testosterone-crazed boys who bang into each other speeding twenty miles per hour and cudgel each other with sticks, and you've got a dangerous mix. Those raging hormones and raw emotions conspire to attack whatever crosses their path. Add No Doz, Ripped Fuel, or Sudafed—even energy drinks—to kids already pumped with adrenaline, and that accentuates the intensity and ferocity with which they go after each other. The ice becomes a romper room of rage.

Small wonder somebody usually gets hurt. The U.S. Consumer Product Safety Commission estimates hospital emergency rooms across the country treated 42,669 young hockey players (ages 5–24) for injuries in 2000. The game is dangerous, even when played within the rules, and kids swaddled in foam and plastic armor remain vulnerable.

Jefferson's own disabled list read like an honor roll:
• Shacks: broken hand, ankle sprain:
• Duncs: bruised thigh, concussion;
• B.J.: bruised thigh, pulled groin;
• Van B: bruised ribs;
• Jimmy: neck spasms;
• Dillon: separated shoulder;

- Bernie: pulled groin, hyperextended elbow, and, after the Chaska game, separated shoulder.

That tally didn't include the bruises they compared like tattoos in the dressing room or the aches they iced after games when they answered Thomas's routine call, "Who needs ice?"

But hockey's injuries run far more serious than bruises. That season, a "clean" hit at center ice nearly killed Blaine wing Dan Holmgren. The check caused internal bleeding in his left thigh. He nearly died several times in the ambulance on the way to the hospital. During a five-hour surgery to repair a damaged vein, he needed twenty pints of blood. Blood stained the ice when an opponent accidentally skated over the right arm of Breck's C. J. Nibbe and gashed his tendons and an artery. In the three weeks following White Bear Lake's upset of Jefferson, the Bears' goalie Eric Aarnio suffered two concussions. His teammate, forward Matt Kleidon, also sustained a pair of concussions. Jesse Polk, a Hastings standout, broke his neck when checked into the boards during a Select-15 hockey game. Between 1996 and 2001, two Minnesota high school players have been paralyzed in hockey games.

––––––––––

To hear the teenager with the closely-cropped brown hair tick off the special features of his twenty-seven-thousand-dollar Permobile, you would think he was hawking a Swedish muscle car. The carbon composite frame rides on two pneumatic, twelve-inch front tires with individual shock suspension. The larger back wheels sport sturdy plastic spokes. "Two twelve-volt car batteries can carry a six-hundred-pound person around all day," the nineteen-year-old boasts. That's enough juice to nudge the young man's bony, six-foot frame from zero to seven miles per hour in the length of a blue parking space.

With a shift of his wrist, Holt Bennington tips back, his head cradled by a special head rest, elevates his unscuffed orange and black sneakers, and raises the entire seat. He is clearly showing off now, a slight grin cracking his face. "It's exactly like being in a dentist's office chair."

Except that Holt can't spit and walk out.

The kid who used to run to his friends' houses like Forrest Gump now throttles his fancy Swedish wheelchair around the lower level of his family's new house, the one they built after his accident. The Benningtons used to live in town by the high school, where Holt could walk home for lunch. But then the two-story colonial's front staircase became an insurmountable roadblock. To accommodate Holt's newly-acquired needs, the family designed this house in a Shakopee subdivision carved out of cornfields. A ceiling lift runs from his hospital-style bed to the bathroom, where he can slip his Permobile over a special commode. An elevator shuttles him upstairs to the kitchen. The garage shelters a sixty thousand dollar, custom-fitted '98 Dodge Grand Caravan Limited Edition with a knob on the steering wheel, fuzzy dice hanging from the rearview mirror, and cabinet speakers under the back seat.

Seated in the lower level rec room between the pool table and fire-place, Holt playfully beeps his chair's horn. Sports memorabilia surrounds him: a framed Dallas Stars jersey signed by the '99 Stanley Cup champions, Brett Hull's St. Louis Blues sweater, a Philadelphia Flyers jersey bearing Shjon Podein's signature, Flyers' captain Eric Lindros's game stick, and, over the fireplace, a poster of the '80 Olympic team autographed by Herb Brooks. There's a Wheaties box picturing fifteen-year-old Holt in his red Shakopee Sabers jersey, No. 25, his long brown bangs parted over a take-on-all-comers smirk. On the opposite shelf rests a black CCM helmet, creased along the top. "It's not supposed to dent like that," Holt says.

The fifteen-year-old Holt Bennington was a thrill-seeking kid drawn to hockey for its high profile and danger. He had skated since he was two. By his own admission, he had rock hands, but he could skate and check. At 5' 11" and 175 pounds, the sophomore defense-man was the biggest player on the Sabers varsity and perhaps its biggest hitter. "I wasn't looking for a scholarship; I was more into picking up chicks and trying to be a tough guy," Holt says candidly. "I played hockey because it was a good way to take out my aggressions in a public place, where I didn't get into trouble for it."

He liked to play rough, but he became a victim of his desire.

On January 15, 1998, in the third period of a junior varsity game between Holt's Sabers and the LeSueur–St. Peter Bulldogs, Holt's defensive partner got caught pinching on the Bulldogs's breakout.

Holt retreated, skating backwards, but a LeSueur forward slipped behind him and collected a cross-ice pass. Holt wheeled and raced after the forward—he pivots his chair to reenact the play. He leaned in to check the attacker, and they both lost their skates. Holt hit his stomach near the top of the left circle, and the LeSueur player landed on top of him. They slid fifty feet into the end boards, where Holt's CCM helmet absorbed the full impact of their combined weight.

Everything splashed white. Holt thudded off the boards, his nose in his chin strap. He watched the other player skate away, but he couldn't move. His glove had come off, but he couldn't feel the ice beneath his hand. His body tingled. The impact had crushed his spine, jammed the fifth and sixth vertebrae side by side, and partially severed his spinal cord. The medics strapped the Sabers' hard-hitting defenseman onto a body board and carried him off a quadriplegic.

After four years and multiple surgeries, Holt has learned to cath himself, to drive with the limited range of his left hand, and to eat with a metal splint strapped to his forearm. He still needs help getting out of bed. His right arm dangles limp as a broken wing.

But he's not bitter toward hockey. "I would still play," he says.

Matter of fact, he's grateful his accident happened playing hockey. Had he hurt himself jumping into pools off roofs, doing double backflips off trampolines, turning cartwheels off bannisters, or any of the other crazy stunts he used to pull, he probably wouldn't have received the outpouring of support, the hospital visits from the Stanley Cup and Kirby Puckett, the sports memorabilia decorating his rec room, or the donations that paid for his customized van. "I don't think I would've had any of the help I have if I'd broken my neck screwing around. Happening with this thing people have all this passion for…" his voice trails off.

His was a freak accident, not the game's fault. Yet, his accident wouldn't have happened on the tennis court. Holt played hockey rough, but he didn't play dirty. "I was out to kill, but I wasn't out to hurt," he explains. "Get the guy off the puck—that was my job." Holt bought into hockey's violent culture—and paid a heavy price.

He doesn't begrudge the game's violence but believes some high school players push their aggression too far. "They feel they can do anything out there if it doesn't get penalized," the nineteen-year-old observes. "They don't just throw a check but say, 'You fuckin' pussy' and jam their stick to the crotch.

"Players encourage that. They say, 'Nice hit, way to knock that guy down.' Kids will be kids, but coaches need to tell kids that if they throw sucker shots, they'll be benched. Teach them that's not the way the game is to be played. The coach is responsible. If he sees that kind of play, he has to stop it."

————

Holt got hurt in an otherwise unmemorable junior varsity matchup. Page back farther in the state's history to an epic final. It's 1969. The state tournament debuts at Bloomington's Met Center. Willard Ikola's Edina Hornets have gained entrance to the Big Dance the past two years but haven't snuck past the first round. This year, Ike's best team to date has stormed into the championship game, outscoring foes that season 142–19. For the first of what will be many times, Ike tests the luck of his houndstooth hat in a state final.

Edina faces the tiny hockey powerhouse from Warroad, a town of fewer than two thousand souls just a short cast south of the Canadian border. The state's top-ranked team, the Warriors are powered by an Ojibwe kid named Henry Boucha. Even though the offensive-oriented defenseman has only played in the Twin Cities once before, five years earlier when he fetched Warroad the state Bantam title, the city folks all know how to say his name, BOO-shay. They have heard the stories coming out of the Northland. Kid can skate like the wind. Shoots a cannon—put a puck through the wall in Thief River Falls; his slapshot bent the goalpost in Grand Rapids. The second coming of Bobby Orr.

Boucha, who played nearly every minute, scored the game-winner in Warroad's opening game against Minneapolis Southwest. Then he scored the game-winner unassisted against Northern rival Roseau in the semifinal game to put the Warriors up against Edina for the title. The state wrapped its arms around this Minnesotan treasure. The underdogs from Warroad entered the championship game as huge emotional favorites.

On February 22, 1969, Warroad delighted the record crowd of fifteen-thousand-plus at Met Center by jumping to a 2–1 lead. Boucha assisted on the go-ahead goal. In the second period, Edina scored two quick goals to pull ahead 3–2. Then Boucha carried the puck up ice on an end-to-end rush. The Edina goalie deflected his shot from the blue line. Boucha chased his rebound into the corner and sent out a centering pass.

Jim Knutson cornered him. The Jim Knutson who would go on to play at the University of Minnesota, where a young Tom Saterdalen was the coaches' gopher. The same Jim Knutson who thirty years later would write a letter of complaint to Saterdalen after the Jaguars coach cut his son, a senior. The Jim Knutson who owns the most famous elbow in the state.

That Jim Knutson, then a senior defenseman for the Hornets, bludgeoned Boucha. Boucha's head banged off the glass. He crumpled to the ice. A sickly silence blanketed the Met Center.

The Warroad coach skidded out to aid his star. Knutson's blow had crushed Boucha's eardrum. When Boucha finally gained his feet, the ice looked lop-sided. He was taken to the hospital, where he spent the next three days.

In an emotional tribute to their assaulted star, the Warriors rallied to tie the game and battled Edina into double overtime, but, without Boucha, they couldn't put away the Hornets. Ike's Edina High captured its first state title.

On the game's pivotal play, the officials made no call against Knutson.

Thirty-two years later, you run into Henry Boucha at the state tournament Hockey Expo. You ask him, "Should they have called a penalty?"

He doesn't answer right away. He picks up a copy of Mary Halverson Schofield's biography *Henry Boucha: Star of the North* and flips to a photo snapped by a spectator. In the grainy black-and-white image, Knutson plants his right elbow squarely against Boucha's head.

"I felt bad for him," Boucha finally says in his soft voice. "Everywhere he'd go, he'd get booed. Ikola wanted to win so bad; those guys were under a lot of pressure."

Elsewhere at the Expo, several booths down from Boucha, a throng of acne-studded boys clusters around a TV screen, those at the edges straining to see the succession of fight highlights. The greasy-haired guy peddling the video trumpets with carnival barker flair, "Lookit that uppercut! Watch this one, watch this one, here comes a right—there!" The boys cheer.

Despite the NHL's sporadic attempts to reign in goons, fight reels like this one and hit highlights flashed on jumbotrons become training videos. If violence is part of the game, then fighting is an essential ingredient in the NHL's product. Come playoff time, even skilled players become hatchetmen intent on wiping out the opposition's top talent. See New Jersey Devils captain Scott Stevens KO Philadelphia Flyers captain Eric Lindros to secure the Eastern Conference championship last year. It is Lindros's sixth concussion in two years. The fans roar. Think the kids don't notice?

In 1999, a fifteen-year-old youth hockey player in Illinois was charged with felony aggravated battery for slamming an opponent into the boards seconds after the game's final buzzer. While the paralyzed victim watched from his wheelchair, an Illinois judge found his assailant guilty of simple battery and sentenced him to 120 hours of community service.

Then there are the sticks. During the fall of 2000, the Boston Bruins' Marty McSorley stood trial for assault with a weapon after cracking the Vancouver Canucks' Donald Brashear in the right temple with his stick. His defense? He was trying to hit Brashear in the shoulder to provoke a fight. The British Columbia judge didn't buy it. He found McSorley guilty and sentenced him to eighteen months probation. The NHL fined McSorley a record seventy-two thousand dollars and suspended him for a season.

That was but the latest in the league's sordid history of stick attacks. In 1988, Dino Ciccarelli, then of the Minnesota North Stars, spent a day in jail and paid a one-thousand-dollar fine for clubbing Toronto's Luke Richardson. Two decades earlier, Boston tough guy Ted Green swung his Sher-Wood at the St. Louis Blues' Wayne Maki in a preseason game. Maki ducked and swung back,

252 • Blades of Glory

shattering Green's skull. The NHL suspended Green for thirteen games—a moot penalty since he spent that time in the hospital fighting for his life—and sat Maki for thirty days.

Henry Boucha, his eardrum healed, became the Detroit Red Wings' rookie of the year in 1972–73. On January 4, 1975, back at the Met Center, this time in a North Stars uniform, Boucha mixed it up with Dave Forbes, a weaker player trying to impress Boston's brass as a big, bad Bruin. Coming out of the penalty box, Forbes jabbed Boucha in the right eye with the butt end of his stick. The blow shattered Boucha's eye socket and damaged some of the muscles that controlled his eye's movement. Charged with aggravated assault, Forbes escaped his trial with a hung jury. Boucha sued the Bruins and the NHL. He won a financial settlement but, saddled with double vision, he could never play the game the same. He retired in 1977 at twenty-six.

Meanwhile, only two months after his probation had expired, Bernie swung away. He chopped at opponents' ankles, calves, and necks, yet officials merely reprimanded him with two-minute minors, until Chaska, when the refs ejected him for his vicious two-fisted stick assault. Under MSHSL rules, that meant he was grounded for another game, the same punishment meted out to players who wore necklaces under their uniforms.

———————

Adam Dirlam's mom shouts from the stands, "Play the body!" A moment later, Adam crushes another mother's son with a forearm shiver inside the Jefferson blue line and poses over his crumpled foe like a lion over its kill. *Attaboy, Adam!*

Karen Bender flinches whenever her son Nick gets checked. Sometimes she screams out loud. "I nearly had a heart attack when they started checking in Peewees," she says.

When it is your kid on the other end of the check, some other primal instinct, this one to protect one's young, can take over. That instinct submerged Thomas Junta into a rage so severe it ended in youth hockey's ugliest incident.

When he saw his ten-year-old son take a check then an elbow to the nose—in what was supposed to be a no-checking scrimmage—

Junta derided the father on the ice for not controlling the players. That father, Michael Costin, reportedly snapped, "That's what hockey is all about." Afterward, Junta beat Costin to death, and, in the now infamous trial, was sentenced to six to ten years for involuntary manslaughter.

In addition to this most notorious incident, a score of other violent outbursts by parents and coaches over the past two years have sullied hockey's name. In Manitoba, an assistant coach of a Minnesota All-Star team playing a Peewee tournament leaped over the boards and wrestled the ref to the ice for failing to call a penalty when the coach's son got checked after the whistle. In Duluth, a judge gave a father a tongue-lashing and banned him from the rink for threatening a coach. A Brainerd, Minnesota, dad was similarly banned for making threats. In Staten Island, New York, following a game for eleven- and twelve-year-old boys, a father bloodied the nose of his son's coach with a stick because his son had not improved over the season. In Euless, Texas, a mother shoved a child for heckling her son, then tussled with another parent. A Texas father jumped out of the stands during a high school tournament and put an official in a headlock on the ice. In Oakdale, Minnesota, the goalie of the Tartan High girls' team and her father were charged with disorderly conduct after shoving and punching opposing fans who taunted them in the lobby after a loss.

In 1998, during a chippy game between Elk River and Champlin Park, the Elks' coach Tony Sarsland warned his players not to take any more retaliation penalties. Thirty seconds later, one of his wingers threw a punch after getting checked. The player avoided a penalty, but when he returned to the bench, the feisty Sarsland got in his face. "I'd like to take you out behind the building and break your fucking nose," the coach growled. Still steamed after the game, Sarsland cocked his clenched fist inches from the boy's chin in the dressing room and threatened, "If you ever do something like that again, I'm going to break your fucking jaw." The Elk River administration suspended Sarsland for ten days.

———

In March 2000, the American Academy of Pediatrics recommended that USA Hockey and other governing boards ban checking among players under sixteen. The nation's largest group of pediatricians cited a study that blamed checking for 86 percent of youth hockey's injuries. Two weeks later, a Montreal physician seconded their motion in an effort to reduce spinal injuries. He was backed by a study that found 243 amateur hockey players in Canada suffered spinal injuries from 1966 to 1996. Six of those injuries proved fatal. While many Minnesota youth and high school coaches conceded that the game had grown more violent, they defended the physical contact at the Peewee and Bantam levels as necessary to teach kids how to take a check. Minnesota Hockey required Peewee teams to sew STOP patches on the back of their jerseys to remind players not to check from behind. The following summer, the USA Hockey Annual Congress defeated a proposal to ban body checking at the Peewee level.

————

In the lobby of the Chaska Community Center, Jefferson parents muttered about the insolence of Chaska kids, but Duncs was all smiles. "I like games like that," the rough-and-tumble center said, meaning those games when the refs let them play smashmouth hockey. Of course, it didn't hurt that the final score was 6–1 in the Jaguars' favor. Duncs was ready to enjoy another chew on the bus ride home.

Bernie skipped the bus ride. He headed to the emergency room to have his shoulder examined. Kelly, the team manager, had to help him out of his equipment. Bernie wasn't smiling on his way through the lobby.

Nor was Sats. As usual, he and Thomas boarded the bus last. On the ride back to school, the coaches pondered Bernie. Do they bench him beyond his one-game suspension? Kick him off the team? They had hoped his teammates would reach him, but so far none had.

————

Back at BIG, among the team photos that decorate the Hall of Fame, there's a faded painting of Bill Masterton. Posed in his North

Stars uniform, the right-handed shooting center holds his stick to the ice. He is bare-headed, having played in the era when the pros mocked as sissies opponents who wore helmets. His short brown hair is neatly combed.

Midway through the first period of a game played January 13, 1968, a check ended Masterton's life. Masterton carried the puck into the Oakland Seals' zone, optioned a backhand pass to his wing—and was double-teamed by the Seals' defensemen. Their hit sent him backwards, and his head bounced sharply against the Met Center ice. Masterton never regained consciousness. The twenty-nine-year-old left behind his wife, Carol, and their two small children.

Masterton's No. 19 suspended from the Met Center rafters served as a grisly reminder of hockey's dangers. Even today with headgear mandatory and technological advances making helmets more protective, the risk of serious head or spinal injury isn't eliminated. Ask Eric Lindros, who was wearing a helmet last year when Scott Stevens handed him his sixth concussion. Ask Holt Bennington about his dented CCM.

Masterton's specter hovers over hockey rinks from Bloomington to Warroad. They tore down the Met Center, but they can't exorcise the fear that still haunts mothers in the stands at BIG and elsewhere across the state whenever their sons get nailed.

CHAPTER EIGHTEEN

REIGNING IN THE CONFERENCE

Before the Chaska game, Sats had enlisted the archives to inspire his team. The coach let Tommy pick out one of the Jefferson classics. After the last bell of the day, the '01 Jags shucked off their backpacks and settled into the desks of B201. Studying this history beat tracking an algebra equation or listening to an economics lecture.

Before he rolled the tape, Sats leaned against his desk. "Who's frustrated?"

Most of the guys raised their hands.

"Why?"

"I didn't score," Tommy said.

"My passes were jinxed," Bernie said. "And I hit two pipes."

"When you guys start practicing as hard as you can, that won't happen," Sats said.

He paused, slipped his right hand into his pocket. "At church yesterday I spotted something in the bulletin that said, 'Remember, it takes twenty-one days to establish a habit.' I started thinking, why did I see that message yesterday? I realized, twenty-one days from today, sections start. If you go out and bust your ass for twenty-one days, you'll have developed a good habit."

His left hand sliced the air to emphasize the point. "Winning has got to be a habit."

Winning had become a habit for the '89 team, captained by Tony Bianchi, which lost only three games all season. Their highlight video, narrated by a local television sportscaster, riveted the '01 squad.

No. 22 scores a pretty goal in the Tournament's quarterfinal game. "That's Dave Dahlberg," Duncs said.

One of the assistant captains scores. "Sweet. Who's that?"

"Sean Rice."

Another goal.

"Rice again."

In the quarterfinal game, Jim Broz smashes an International Falls forward against the Civic Center's clear dashers. "Bitch!"

The camera shows Sats pacing in the dressing room, his youngish face dominated by large, plastic frame glasses. The '01 players laughed.

But when Tony Bianchi sneaks the puck past the Rochester John Marshall goalie with less than four minutes remaining to tie the championship game, they felt the goosebumps rise under their Jefferson letter jackets.

That was the effect Sats intended. He worried they had lost focus. Following the team's troubleshooting meeting, they had rallied to beat Eden Prairie, but then they lapsed back into *laissez-faire* play against Rosemount and Eagan. If they didn't rise up to their ability, they would sabotage their chances. Sats wanted to salvage something from the season, and he decided to focus on winning the Lake

Conference. Maybe they could translate that into a Tournament run. As he had told them at the start of the year, all twelve times the Jaguars had won the conference title, they had gone on to State.

To get there, they had to win their last six regular season games—all against conference opponents. Once the screen went black and the lights came up, Sats offered a final petition. "We have six games left, but we have twelve games left," he said, adding the three section playoff games and three Tournament games needed to capture the state championship. "You guys have got to believe."

———

Amen. Following the Chaska scrum, the Jaguars focused their physical game against the Eastview Lightning and played like converts. Tommy fought for the puck high in the slot and fed B.J. down low. Nick worked the puck off the boards and around the net to Duncs in front. Tommy sailed coast to coast, bulled his way through both D, shot, then poked in his rebound. Eastview's powerplay got one by Jeremy, but Van B quickly converted a pass from Duncs. Then Duncs flattened a Lightning D behind the net and slipped the puck to Jimmy on the other side. They busted their asses like good boys—not letting the ephedrine take over their emotions—and skated away with a 5–2 win.

The Jaguars had missed Bernie on the powerplay and penalty kill. He served his suspension in the stands, his right arm in a sling. After the game he did not join the team in the dressing room but disappeared into the crowd.

———

Tuesday night, February 6, 2001, was Senior Night. Under the direction of Steve Duncan, who chaired the Senior Night committee, the senior parents decorated BIG accordingly. When the bus dropped off the boys, a photo collage greeted them in the lobby. Against a glittery backdrop, their parents had arranged an enlarged color shot of each senior player with his parents as well as one for Kelly, the manager, and the three senior cheerleaders. They had printed special keepsake programs for the evening adorned with each senior's graduation photo and a few words on what Jefferson Hockey had meant to their lives. They taped large, colorful posters for each senior player behind the Lakeville goal and positioned blue and white balloon bouquets throughout BIG. The boys' moms and dads proudly wore their sons' jerseys. It was a night to reminisce.

After the first period, all of the players except for the seniors retired to the dressing room. Tommy, Nick, Duncs, Timm, Jimmy, B.J., Shacks, and Brett Shelanski, the senior goalie who had played j.v., shed their helmets and gathered at the team bench. The boys' parents huddled on the opposite side by the penalty box. "Parents, I'm sure you'll never forget those 5:00 A.M. skates and all you've done to make it possible for your sons to be part of the Jefferson tradition," Pat Dillon, Nick's dad, began over the P.A.

One by one, he summoned the seniors. The Jaguars' '01 captain slowly skated the width of the rink to meet his parents. Mary and Kelly Gilbert stepped out of the penalty box onto a carpet spread on the ice. Tommy presented a rose to his mother, who rewarded him with her wide-toothed smile. She loved watching her son play and would've gotten up at any hour to do so, even for a practice. Kelly beamed beside her. They had watched Tommy, the little boy idolizing the star next door, grow to become the star himself, captain of this elite team. Hockey promised him a bright future. They smiled for the photographers.

Tommy took his place with his parents along the blue line to watch his friends meet their parents. In the keepsake program, he had written, "Most of all, I will always remember my teammates I played with since Squirts." The boys had become Tommy's brothers. They had played nearly eight hundred games together, and now it had come down to the final four of the regular season, the number Sats circled on the green board before the game. They were guaranteed only one more beyond that. It depressed Tommy to think about that. They lined up on the blue line like they did for the national anthem, yet that sounded a beginning; this signaled a closing. They had forged a family that was about to split up.

Karen Bender gave Nick a big hug and a warm kiss on the cheek. She wanted to squeeze enjoyment out of each short moment left.

The moment flooded her with feelings of love for her son, of whom she was so unbelievably proud, this boy whom she taught to be kind and who had become so compassionate yet still competitive. This boy whose confidence had blossomed. This boy who had grown into his role as alternate captain and team leader. Those emotions flowed through her embrace.

Mike Coffman also hugged his son. Hockey had given them a bond, an understanding. From the days Mike coached Nick's Squirt C team to today, Nick had made such huge strides. Mike had looked at his son's graduation picture in the program and seen the toddler who had toted around one of Mike's hockey sticks grown into the handsome young man in his Jaguars jersey, the *A* stitched on his chest.

Deb Irvin watched the hugs and knew her turn was next. She knew about good-byes, having buried her sister only two months earlier. These women had been so kind. She came home from the funeral to find her house cleaned and a note from Karen and Merrelyn. They had left cheese and wine chilling in the fridge for her to pass some quiet moments with Dave. You couldn't replace friends like that.

Dave Irvin's chest swelled. He remembered another night at BIG. As the girls' team headed onto the ice for practice, Duncs came over to Dave, their coach. They hugged, and Duncs planted a kiss on Dave's cheek, telling him—right in front of the girls—that he loved him. Dave had married a wonderful woman and gained a one-of-a-kind son.

Steve Duncan, in his No. 22 jersey, didn't have to compete with Dave; he felt secure in his son's affection for him. That was the kind of caring young man he had matured into. Duncs had given him so much to remember on and off the ice. Steve knew he would watch his son play hockey next year somewhere. The lump in his throat came from knowing that he had only a handful of games left to watch him play in his Jaguars jersey.

Merrelyn Lorenz waited alone in the penalty box. The night was yet another reminder—in a succession of reminders over the past four years—of Bradd's absence. If only he could have been there that night to stand with her. If only he could've cheered Timm's play. If only he could've seen his graduation picture, the little boy who used to run around their basement in his goalie equipment here posed in his Jaguars' dress whites, his customized mask at his side. If only Timm could hear his father say how proud he was of the person he had become. If only....

She had thought about that night all day, from the moment she awoke alone through dinner with Timm at Famous Dave's, but she hadn't mentioned anything to Timm. She hadn't wanted to distract him. She hadn't wanted to take his mind or emotions away from that night's hockey game.

Thank God for these other women. They had welcomed her as though her son had been one of theirs. They recognized the hockey in her blood. She and Debbie Earl had bonded as goalie moms. Her best friends had always come through hockey. So, too, had Timm's. She couldn't bear to think about leaving them for Colorado, even if that was home.

Timm laid the rose in Merrelyn's hands and returned her solo hug. He had tried not to think about it, tried to put it out of his mind during the day at school, but there it was again, his father's absence filling the arena. His mother would ask him when he got home after the game, "Was it hard?" Yes. Of course. He missed him all the time. When he drove to school. When he studied for tests. When he ate dinner. But most of all, when he played hockey. There was an empty spot in the stands, a spot he could never fill. Yet down there on the ice, shoulder to shoulder with his teammates on the blue line, the emptiness didn't feel quite as big. They steadied him from pitching into the void.

————

The Jaguars had played flat the first period. The score stood at 1–1. Lakeville had come at them hard, and Jefferson had stumbled with its breakout, fumbled the puck going into the attacking zone, bumbled its chances. Once the ceremony ended and the seniors had rejoined their teammates in the dressing room, Sats chastised them for their poor first period. "I don't know how far you guys want to go. You haven't picked it up since Eden Prairie. You're not going to get there if you keep playing like this."

They responded with their best period of the season. They bullied the Panthers off the puck and poured eighteen shots on the net. Six found their mark. Five of those goals came from seniors Nick, Duncs, Tommy, Jimmy, and B.J. For his part, Timm shut down an early Lakeville threat.

Bernie watched from the stands, his arm still in a sling.

The game ended Jefferson 8, Lakeville 1, a Senior Night to remember. Afterward, the boys' parents swilled champagne at Billabong in a reunion with last year's senior parents, who had returned for auld lang syne.

As the game had worn on, Sats and Thomas lightened up behind the bench and relaxed their criticism. The mood turned upbeat. Players joked between shifts. They laughed their way to the dressing room. Sats whistled for their attention. "Hey, guys, that was a little better mindset. Wasn't that fun?"

In the rematch with Kennedy, which Jefferson barely won in overtime, the fans sang "Happy Birthday" to Timm, who turned eighteen the next day. His mom took him to see the Return of Mario. Amazingly, the upstart Minnesota Wild shut down Lemieux, one of only seven teams able to do so that season. With Minnesota closing in on its improbable 4–2 victory, Timm and Merrelyn stood the last two minutes and rocked the rink along with the other 18,825 fans. Timm's first impression of the Xcel left no doubt in his mind that come March, when the fans hit their feet, he wanted to be down there on the ice with his Jefferson mates.

The talk in Jock Hall, the carpeted strip behind the auditorium where the varsity athletes hung out and freshmen girls were afraid to walk, was about Duncs's takeouts. Duncs had one hundred so far in twenty-two games, an average of 4.5 per game. The player who wore the team's December and January "Hit Man" T-shirts often had six or seven takeouts in the big games. If he could average 7.2 over the last two regular season games and the six section and tournament games, he would break Kelly Hultgren's '89 season record of 157. There wasn't a guy sitting on the bench in Jock Hall, teammate or otherwise, who didn't think Duncs could do it.

With two games left in the regular season, both critical in the conference race, Sats wanted his players to shift into a playoff mind-set. He demonstrated in practice how they should lie down to block shots, stacking their shin pads and placing their sticks toward the middle so shooters had to go around them to the outside. The natural inclination was to go down the other way, stick to the boards, to protect oneself.

"You could get hit in the stomach or chest that way," Nick pointed out.

Sats turned on him. "You just said you'd do anything for these guys. That's what they do to win the Stanley Cup. It's that time of year. You've got to start playing that way. Do it for these guys." He gestured with his glove to the other Jags. "I've never seen a guy get hurt doing that."

"I did," B.J. said. "Against White Bear Lake. I hurt my knee blocking a shot."

"That's not hurt," Sats said. "I mean being taken to the hospital."

They drilled doing it Sats's way, but Nick couldn't resist the temptation to slide into the shooter, taking him out the way a baserunner broke up a double play.

Sats showed them the '94 highlight video. Over half of that team's regular players graduated to pro hockey. Those guys had been the ones Tommy and Duncs and Nick had pretended to be. They listened to senior Mike Crowley say, "Growing up, seeing teams be successful, that makes you want to be successful." They watched Crowley ice the dynasty's three-peat with a beautiful third period goal. They felt the hair rise on their arms.

All Tommy could think about was hockey. Nothing else mattered. His girlfriend understood. "I'll just leave you alone for the next couple of games," she said.

The day before a game, Tommy couldn't study. Game days he napped after school. In class he doodled the section playoff brackets on his folder, envisioning various scenarios. He felt the pressure as a senior to impress upon the younger guys that once the playoffs started, a loss ended it all. He felt the pressure as captain to be a good leader. *From one to whom much is given, much is expected.*

On Tommy's notebook, Jefferson always won, but a recurring nightmare plagued him. Sometimes he woke with the game so real that he stared in disbelief and dejection at the ceiling he couldn't see until slowly his mind cleared. It hadn't happened. Then, he would fall asleep, and it would happen again. They would lose the section championship to Holy Angels.

———

The day after the Chaska brawl, Bernie showed up at school with his arm in a sling. He told his teammates his right shoulder had suffered a second-degree separation and that the doctor had suggested he sit out two weeks, maybe longer. Amber, the team trainer, routinely asked him for a note from the doctor. Under league rules she needed that to be able to start working with Bernie on his rehabilitation. He didn't have one. She pestered him for the note the next day and the next. They lost three days of physical therapy. Finally, on Saturday, Bernie produced a note, but it did not specify a "second degree separation" nor prescribe two weeks of rest. The doctor had simply written that Bernie could return when the pain in his shoulder became "tolerable." After examining his range of motion, Amber figured he had a lesser first degree separation.

Coach Thomas suspected Bernie had feigned the severity of the injury to win sympathy from his teammates and mitigate their anger at him for losing his temper and taking a stupid penalty.

Bernie admitted he had grown tired of the daily practices. Other players watched practices while injured. Bernie skipped them. "Practice sucks," he said. "There's nothing I'm going to learn after three years."

His teammates were hurt by what they interpreted as Bernie caring only for himself. One day in the dressing room, Jimmy complained about a caption Bernie had written for the school yearbook, which he helped edit. On the hockey team's page, accompanying the largest photo, one of Bernie getting pulled to the ice, Bernie had composed, "It takes several defenders to take down Bernhagen because of his superior offensive skills." Jimmy shook his head. "When he jerks off, he probably thinks of himself."

Sats had encouraged his captains to intervene, but they hadn't stepped up. So he organized a private meeting in his room between Bernie and the captains, as well as Dillon and Adam, the only two other juniors Bernie respected. Sats had done this before—cranked up the peer pressure—with kids whose drug use was dragging down the team, but never to confront explicitly another player's attitude. With the season nearing its climax, he counted it as his last hope—or Bernie's last chance.

Tommy, Duncs, Nick, Dillon, and Adam faced Bernie after school in B201. Enough, they said. The temper tantrums in practice, the tirades on the bench, the arguing with coaches, the berating other players, the stupid penalties—all that had to stop. If Bernie wanted to win the Tournament this year like they did, they needed him to play for the team and to show a positive attitude.

Tommy told Bernie his bitching and bickering hurt the team and their line. It also hurt Tommy, personally. It took the fun out of the game and could spoil his chances in front of scouts. "You've got one more year; I don't," Tommy said.

For once, Bernie sat speechless. He listened to his teammates' concerns. His eyes moistened. Perhaps they had reached him.

———

On Tuesday, February 13, the day of the Apple Valley game, a freezing rain greased the roads. Driving turned into sledding.

On his way to school to get ready for the game, B.J. wiped out. A car cut in front of him on 102nd Street, not far from the school, and B.J. hit the brakes. The back end spun into a snowbank, and his Blazer flipped. Several times. When it finally came to rest, the windows and windshield were smashed out, and the roof was crumpled. B.J. hadn't been wearing his seatbelt. Yet, somehow, he wasn't hurt. He managed to crawl out of the battered Blazer without a scratch.

He considered himself lucky. When his mom arrived at the scene, she credited a higher source for her son's safety. "First thing I did was take the St. Christopher medallion out of the car to put into the next one," she said.

Once the Bloomington police officer had gathered the information he needed, B.J.'s parents asked if he could go over to the school to get ready for the hockey game. The officer, noting B.J.'s letter jacket, asked, "What number are you?"

"Sixteen."

"You scored the tying goal last Saturday night," the officer said. "I'll drive you over myself. Hop in."

That night, the Jaguars would need all of B.J.'s luck to get by a swift and motivated Apple Valley team. Not only could the Eagles—seven-time conference champs themselves—spoil the Jaguars' conference drive, the two teams could face each other in the section playoffs, and both would want the psychological advantage of having won this game. In their previous meeting, the Jaguars had barely finished off the Eagles 2–1 on Nick's game-winner. Bernie had scored a pretty goal early but missed on a breakaway. Perhaps his return to the lineup for the rematch would prove to be the Jaguars' lucky charm. He had been cleared to play, but Nancy wished he wouldn't. She thought he was rushing his return and feared he risked hurting himself worse.

Apple Valley played like a team possessed. They skated hard, cycled the puck, and bottled up Jefferson's breakout. The Jags seemed to be playing catchup. Nick netted a rebound off one of Duncs's shots, but the Jefferson pep band played the Apple Valley school song twice.

Down 2–1 at the first intermission, Sats paced among the orange peels. "That was terrible, just terrible." He left to compare notes with his assistants outside the door.

Bernie iced his shoulder. "This guy lets everything bounce off his pads. There's a rebound on every shot."

Sure enough, in the second period, Shavvy banged in a rebound off a Bernie shot to tie the game. With less than a minute left in the period, Nick fed Tommy, who buried his shot to put the Jaguars up 3–2.

Five minutes into the period, Duncs nailed an Apple Valley defenseman chest to chest. The blow knocked him down. He lingered a moment on the ice, then limped to the bench. He remained dazed the entire second period but didn't miss a shift. Amber checked him out in the dressing room between periods and reported he was "talking dumb," but Duncs stayed in the game.

In the third period, Apple Valley beat Timm to tie the game at three.

Two shifts later, with less than 3:30 to play, Bernie mixed it up with an Eagle in the Apple Valley end and axed him across the side of his neck. The Apple Valley player dropped. His helmet flew off. He flopped like a fish on a dock. One of his teammates rushed to his side. Amber hurried out to tend to him. Suddenly, as the ref escorted Bernie to the penalty box, the boy stood, gave Bernie a little wave, and skated to his bench.

The fans booed him for faking an injury. Worse, though, had been Bernie's retaliation. Sats clenched his jaw. He couldn't believe it. First game back since being ejected for hitting a guy with his stick, and Bernie whacks another with a vicious swing. Only a week earlier his teammates had told him to shape up. Later, Sats would say, "Remember the last item when we talked about setting goals, being willing to change behavior?"

Sats shook his head. His tortured superstar had taken yet another stupid retaliation penalty, putting the game, the conference title, even the team's playoff hopes, in jeopardy.

The Eagles' powerplay sniffed victory, but the Jaguars fought off the attack. Just as the final seconds ticked off Bernie's penalty, Duncs poked the puck away from Apple Valley's left D on the penalty box side of the rink. He carried the puck up ice past Bernie waiting by the door to jump back into the game, but stalled at the Eagles' blue line. Bernie, racing behind Duncs, scooped the puck off the side boards and took a shot from a bad angle down low. His rebound bounced to the goalie's left. Bernie swooped behind the net and whipped the puck out front, a perfect setup for Duncs, who one-timed a blast through the Apple Valley goalie.

The scoreboard read, Home 4, Guests 3, with 1:12 remaining.

Duncs slid on one knee and pumped his right arm. Bernie and his linemates skated him down and gathered Duncs in a hug. His head woozy, Duncs's heart had carried him.

Afterward, he slumped in his corner of the dressing room, leaned his head back against the wall, and closed his eyes. "That's the worst concussion I've had."

Deb and Dave Irvin waited for Duncs at the top of the bleachers. Steve Duncan waited down below. When Duncs finally emerged with his bag slung over his shoulder, they took turns congratulating him and asking him how he felt. "Who's the President?" Dave asked.

"Bill Clinton," Duncs said, his eyes still not completely focused.

Sats also felt like he'd had his bell rung. Apple Valley had shown it was a team to worry about. Had the Eagles not missed the net with three perfect scoring chances, they would've dumped the Jaguars 6–4. Goodbye, Lake Conference title. Jefferson couldn't count on them choking again in the playoffs.

Then there was Bernie. Sweet, stupid Bernie. He had risked the game, then won it. How do you solve a conundrum like this kid?

––––––––

At practice the next day, Sats collected twenty-five cents from each player for the Quarter Drill, a three-on-three round robin among five teams. He paid the winning line a buck apiece and the winning goalie $1.25. But when it came time to award the prize money, he realized he was a quarter short.

"Who didn't pay?" he asked.

Timm coughed, "Earl."

"Jeremy? We solved the mystery. Usually I give the goalie $1.25, but I guess I'll give that now to the center of the winning line."

That meant Bernie. "Yeah, it goes to the center," he said.

"Or maybe I'll split it among his teammates," Sats teased.

"Screw my teammates," Bernie said.

"That's Bernie's motto," Tommy said. "'Screw my teammates.'"

————

Two days before Burnsville, the final regular season game of the season, Sats rubbed the boys' noses in a tape of the second period from their first meeting. They watched the Blaze score three unanswered goals and endured Reed Larson's analysis of their flaws. Larson, an NHL All-Star out of Minneapolis Roosevelt High, pointed out to the Channel 14 audience that Burnsville repeatedly beat Jefferson to the puck and outplayed the Jaguars physically—with only two seniors. "You should be embarrassed," Sats said. And they were. They stank.

The theme for practice the next day was, "The harder you work, the luckier you get." Sats had them shout this in unison during the agility drill. They practiced with intensity. Especially the seniors, who realized that time was running out on their season. Sats yelled at them to shoot on net and to hustle. They skated hard and dove for pucks. No reason they shouldn't bust their asses for the few hours left of practice, Tommy had told them.

Afterward Shavvy, who skated well, commented, "This was a good practice. I think it's an omen."

Saturday broke cold. By midafternoon, when the Jefferson bus pulled up to the Burnsville Arena, a wooden structure whose shape and color resembled a loaf of Wonder Bread, sunny skies had warmed the air to the day's high of 7°F. The players shivered in their jerseys on the walk inside.

The game started late, due to an injury delay in the preceding j.v. game. A Burnsville player who had recently suffered a concussion was stricken by convulsions after being checked into the boards. He was taken off the ice on a stretcher.

Before the Jaguars had boarded the bus, Sats told his boys in front of the green board, "If you win today, you tie the Jefferson record for most regular season wins: twenty-two." The '93 champs who finished the season undefeated won twenty-two regular season games before the league added three games to the schedule. The players seated on the benches before Sats and perched on the lockers behind them mulled over that possibility. "You also have the chance to win our thirteenth conference title."

Eden Prairie played Apple Valley that evening. If both Eden Prairie and Jefferson won, they tied for the conference title. If Jefferson won and EP lost, the Lake Conference was theirs outright.

"I'm putting some pressure on you, yeah, but I think pressure's good in the right direction. When you guys play in front of eighteen thousand in the old Civic Center, you're going to have a little pressure on you. We might as well see how you respond."

They responded. But John Barger, Burnsville's coach, must have delivered a rousing pregame speech himself, because the Blaze also came out roused. They played with the confidence of knowing they could beat Jefferson. The two teams raced up and down the ice in a thrilling, high-tempo game.

Knowing his team lacked depth, Barger left his top line with Mike Franks and T.J. Jindra—the pair that had undone Jefferson last game—on the ice for the first minute and a half through both Bernie's and Duncs's lines. With Franks and Jindra resting, Jefferson's third line opened the scoring when sophomore Brad Peterson threaded a shot between the goalie's legs.

Barger tried flying his wings to sneak one past the Jefferson D, and at 7:18, it worked. A wing got behind Adam and Stark and beat Jeremy on the breakaway to tie the game.

The two teams battled it out in the tight, close arena, packed to its low, wooden rafters. A shot from the point skittered between the Burnsville goalie's legs and came to rest several tantalizing inches from the goal line. The goalie froze, thinking the puck was underneath him. Nick raced a Burnsville defenseman to the puck, fought off his check, and reached his stick past the goalie to will the Jaguars up 2–1.

The wily Barger switched goalies to give his team the chance to regroup. They played even the remainder of the period.

In the Jefferson dressing room, the players crammed shoulder to shoulder on the benches to see the strategies Sats diagramed on the white board. He implored the guys on the bench to shout out to the D on the ice whenever Burnsville tried to fly its wings. "This is sudden death hockey starting today," he said. His voice strained. This was as intense as they had seen him all season. "This is for the Lake Conference title. You've got to play intense!"

Three minutes into the second period, Bernie, playing one of his smiling performances, lifted a Burnsville player's stick to swipe the puck and rifled a pass onto Tommy's tape across the zone. Tommy fired, and Peterson knocked in the rebound. 3–1, Jefferson.

In the dressing room between periods, Duncs looked whipped. Sweat dripped from the foam pads in his helmet. When he removed it, his hair was drenched. He had played two periods all out—killed penalties and anchored the powerplay—but still had one to go. The fatigue showed in his face. He sighed and rolled his eyes.

Sats, his voice already hoarse, exhorted his boys, "Guys, you're fifteen minutes away from 22–3. Let's go!"

Duncs walked to the water fountain and washed down another Ripped Fuel pill. Jimmy downed another himself.

To start the third, Bernie's line hit the ice to the theme of Monday Night Football thudding over the loudspeakers. Then AC/DC screamed "You Shook Me All Night Long" until the official dropped the puck. Bernie won the draw and passed back to Stark, but Franks swiftly intercepted his pass and split the D. Jeremy denied the Blaze star, but this game was far from over.

The Jefferson cheerleaders clapped their mittened hands in the front row. "We've got spirit. S-P-I-R-I-T, spirit. Let's hear it."

Going the other way, Bernie rushed coast to coast, deked the goalie, but just as Bernie was about to slide the puck into the open-glove side, the goalie stretched out his arm and robbed him.

Moments later, Bernie slashed a Blaze player who jostled him in front of the Jefferson net. Even though the ref called coincidental minors, the Jags were at a disadvantage without Bernie on the ice. It took Jindra little over a minute to swing wide around Van B, then beat Jeremy high to pull within one. The clock showed 1:38 remaining, easily enough time for the Blaze to tie it.

Jefferson poured on the pressure. Tommy fed Shavvy on a two-on-one, but Shavvy shot wide. Next shift, Duncs juked around the D and ripped a wrist shot on goal, but it was right into the goalie.

With twenty-nine seconds left, Barger changed goalies again to rest his top line. He had dressed three goalies for the game to be able to take advantage of the automatic timeout.

But he ran out of tricks, and the Blaze ran out of time.

The last regular season game for seniors turned out to be a career day for a Jaguar sophomore. Brad Peterson's two goals had secured at least a share of the conference title. The kid Sats had demoted to j.v. midseason had become the unlikely hero. That afternoon, Brad's dad clapped at the final buzzer.

After they showered back at school and grabbed a bite to eat, Duncs, Nick, and Timm headed to the Eden Prairie–Apple Valley game. Tommy called Duncs on his cell phone to get the score.

"They lost 3–2. We're the champs."

They didn't know that yet in the cramped dressing room at Burnsville immediately after their own win. They just knew they had left their hearts out there on the ice in a tough game, and it had been good enough to ink at least a portion of another Lake Conference title on the Jefferson gym wall.

"This means we're headed to State," said Adam. He had become a student of Jefferson history.

Sats was buzzed. After a brief heads down, he shouted, "Great job, Blue!" He pumped each guy's hand. Then he opened his mouth and roared, "It's playoff time!"

CHAPTER NINETEEN

SHE GOT GAME

If you were made of sugar and spice and everything nice, you dreamed of being a Jefferson cheerleader. As a second grader, you wore a miniature cheerleader jacket and attended the Saturday clinics the high school girls offered and practiced your cheers in the kitchen. You knew the competition was cutthroat—that year nearly a third of the ninth grade girls tried out—but you also knew that those who made the cut enjoyed celebrity popularity. Even post-Title IX, glory and adulation waited not in a smelly uniform but in a pleated skirt and knit sweater.

Ever since Sarah Kraft could remember, she had loved hockey. Her mother took her to Jaguars hockey games. Sarah considered the high school stars who won three state championships "the greatest people ever invented." A figure skater, she eagerly anticipated her moment in the spotlight, "I couldn't wait until I was a senior and down there cheering when the boys won state."

Then life changed in Bloomington. When Sarah was in fourth grade, the Jefferson youth hockey program organized girls' teams. Sarah jumped at the chance to play. She envisioned new possibilities for herself.

One day in phys ed class at Olson Elementary, Nick, Duncs, and Tommy boasted with prepubescent braggadocio, "We're going to be captains of our hockey team in high school."

Plastic floor hockey sticks in hand, Sarah and her friend Kendra Ottum countered, "We're going to be captains of our hockey team."

"There's not going to be a girls' hockey team," the boys said.

"Yes, there is."

And what do you know? By senior year, Sarah was a vivacious and pretty young woman who liked dark eye shadow and the Minnesota Wild's eighteen-year-old rookie sensation Marian Gaborik; Kendra was a confident All-Metro soccer player with exceptional athletic ability. Together, they captained the '01 Jefferson girls' varsity hockey team.

They had Duncs's mom to thank. Deb Irvin saw the fun her son had playing hockey and wanted some of that fun for herself. Even though she could barely skate, the then thirty-six-year-old mom and her sister assembled a ragtag team in the Minneapolis Women's C-Division. Going up against younger and more skilled college club teams, they didn't score a goal until their seventeenth game. They finished their first season winless and in last place. They had a blast.

In successive years, they parlayed their enjoyment into steadily improved skills. By their fifth season, they won the state championship. The season was all smiles.

Deb wanted to share the fun with younger girls. When the surveys she mailed to Bloomington families came back showing strong interest, Duncs's mom successfully lobbied the hesitant school board to support and sponsor girls' hockey as a varsity sport. The Booster program organized Under 10, Under 12, and Under 15 teams. Sarah Kraft and her playmates traded their white skates for black.

Deb had talked her husband, Dave Irvin, into coaching her women's team. A goalie himself in high school, Duncs's stepdad had coached Duncs as a Squirt and Peewee and was the Booster goalie coordinator when Deb started playing. He fell in love with coaching girls. "They haven't been playing since they could walk like the boys," he said. "They want to learn the game, they work hard, and they appreciate everything I teach them." Dave became the natural choice for head coach of Jefferson's first girls' varsity team in 1997–98.

By the time Sarah and Kendra reached their senior year, the female Jaguars had laid the foundation for their own tradition of success. They had made three straight trips to the state tournament, finishing as runnersup in 1999, and hung three team photos in BIG's Hall of Fame. Yet the girls still yearned for the respect bestowed upon their hockey brethren.

———

Before they could vote, women played hockey. As early as 1916, the University of Minnesota organized intramural teams that skated in calf-length dresses. The Depression and the War thwarted the growth of women's hockey until Title-IX legislation mandated equal athletic opportunities. That gave rise to a few fledgling efforts in the '70s, which popped up and withered. It wasn't until the '80s that female hockey teams gained a foothold. In the '90s, the game took off. The number of girls and women playing hockey in the United States rose from fewer than six thousand in 1990 to more than thirty-seven thousand by the close of the decade.

They wanted to play the traditionally male sport for the same reason the boys wanted to play: love of the game. As Deb Irvin discovered, the hockey virus was gender blind. "Hockey is a game that once you play it, it gets in your blood—doesn't matter if you're a boy or a girl," Dave Irvin said. "Once anyone experiences those thrills, they want to do it over and over again."

Minnesota became the first state to recognize girls' hockey as a varsity sport in 1994–95 with twenty-four teams and the first to host a girls' high school hockey tournament. Until that point, a couple of exceptional female players had starred their way onto boys' varsities, but finally the girls had a league of their own. Just six years later, 120 girls' teams vied for a spot in the eight-team state tournament.

The old male guard didn't cheer the women's movement on ice. At school board and hockey association meetings across the state, men opposed what they perceived as an invasion that threatened boys. The result was blatant discrimination—a 1991 Minnesota Department of Education survey revealed only 35 percent of Minnesota high schools were in compliance with state and federal laws that required equal athletic opportunities for both genders. The boys resisted sharing the ice with girls.

That mentality might have kept hockey sticks out of the girls' hands had it not been for the Mighty Ducks bill, the watershed state legislation in '95 that provided communities grants to build new ice rinks or renovate existing ones. With enough ice for everyone, resistance softened but did not completely dissipate. Respect across gender lines would be harder to win.

Despite being the fastest growing sport in America, female hockey had not been able to generate the same interest in fans as it had in participants. Women hockey stars even at the top level remained virtually anonymous. After the United States won the gold medal in the Nagano games where women's hockey debuted as an Olympic sport, U.S. forward Karen Bye said, "We walk through airports in our USA jackets and people ask if we're on the basketball team."

———

While the boys competed in the Holiday Classic, the Jaguar girls played in their own elite holiday tournament, the Kaposia Classic. Before the Jaguars took on the Hibbing Bluejackets in the opening game, the pregame pomp and circumstance assumed an NBA ambiance. The arena lights dimmed. Beethoven's Ninth blared over the P.A. Strobes silhouetted a player enlarged against a screen. Fog pumped across the ice. The girls stepped from behind a white sheet hung over the bench amidst a dazzling array of flashing multicolored lights. Spotlights chased them around the ice.

The special effects were squandered on only a few fans. The family and friends scattered throughout the bleachers would hardly have needed reservations for a table at Billabong. Duncs was there to cheer on his girlfriend, the Jaguars' talented defender Gianna Gambucci. Otherwise, hockey fans stayed away from the tournament *en masse*.

Comparisons to men's hockey cursed women's hockey. The girls and women didn't skate as fast; their shots were weaker. Under the no-checking rules, they didn't deliver the same bone-crushing hits. In short, female hockey lacked the testosterone that animated the men's game. Though played under the same name, it wasn't the same game.

In the Kaposia Classic, diminutive Hibbing forward Andrea Nichols snaked her way through the Jefferson defenders and deposited the puck in the back of the net. Such play challenged spectators accustomed to watching male hockey. Just when they expected the smaller puck carrier to be flattened by a larger player, the defender merely brushed her or lunged for a pokecheck. The anticipated collision rarely occurred.

Female hockey is physical the way basketball is physical, yet the checking ban opens the ice to skating, stickhandling, and playmaking. The women rely on teamwork and fundamentals. Critics dismiss the differences as inferior. Ironically, women are playing hockey the way men used to, before size and strength supplanted grace and creativity. Girls and women resurrected the game rued as lost by the old guard purists, the game where finesse prevailed over force.

Girls and women are not only redefining the sport, they are rewriting the definition of an athlete. That rankles those who believe jocks wear jocks. "Hockey represents a stereotypical male sport, one that's coded as a 'combat' or contact sport," says Mary Turco, a Dartmouth professor in women studies and author of *Crashing the Net: The U.S. Women's Ice Hockey Team and the Road to Gold*. "Traditionally, we've viewed that athlete as a superior athlete. If you give credit to females for being excellent in that sport coded as male, then it becomes just human, and it's devalued. There's resistance to giving the same value to a sport if women do it."

By breaking into a traditionally male sport, females busted open a Pandora's Box of identity issues revolving around gender and sexuality. For the adolescent American female, identity and body image are inextricably intertwined. The physical virtues hockey rewards—speed, power, strength, and physicality—run counterculture to traditional female training to be gentle, quiet, timid, demure, petite, submissive, and polite. Ambition and competitiveness subvert sugar and spice. Body image struggles between the muscular athlete and the anorexic supermodel ideal. Thus, the girls coming of age as hockey players face considerable confusion.

Those who have stepped outside the boundaries of society's feminine norm get labeled "dykes." That misperception is enough to keep some girls from going out for hockey. They fear being labeled; they fear being propositioned. Homophobia, usually rampant in male locker rooms, bars some girls from the women's room.

At the same time, the girls are treated as objects of male sexual desire. Coming out of the BIG dressing room one day after practice and walking past the girls lined up in their hockey gear ready to take the ice, Sats said to his players, "Watch your hands, guys."

––––––

The Jaguars started the season ranked No. 2 in the state, but they lost four of their first six games. They entered the Kaposia Classic on the skids. A fourth consecutive trip to the state tournament looked unlikely.

Larissa Luther hit her personal low over the Christmas break. Tall and tomboyish, she was a fierce competitor who didn't know what it meant to quit. The senior had a strong shot, solid skates, and the drive to go through another player to get the puck. She could play forward or defense and was equally good at either end of the rink. Junior year she left her old school to outrun a bad situation. She picked Jefferson because that was where she could win a state championship. When she called Dave Irvin to introduce herself, he said, "I know who you are. We would love to have you."

Larissa's talent and drive, however, had not translated into success. Like Tommy, she thought she could win games single-handedly.

She skated end to end without passing to open teammates. On the powerplay, she shot whenever she got the puck instead of working it around. Like Bernie, she sometimes got frustrated and took penalties that handicapped the team.

Her first year at Jefferson, Larissa had struggled for acceptance from her teammates, but it hadn't been forthcoming. Hers was a strong personality on the ice and in the dressing room. When she was in a bad mood, she sometimes lashed out at others. That intimidated the other girls and caused more than one divisive fight. She was used to being the star, but the year she transferred, Jefferson already had a star in Bethany Petersen. Larissa also had to share the limelight with Joccie Cookson, an All-State junior transfer from Edina.

Larissa had hoped things would be better senior year, but they went the other way. On a college recruiting trip out East, she and another standout teammate got caught partying. The MSHSL suspended them for two weeks. Their teammates condemned their infraction as selfish. The team lost two games it should have won while Larissa and the other girl sat out.

Two weeks before Christmas, Larissa snapped. Against Burnsville, she took a penalty with Jefferson on the powerplay. She argued the call all the way to the box in language that would make a sailor blush. The referee handed her a ten-minute misconduct. She proceeded to throw what one teammate described as a "hissy fit." The referee tossed her out of the game, which carried an automatic suspension for the next game. Hockey, which had been there for her since she was four years old, seemed to be failing her.

It got worse. Timm broke up with her that weekend. They had dated for seven months. Larissa sank into a depression. She became physically ill. Life looked grim.

The team's troubles had taken their toll on the *esprit de corps*, but Larissa's downfall seemed insurmountable. Even though she might not be able to win games single-handedly, she could personally sabotage the season. With Larissa slumping after the spiritless loss to Hibbing, the team seemed doomed.

Five weeks later, the girls beat Burnsville in the final regular season game to clinch their first Lake Conference title. The victory capped a remarkable turnaround.

No one was more excited than Dave Irvin. He happily accepted congratulations from other parents that night at Billabong after the boys' game. Poised to begin section playoffs, the human resources manager for Toro admitted he couldn't concentrate on his job. "Hockey is all I can think about right now," he bubbled.

Handsome and fit with brown hair and warm eyes, the mustachioed Irvin looked like Tom Selleck on Slimfast. From the bench he shouted instructions to his players and badgered ineffectual officials, but the girls could sense he cared about them. His compassion and competitiveness had engineered the girls' amazing transformation. One woman intimately familiar with the girls' individual problems declared, "He's a miracle worker."

Undone by the Hibbing loss, Dave had sought counsel from his mentor. "I can't stand that we're losing with this much talent," he confided in Sats.

Sats passed along some advice John Bianchi had given him, "You can't care more about it than the kids."

"Too late for that," Dave said.

Dave told his girls the way they had been losing wasn't acceptable. He needed maximum effort from everyone. Each girl must commit to the team. He changed the forecheck. He banned the boombox and headphones from the dressing room before the pregame skate. "For two hours, it's a hockey game, not a rock concert," he told them. "Let's focus on hockey."

The girls complained. Dave wasn't sure what to expect. After the recruiting trip fiasco a month earlier, they had staged a "Come to Jesus" meeting when the captains had exhorted the girls to put the team first. That had not stopped the slide.

This time, the test came in the Kaposia Classic consolation championship against Edina, who had beaten the Jaguars in the season opener 6–3. On New Year's Day, the Jaguars resolved to play as a team. They trounced Edina 4–1 and aced the test.

More importantly, Larissa bought into the team concept. In the game where she got ejected, Larissa had been surprised to see her teammates come from behind to win in overtime—without her. That victory summoned her to become a team player.

She talked to Dave about trying her hand in goal, where the team was vulnerable. Even though she had never played goalie, she trusted her athleticism and instincts would carry her. With the Jaguars' regular goaltender slumping over the holidays, Larissa told Dave, "Coach, I'll do whatever you want because I want to win a state championship in the worst way."

Her first practice—using equipment she borrowed from her older brother Landon, who had played goalie for White Bear Lake—Larissa looked like she had grown up in goalie pads, but Dave was reluctant to sacrifice his second-leading scorer to the nets. He told Larissa, "If we do this, you have to commit to this. You have to trust us."

"I'll do whatever it takes," she said.

Dave began the experiment slowly, taking Larissa off the power-play to see if the team could produce without her. Larissa accepted that decision, and he saw that her transformation to a team player was for real. "My heart went out to her," Dave said. "This kid was going to help us win a state tournament."

He finally started Larissa in goal mid-January, and Larissa's selfless gesture proved a flashpoint for the team. "She made us each want to give something to the team because she was giving something to the team," said Sarah, who spent hours on her own time firing pucks against a BIG wall.

The Jaguars didn't lose again after the Hibbing game and rode an 11–0–1 streak into the section playoffs. The team had come together.

On Valentine's Day, girls walked the Jefferson hallways wearing soft red sweaters and carrying pink carnations their sweethearts had sent them. Candy hearts inscribed "hubba, hubba" and "lover boy" littered the carpet. Sats snuck out during his prep period to buy flowers for his wife.

Kendra Ottum, who had matured into an attractive young woman and solid defender, spotted Tommy seated at a table in the cafeteria during fourth period. She wore a blue bandana over her blonde hair, a tight Jaguars T-shirt, and royal blue sweats hiked up over her muscular calves. "You going tonight?"

The girls played Buffalo in the Section 5 semifinals. Despite their success, the female hockey players still lagged behind the cheerleaders and danceline in the school's social class system.

"No, it's Valentine's Day," Tommy said. His girlfriend was going to fix him dinner.

"That's what everyone is saying," Kendra said. "My date tonight is with the Buffalo girls."

————

Jefferson beat the Buffalo girls to advance to the section finals against the Wayzata Trojans, coached by Mr. Hockey '88, Larry Olimb, and Amber Hegland. (Amber became the first girl ever to skate in the boys' state tournament, playing for Farmington in the '94 Tier II edition.) Wayzata had beaten the Jaguars—minus Larissa—1–0 in their only other meeting early in the season.

Following warmups, adrenaline charged the atmosphere in the Jaguars dressing room at the Richfield Arena. The girls' chatter bounced off the red-and-white cinder block walls. The team manager passed out sticks of gum. A black boombox, which had made a comeback, blasted Def Leppard's "Pour Some Sugar On Me."

Sarah turned down the music for Dave's pregame speech. Some of the girls wrung their hands. Some squirmed in their breezers. Some pulled back their hair, waxed the tape on their sticks, or chugged Powerade. They punctuated his remarks with amens and alleluias.

"Everybody's a team right now," Dave began in his firm voice.

"Uh-huh."

"I know you've all got butterflies right now; you would be weird if you didn't," he said. "But we expected to be here."

"That's right."

"You're the best team in the state—"

"Uh-huh!"

"Tonight's the time to show it."

"That's right!"

"We want to kick some ass tonight."

"Yeah!"

Sarah read a letter to her teammates: "I don't get another year to make our dreams come true....Let's show them tonight who we are....God has blessed us, turned our season around and made us victorious."

They huddled together in the center of the room. "Break their hearts, you guys," Kendra said.

Then, à la the Mighty Ducks, they quacked in unison: "Quack, quack, quack—Go Jaguars!"

A voice screamed, "Jefferson, what time is it?"

Together, "Time to get a goal!"

"What time?"

"Time to represent!"

They hugged tight.

A sign taped by the door read: "Let's do it for J. R....Remember, he's watching." J.R. Riekens, the team's bus driver, had died of lung cancer two months earlier. Last year, he had dressed in a tuxedo to drive the girls to the state tournament. Following his funeral, the team had shown up for practice at BIG teary-eyed.

Each girl tapped the sign with her glove on her way out.

The Jefferson pep band welcomed them onto the ice. The cheer-leaders shivered their mylar pompoms. Squirt-aged boys in Jefferson jackets shook homemade signs. The school librarian, in a Jefferson jersey and stuffed jaguar head, waved her oversized PRIDE paw.

The boys' varsity sat together in their letter jackets. Tommy had organized the outing as a team-building activity. It wasn't for love of the girls.

Early on Larissa had some trouble controlling a rebound, and the guys joked they should yell, "You'll never be as good as Timm"—but they didn't. The Jaguars' leading scorer Sharon Cole put Jefferson up 1–0 three minutes into the game. The guys teased Jeremy that Sharon had played Squirt A in the Kennedy Booster program when he was on the Squirt B team. Jefferson dominated the first period and Joccie Cookson added two goals, but the guys agreed that their Peewee A team could've beaten the girls' varsity.

In the second period, Kendra slid a pretty pass from the top of the circle to Marnie Prall in the slot on the far side. Marnie one-timed the pass into the net to stretch the Jefferson lead to 4–0 but fell down when her linemates hugged her. The guys laughed.

By the time a group of small girls in Jaguar jerseys standing beside the Jefferson bench started the final countdown: 10, 9, 8…most of the varsity boys had split to watch porn videos at Duncs's house.

Following the awards ceremony and post-game photo, the girls gathered back in the dressing room. Dave congratulated them. "I'm extremely proud of you guys and where you've come from since the start of the year. If you don't win another game, I will think back on this year and be proud of you. But we have some unfinished business. We're not leaving St. Paul without a trophy."

They tugged off their jerseys and unlaced their skates. One girl said, "Know what this means, girls?"

What? Work hard this week, maintain focus? Or, did the victory mean they had the chance to win the championship that previous teams had missed? Or, that they might earn the elusive respect?

No. The girl shouted a phrase never before uttered in the presence of the dressing room urinals: "Time to go shopping."

She meant for the tournament banquet. The Jaguar girls fashioned themselves the hottest team in the state. They planned to make a statement to that effect at the banquet in prom-caliber dresses. They would go Barbie rather than butch. Look out, Bloomingdale's.

The MSHSL scheduled the girls' hockey tournament at the State Fairgrounds Coliseum, a glorified horse barn that seated 5,600, while the Xcel Energy Center hosted the state high school girls' dance competition. Bottom line: when it came to girls, dancelines outdrew pucksters.

The Jaguars ate their first pregame meal at Mancini's, a St. Paul state tournament landmark, but the steak didn't sit well with Sarah.

She vomited during the first intermission, then went out and scored the game's first goal. Joccie added a pair of goals, and Larissa recorded a shutout. Over at BIG, where the boys played their first section play-off game, Art Seplak announced, "Final score from the State Fairgrounds Coliseum, Jefferson 5, Forest Lake 0. The Jefferson girls advance to the semifinals Friday night." The fans clapped politely.

Sats forbade the boys from attending the girls' 9:15 P.M. semifinal game because he wanted them to be well-rested for their section semifinal game Saturday. The girls felt slighted. Sarah called Sats at school Friday and chewed him out. He relented partway, granting permission to attend the first two periods. Duncs, Nick, Timm, and Brett Shelanski watched Jefferson defeat Chaska 4–1.

The February 24 state final pitted the Jaguars against the top-ranked Blaine Bengals. No team had been able to beat the 25–0–1 Bengals, including the Jaguars, who were on the short end of a 4–3 contest in November. Blaine's All-State wing Tiffany Hagge had scored a hat trick, but the Jaguars knew the season's final game would be distilled to a showdown between the two goaltenders, Larissa and Jody Horak.

Coming into the tournament, Jefferson had allowed more goals (34) than any other team but one in the tournament's five-year history, an average of 4.25 per game. Larissa had helped rewrite that history, giving up only one goal in the first two games. The Jaguars had not lost in the ten games she had patrolled the pipes. She had posted a 1.17 goals against average and recorded three shutouts.

Still, those were modest numbers compared to Jody Horak's résumé: undefeated in 28 games, 0.65 GAA, 16 shutouts. If it's true you're only as good as your last game, Jody was perfect—in the semis, South St. Paul had outshot Blaine 26-13, but Jody had blanked them. The state's top netminder had a lock on the Senior Goalie of the Year award regardless of Saturday night's outcome.

The Jaguars had seen the papers, Jody's picture splashed all over them. The *Star Tribune, Pioneer Press, Let's Play Hockey, Minnesota Prep Sports*—Jody had graced more covers than Gisele. Jefferson knew one player stood between them and the state championship: Jody Horak.

Before the pregame skate, the referees stopped into the Coliseum dressing room to encourage a clean game and review some logistics of the Channel 9 statewide television broadcast.

"How do you fit a commercial into ten seconds?" Gianna Gambucci asked.

The referees smiled. "They're quick."

Dave diagramed on the white board a pass around the net wide to the strong point—or the weak point if open—to catch Horak off balance. He told the girls to shoot, that their best chance to beat Horak was on a rebound.

Sarah read a letter: "Each of you has touched my life. I love you all and wish you the best of luck." The girls clapped.

A father panned the dressing room with his camcorder for the season highlight video.

One of the managers brought in a teddy bear that J.R.'s wife had given to the team. The girls passed it around. They wore J.R.'s initials on their chests.

"Listen up." Dave stood before the nineteen girls seated in the green folding chairs after their warmup. "The St. Paul paper is all about Jody Horak and Blaine. I don't think they even know where Jefferson is. What a nice story we'd give them to send Blaine home with a second place trophy."

Larissa peered through the cage of her white mask emblazoned with a blue flame. She knew to make that story come true she would have to outduel the competition. The University of Minnesota had already signed Horak to a scholarship. Larissa's future—most likely as a defender—remained unknown. She was about to start only the eleventh game of her career in net. Against perhaps the best team in the nation.

The girls huddled in the center of the room.

"Break their hearts, ladies," Kendra shouted. "Break their hearts."

They bumped chests. They banged their sticks on the metal air ducts. They jumped up and down. They screamed and whooped. Underneath the Coliseum bleachers, the goosebumps prickled their skin.

————

Larissa wanted that first shot to prove herself, but she had to wait over three minutes for it. When the Bengals snapped a clean shot from the circle, she steered it away with her blocker. That was it. She was engaged. She was hot.

A minute later, Tiffany Hagge raced in along the right side, slipped the puck between the defender's skates, and fluttered a wrist shot to the far side. Larissa couldn't raise her blocker in time. The Bengals jumped first onto the scoreboard.

The Jaguars fought back, but couldn't beat Horak.

Down 0–1 after the first period, Dave reminded the girls that Blaine had beaten South St. Paul in the semis by scoring only one goal. They determined they would not let that happen to them.

The Jaguars finally discovered Horak's humanness on a powerplay opportunity early in the second. Sharon Cole and sophomore wing Allison Turgeon closed in on a two-on-one. Horak blocked Sharon's shot, but the rebound bounced wide to Allison. She flipped the puck over Jody, who lunged and got a piece of it, but not enough. At 3:13, Jefferson tied the game one-all.

The Jaguars hugged Allison, then skated to the bench to slap their teammates' gloves and down the ice to tap Larissa's glove. Horak sat up and smacked her stick on the ice.

Three-and-a-half minutes later, Joccie broke in on the left side as part of a two-on-one. The defender cut off the pass to Sarah, so Joccie angled toward the net. Horak shoved out her stick for the pokecheck, opening her pads. Joccie stuffed a backhand between her skates. Jefferson 2, Blaine 1. Horak slumped against the crossbar; Sarah hugged Joccie.

The Jaguars nursed their lead into the third period. Across the rink from where Duncs, Nick, and Timm watched, a "Let's Go, Blaine" chant rippled through the Bengal side. The Jaguar cheerleaders responded, "Let's go, Jaguars." Fans on both sides rose to their feet to exchange cheers while the action on the ice swung back and forth.

The final half of the third period, the Bengals poured on the pressure in the Jaguars' end. With three minutes left, Larissa squared off on a shot in close, stopped it with her chest, and smothered the rebound. The Bengals pulled their best player in favor of an extra attacker, but Larissa stoned them. On twenty shots, they managed to sneak only one past her.

Larissa, the upstart challenger, had dethroned the champ and set a tournament record by allowing a mere two goals in three games. The next day, Jody Horak would be lauded *Let's Play Hockey*'s Senior Goalie of the Year. She had already been named the *StarTribune*'s co-Metro Player of the Year (along with Renee Curtin, Ms. Hockey), but Larissa would be named the Metro Player of the Week in the season's final week, the one that mattered the most.

The Jefferson faithful were on their feet to count down the game's last seconds. Dave realized that his team was about to win its first state championship. Joy and pride surged through him.

When the final buzzer sounded, the Jaguars' bench emptied. Larissa turned the net upside down and scrabbled under it, but her teammates wouldn't be denied the traditional hog pile celebration. They climbed inside—led by Joccie—and piled on top of her like teenagers stuffing themselves into a phone booth.

Young girls wearing Jefferson jerseys watched in wonder. It didn't matter to them that the Coliseum was two-thirds empty or that only a fraction of those who watched the boys' Tournament tuned in to Channel 9 that night. What they witnessed on the ice was enough to inspire their own dreams for themselves. They wanted to follow in Sarah's and Larissa's skates to their own state tournament.

By the time Dave arrived in his street shoes, Larissa was on her feet, her mask off. He wrapped her in a bear hug. For a moment, coach and player stood locked in a timeless embrace, wordless. Larissa thanked Dave for the chance to play goalie. "This makes it all worth it, doesn't it?" he said into her ear above the din of the crowd's cheers. "Ever think it would feel this good?"

———

Inside the dressing room after accepting the first place trophy, Sarah blasted the boombox. The girls hugged and shouted. Tears streaked their faces. Someone said, "You guys, I don't want to go home."

When the players and Dave finally emerged onto the concourse, a throng of family and friends waited for them with flowers and applause. Dave's brother held up a copy of *Minnesota Prep Sports* with a cover shot of Jody Horak and the headline, "Can Anyone Penetrate Blaine's Defense?" He shouted happily, "There's the answer to that question."

Gianna walked down the ramp into her father's arms. Gary Gambucci had starred at Hibbing High and later played in the NHL and WHA, but he'd never had the chance to skate in the state tournament. The four years he played varsity, his team lost the section playoff to the International Falls '60s dynasty. Gary had waited thirty-seven years to experience the thrill of winning a high school hockey championship. When he saw his daughter with the gold medal around her neck, he broke down and hugged her close. The moment was worth the wait.

CHAPTER TWENTY

BOULEVARD OF
BROKEN DREAMS

Playoff time! And so began the season of broken hearts. The section playoffs whittled away the field of seventy-three AA teams to eight section winners who qualified for the state tournament. With each game along the way, one team's dream died. Eventually, every team's hopes would end with a loss. Every team save one. And every team wanted to be that last one standing. State champions.

The state tournament offered quarterfinal and semifinal losers a consolation round and third place game—cheap condolences, but another game nonetheless. The section playoffs meant sudden death. Lose there, and it was all over for the seniors. Twelve years of early

294 • Blades of Glory

morning practices, late night games, long seasons, summer camps, lifting weights, studying film—finished. History. Before the sound of the final buzzer faded, hockey suddenly became a thing of the past. Even if they played another game at the next level—which most wouldn't—they would never play again with their friends on their home ice in front of their families. That final loss would become the memory that forever framed their high school experience.

On the other hand, if you could survive your section, you lived your dream. To close out senior year at the Tournament—that was the ultimate experience. Nothing compared.

The sections decided which road the seniors traveled.

————

The route from 4001 West 102nd Street, Jefferson High School, to 175 Kellogg Boulevard, the Xcel Energy Center, stretched twenty miles, a thirty-five minute trip in good weather. But the Jaguars couldn't simply hop a bus to St. Paul. First they had to win three section games.

In the various scenarios Tommy doodled on his notebook, the most likely came up Jefferson versus Holy Angels in the Section 5AA final at Mariucci Arena. The brackets showed the Jaguars winning the rubber match to repeat last year's victory and further avenge the loss their sophomore year. Riding their nine-game winning streak into the playoffs, Tommy intended to litter the road to the Xcel with broken dreams.

————

At practice Monday, Sats reported the results of the Section 5AA seeding meeting. "Everyone voted you No. 1 yesterday. You deserve that, but it just puts a bigger target on your chest."

He worked them hard for Thursday night's game. When they gathered for a water break, the players' shoulders heaved. Afterward, in the subdued dressing room, Sats chided them, "Tough practice, eh?"

Tommy smiled, unfazed. "I don't feel pain, Sats."

————

During a scrimmage in practice that week, Bernie controlled the puck high in the slot. He passed back to Eric Lindquist on the point, but the puck eluded the junior defenseman and sailed out of the zone.

"Put it in the corner, not out to the point," Sats yelled.

"Lindquist should've been there," Bernie yelled back.

"Christsakes, that gives them a breakaway. Put it in the corner."

———

The word of the day: poontang. "Know what it means?" Nick asked a friend as they climbed the stairs from phys ed class to the cafeteria for lunch.

"Sure, pussy."

"Wrong." Nick grinned. "A woman regarded as a means of sexual gratification."

He and Duncs passed the time in English class looking up words in the dictionary. These days life began at 2:20, when school ended and they headed back down those stairs to dress for practice.

Nick's confidence was at an all-time high. He had taken seven shots against Burnsville; all seven had been on target, one had scored. After playing defense last year, he felt he was hitting his stride at forward, learning to be creative with the puck and picking his shots. He had improved his forecheck to the point that it was perhaps his greatest strength. He had become an all-around player. He was pumped for the playoffs. These last six games were why he had played the first twenty-five.

———

Timm woke Thursday morning underneath the Led Zeppelin banner in his room at the top of the stairs. On the wall to his left, the NHL's top goalies—Osgood, Roy, Hasek, CUJO, and Kolzig—bid good morning. A bookshelf under the window supported various hardware and photos from his Colorado state champion teams in Bantams and Midgets. They stood tall next to a photo of his dad.

That night Timm would start the first playoff game against Minneapolis South. It was just like last year, when he opened the playoffs with a shutout over Kennedy.

He pulled on his clothes while it was still dark outside. On top of his dresser, a cigar waited. He wanted a special occasion to smoke it. Maybe late Saturday night, March 10, he would torch that stogie.

———

That morning, Thursday, February 22, Kelly Gilbert got up before the boys, unfolded the *Star Tribune*, and flipped through the sports section. "Mr. Hockey candidates named." He found both Tommy and Duncs on the list of ten seniors. Tommy had the chance to join Nick Checco and Mike Crowley, Mr. Hockeys '93 and '94 respectively, in Jefferson immortality. If the Jags went the whole way, Tommy could claim the prize with a strong performance.

When Tommy woke up, his dad told him the news. Tommy wanted to see for himself. He was happy to read his name. But he wasn't surprised. Considering the way he had played that season, he expected the nomination.

At school, his classmates once again called him "Mr. Hockey."

———

The phone woke Deb Irvin. It was Steve, her ex. "Have you seen the newspaper?"

No, she hadn't.

He told her. They shared a moment of mutual pride. Timm had already picked up their son for school.

The phone rang again. "Mom," Duncs began, his voice bursting.

"I know," she said.

Tommy had told him. "I can't imagine it," Duncs said. "This is what we all dream about."

"Well, go rip it up tonight," Deb said. "You'll have to put on a show."

———

Back in 1955, Minneapolis South had battled Thief River Falls in a state tournament epic that took eleven sudden death overtimes to decide. Almost fifty years later, the urban hockey landscape had changed. The once rich city tradition had become impoverished to the point where the Minneapolis school board put hockey on the chopping block in 2002, sparing the sport only at the last minute. Most of the players on the '01 Tigers varsity would not have survived tryouts for Jefferson's j.v.

The mood in the Jaguars' locker room at school was understandably relaxed. Stark rubbed a puck across his freshly taped blade. Jimmy reclined on top of the lockers, headphones plugging his ears. Sats distributed gum; Tommy selected green. Nick dropped two Ripped Fuel tablets onto the wool cap atop his locker.

Timm sat on the bench directly in front of the green board. He stared at the small brown tiles on the floor and spun his Columbia blue wool cap on his right hand while Sats gave his pregame talk: "You've been playing under pressure and playing well. That's because you're a good hockey team."

The Jaguars boarded the team bus for the seniors' final pregame ride to BIG. The air was cold, the stars sharp in the clear sky. Since the section semifinal would be played at a neutral site, tonight would be the seniors' last game of several hundred played together on their home ice.

In dressing room D, Duncs pulled on his good-luck Polo crew socks. He had worn the same pair under his skates all season. He hadn't washed them, just shoved them back into his bag after each practice and game. The socks started the season new and white; now they were ragged and brown. Duncs was ready to rip it up.

Timm kissed his equipment.

After heads down, Sats said, "This is the start of our second season. I know some of you have been waiting for this, to get back to the play-offs since we lost those two games last March. Here's your chance."

———

Timm crouched, head upright, body taut. The linesman standing at the center faceoff dot raised his arm toward the South goalie, toward Timm. Timm nodded. The linesman dropped the puck. Playoff time!

Jefferson's speed made the Tigers look like they skated on peanut butter. Most of South's rushes fizzled in the neutral zone. Whenever one of the Tigers did stick a Jaguar, the South fans released a mighty roar. That wasn't too often. The Jaguars outshot the Tigers 21–7 in the first period, but Jefferson fans spent the first fifteen minutes slapping their foreheads over missed chances.

Finally, at 11:31, Bernie slipped wide past the South D and carried the puck deep into the Tiger zone, then slid a perfect pass to Dillon. Jefferson 1, South 0.

On their first shift, Bernie had found Tommy floating behind the Tiger defense. He launched a bomb from his corner to the South blue line. Tommy caught the pass wide open. The crowd squealed in delight. Nothing but open ice between him and the goalie. Tommy turned—and slipped on his nerves.

Tommy wasn't playing like Mr. Hockey, but Duncs was putting on a show. In the first minute of the second period, Jimmy carried the puck into the Tiger zone with Duncs. The defense pulled Duncs down from behind, but, falling, he managed to get the shaft of his Sher-Wood on Jimmy's pass and deflect it past the goalie. Crisp passes made the play; Duncs's determination finished it.

Bernie had shown up for the playoffs. He figured in four of the Jaguars' five goals. In the third period, he set up Tommy for a short-handed goal and gave Nick a perfect feed for another tally two minutes later. Bernie even went down to block a shot. Whenever the poet graced the ice, the game tilted in Jefferson's favor. He smiled under his wire facemask.

Timm turned away all sixteen of the Tigers' shots for his second shutout of the season, a 5–0 win that advanced them to the next round.

After heads down, Nick called out, "That's one, boys. Five to go!"

Instead of jubilant shouts and back slaps, they undressed somberly. The win had been expected, routine. Something bigger started to sink in. The seniors had just played their last game in the friendly confines.

Bernie circled the dressing room, stepping over the bags and sticks, to hug each one of the seniors he had played with since Mites. Duncs's eyes misted. He stood up to shake Tommy's and Nick's hands. B.J. winced. "It just hit me now. I started playing games here when I was five."

Slowly, they started to leave. Tommy shook Duncs's hand again on the way out.

While the sophomores cleaned the dressing room for the last time, Shacks straddled his equipment bag. "I don't want to leave this place."

Steve Duncan waited for Duncs out in the lobby like he usually did, but it seemed to be taking his son longer than most nights. Wondering where he was, Steve stepped inside to look for him. Most nights, the players walked the length of the rink through the empty bleachers, sidestepping the guys sweeping up the spilled popcorn and crushed Styrofoam cups. That night, Steve spotted Duncs walking across the ice, his bag slung over his shoulder. His cap was turned backwards on his head, his white jersey hung loosely on his frame. Steve watched his son pause at center ice, kneel, and tap the blue faceoff dot with his fist.

He thought of all the faceoffs he had watched his son take at that spot over the past thirteen years. There had been hundreds of games, countless memories. This image would be the one that lingered, burned into his memory. As happened so often when he watched his son on the ice, Steve felt the emotions swell inside him. That moment was a gift. Duncs had given him something to remember all right.

Steve couldn't shape his emotions into words when Duncs crossed the ice, so the next day, he wrote a letter:

To my son, the hockey player,

I couldn't let this time in our lives go by without letting you know how deeply touched I was last night. I hope someday you have the privilege of capturing a moment with your son as I did last night.... You have brought something to the games you have played in that can't be measured in statistics or headlines—you have brought your heart to the game. As your fingers touched center ice last night, I saw how wonderful that is. Thank you for all the memories you have given me, but especially for that moment last night.

Love, Dad.

Eastview knocked off Burnsville. That meant Jefferson faced the Lightning Saturday afternoon in the Section 5AA semifinal. Unlike their games against Burnsville, the Jaguars had beaten the Lightning handily in their two meetings that season, outscoring Eastview 11–4. In their last game, three weeks ago, the Jaguars had powered five goals on twenty-one shots past Orlando Alamano and chased the Fresno kid from the nets after two periods. The Jags could beat the Lightning with one hand tied behind their backs. Back at school after the South game, Sats announced their next opponent. The boys cheered.

Timm, who noted that they had begun the playoffs with a 5–0 win this year just like last year, saw the matchup as an especially good thing. In the semifinal last year, they had romped over Eastview 8–1 for Sats's 500th career win at Jefferson. Sats's nemesis at Eastview, Mike Gibbons, the guy he had nearly punched over the recruiting accusation, had taken the loss badly. Gibbons's Lightning had never beaten Sats's Jaguars. He threw a temper tantrum on the bench, flailing his sport coat to the ground and stomping on it. Coach Gibbons, a square-jawed bulldog, was determined to make a name for his Lightning. He told his team this game against Jefferson was the championship.

Sats didn't want his guys groggy for the 12:30 game from sleeping too late. He imposed an 11 P.M. curfew Friday night and summoned them to Perkins for a team breakfast at 8:30 A.M. After chowing down heartily, Nick got his skates sharpened and hung out briefly at Duncs's house. They got to school by 10:45. Duncs felt rested, ready to play. He couldn't wait for the first shift. He tipped the bottle of Tums he kept in his locker and gobbled four tablets.

Tommy was one of the first ready to head over to Braemar Arena. Dressed in his breezers, socks without shin pads, a blue Jefferson pullover windbreaker, and Michigan cap, he dropped his bag by the door and pulled up a chair in front of the green board to read Sats's scouting report. "1) NO TEAM WORKS HARDER." He had underlined it twice. Still, Tommy was relieved to be playing Eastview. Burnsville had worried him. They were headed toward the scenario he had doodled, that final against Holy Angels. Never mind the nightmares. He read Sats's final point: "9) We must play hard—have fun."

The rest of the guys gathered around. Bernie tipped back in a chair to the right of the board. Timm spun his wool cap on his hand. Duncs and Nick clambered atop the lockers in the back. Nick drained his blue Powerade. Sats strolled out of his office. His face was serious as always before a game, but there was no sense of urgency about him. He reviewed the scouting report, then, hands in his pockets, he looked from Bernie to Timm to Tommy to Nick to Duncs and said, "You guys have played a tough schedule, handled some tough teams. This is when the fun starts. Let's go over there and have fun."

They took a short bus ride through freezing rain. Nick liked playing at Braemar. The past two years, Jefferson had won all of the games it had played there: two Holiday Classics and last year's section semifinal, seven total. His last game there, against Edina, he had scored the big goal that had set up Duncs's game-winner. Nick expected to win this one big, something like 7–1 or 6–2.

Looking past the rain streaking the window, Nick thought ahead to the team's next bus ride....The Jaguars would go on to play the section final at Mariucci Arena, like last year, when the caravan of honking fans had followed the team bus to the University of Minnesota campus. Only this time, instead of warming the bench, he would share the spotlight with Duncs and Tommy and Bernie. Then it would be on to St. Paul, where they would stay at the Holiday Inn across the street from the Xcel and their fans would party for three days....

Sats stopped at the concessions stand for a cup of coffee. The boys headed down to their dressing room. Duncs pulled on his brown socks. Bernie tied his skates. Tommy lashed his shin pads with a pair of black laces.

Nick taped his stick carefully, then studied his work. "How well I shoot depends on how much confidence I have when I look down at my stick and see how well I taped it," he said once.

Timm placed his forehead against the forehead of his mask, clasped his hands behind his neck, closed his eyes, and rolled his personal highlight reel.

Jimmy doled out Ripped Fuel.

They took their warmup and returned to the dressing room. "Heads down," Sats said.

Bernie turned his head with his hands to crack his neck.

Tommy prayed, *Give me strength, God.*

After saying a prayer himself, Sats broke the silence. "Yesterday at practice I was looking at the wall—saw the five pennants up there. You guys go out and continue to work your asses off, and you can put another one up there!"

Timm stood at the door, and each guy punched his blocker glove on the way out. The crowd nearly filled Braemar. Some Jefferson fans had skipped the game in favor of the girls' championship game that night, figuring they would watch the boys' section final at Mariucci. Several hundred crammed the Eastview side. Three times that many stuffed the Jefferson side.

The Jefferson band in its shapeless blue windbreakers struck up a tune.

The white Jaguar jerseys huddled around Jeremy in the net. "Let's come out fired up," Tommy shouted over the crowd. "Let's score some goals, get a lead we can stay with."

Bernie's line—with Tommy and Dillon on the wings—started. Off the opening draw, Eastview raced into Jefferson's end. Jeremy blocked the shot, but couldn't cover the rebound. Eastview's forwards swiped at it once, twice. Andrew Panchenko found the net. Goal! Thirty-one seconds had elapsed.

Standing in the row of parents behind the bleacher seats, Kelly Gilbert thought, *uh-oh.*

"That's fine, boys," Nick said on the bench. "We've just got to go out and get that one back."

Eastview pressed hard in Jefferson's end and iced the puck repeatedly from its own end to slow the pace. The top line seemed to be out the entire first period. Jefferson tried to complete long passes, but they hit skates or hopped sticks. Even though the Jags managed ten shots on net, Alamano turned them away. The Lightning skaters dived to block a handful more.

Bernie and Tommy started complaining on the bench. After fifteen minutes, Eastview led 1–0.

In the dressing room, Timm said, "We've got to stop bitching at each other."

Duncs nodded. "That'll kill us."

"We're not ending our season here, boys," Tommy said.

"Don't worry about that," Duncs said. "Just keep working hard." He swilled some water and spit it onto the floor. "We need some big hits here to get us going."

They could hear the Jefferson band playing in the stands. Sats paced between the orange peels with his hands in his pockets. "You're a talented team. That's why you're here. They want this game. Make short passes."

He peed at the urinal on the back wall and flushed, as though to put the period behind him.

First shift, Tommy lost a battle in the corner. Next shift, he won a battle in the corner, passed the puck out front, but Bernie couldn't get it out of his skates to shoot.

The boys' parents and friends and neighbors and classmates felt their pulses quicken, their palms moisten, their guts tighten. The fathers stood with their arms folded. The mothers crossed their fingers and mouthed silent prayers. The cheerleaders down front kept up a nearly constant routine of cheers.

For one stretch of almost two minutes without a whistle, Jefferson drove the crowd crazy with a succession of hits and chances. When the clock finally stopped, the Jefferson side thundered its approval. The Jaguars had taken control.

With four minutes left and the Senior Line in place for a faceoff, the cheerleaders clapped out, "J-A-G-U-A-R-S!" Steve Duncan knew his son had it in him to will Jefferson back into this game. Now would be as good a time as any to do it.

Seconds later, the puck came up the boards, deflected by a skate. Duncs plucked it onto his stick and rushed down the right side. He had a defenseman to beat. Alamano played the angle cleanly. Duncs fired for the only daylight he could see, a small patch between Alamano's pads. But Alamano closed down the five-hole. The puck bounced off his pad high into the air. Following his shot to the net, Duncs swung, connected, and batted the puck past Alamano to tie the game.

He peeled away from the net, dropped to one knee, and pumped his fist. Trailing the play, Nick saw the referee on the opposite side and just beyond the goal line—in position to see the play unobstructed—immediately wave off the goal. Nick skated over to Duncs and shook his head.

The ref ruled Duncs had played the puck over his shoulder, but the fans thought it had been below the crossbar. One shouted, "Are you fucking blind, ref?"

Steve Duncan grimaced.

Sats didn't protest.

Teachers, neighbors, friends, and classmates would tell Duncs they believed the goal was good. Duncs thought it was legal but skated to the bench and told his teammates not to worry about it. They would get another one soon.

A minute later, Duncs got tripped and drew a penalty. The Jefferson crowd practically tore the roof off Braemar with its excitement at the opportunity to tie the game. Bernie, Tommy, and Duncs worked the puck along the perimeter, but the Lightning killed aggressively and hurried the puckholder. Finally, with just ten seconds left in the powerplay, Nick got off a shot from high in the slot, but an Eastview defender dropped to block it.

With eleven seconds left in the period, Duncs took a faceoff in the Eastview end, but even with the powerplay unit out, nothing came of it. At the buzzer, he butt-ended the boards in frustration.

It occurred to Duncs and the other seniors in the dressing room that they might be about to play their last period of high school hockey. They peeled their oranges pensively.

"Remember the Edina game?" Jeremy said. "We were down, and we won that one."

"Remember how much fun that was and how hard we worked?" Nick chimed in.

"This is how it goes sometimes," Duncs said. "You've got to work hard. Nobody's tired now."

Sats came in. "Guy lives in a house with two Dobermans. Tough? Yeah, they are. He exercises them in the back yard. Every day he feeds the dogs. They love it.

"One day, he sees a new neighbor with an ugly bulldog. The dog gets off its leash, sniffs at the picket fence, finds a hole, and sticks his nose through toward the food. The Dobermans go over and maul the shit out of the bulldog. He runs away.

"Happens again the next day. This time, the bulldog gets up to his neck under the hole before the Dobermans come over and maul the shit out of him."

The story gripped the boys. They watched Sats pacing and gesturing. Tommy retied his skates.

"Next day, same thing. Bulldog gets halfway through, but then the Dobermans come over and maul the shit out of him.

"Then the guy leaves on a business trip. He tells his wife, 'Be sure to exercise the dogs.' When he comes back, his wife picks him up at the airport. He asks her, 'Did you exercise the dogs?'

"'No,' his wife says. 'Funny thing happened. The dogs won't go outside anymore. There's a bulldog out there eating their food. They mauled him, but he wouldn't leave. Finally, they got sick of beating up on him, and the next day, they left him alone.'"

Sats paused in the midst of the orange peels. The room was still.

"What's the moral? We keep kicking ass. We never quit. The guys in those uniforms never quit. You've gotta dive for pucks. You've gotta block shots. You've gotta take hits. Whatever it takes. You've gotta be like bulldogs. We'll make those Dobermans back off and not want to play!

"Now, think about that a bit." He walked out.

After a moment, Nick said, "Seniors, how bad do we want this not to be our last period?"

Tommy stared at the floor.

Duncs rubbed his hands together, glanced at his teammates. "We gotta relax. Nobody's nervous."

The door opened, and the sound of the Jefferson band rushed in. Sats walked to the center of the room. The buzzer summoned them. They reached for their gloves and helmets and sticks. "Wait a minute," Sats said. "You have a decision to make. Do you want to be the bulldog who keeps chipping away? Or do you want to be the Doberman who backs off because he knows he's been defeated?"

"Bulldogs!"

"Do you want to be bulldogs?"

"YEAH!"

They punched Timm's glove and skated out to the chorus of drums, pompoms, and applause.

Eastview made them wait. The prizefighter seeking a psychological advantage, the Lightning stalled in its dressing room. The Jaguars' starting five and Jeremy waited in the ring. Bernie circled at center ice.

Kelly Gilbert had a bad feeling in his gut. *Things aren't going right. Was Duncs's no goal an omen?*

The Lightning finally emerged, roiled as a rodeo bull about to bust out of the gate, but Coach Gibbons held his hand to the chest of the player first in line. Their skates clattered in place.

"Okay." Gibbons pulled back his hand. "Go ahead."

"Hit it running!" The message passed down the line. "Hit it running!"

They ran four or five strides to the gate and leapt onto the ice.

When the puck dropped, Eastview stormed the Jefferson net and banged a rebound past Jeremy. It took only twenty-five seconds. Panchenko again. Nearly a replay of the first period start. Only faster. Swifter. More cutting.

Some guys on the Jefferson bench dropped their heads. Duncs could see in their eyes they were scared; he felt as intense as he ever felt, ready to go all out, do whatever it took to score. Whatever it took to keep the season from ending at Braemar. He felt like he could play five overtimes.

Gibbons sent out his next line to join the celebration. Each arriving player leapt into the growing huddle of black jerseys behind Jeremy, who skated off to his right, a short turn, and returned to stand in front of net, gloves to his pads.

Sats replaced Bernie's line with Duncs's. Duncs, Nick, and Jimmy skated back to offer Jeremy some encouragement.

Merrelyn clutched her hands to her mouth. Her eyes looked grim.

Timm had a sinking feeling going into the third. Now this. It was hard to sit by, powerless, not able to play. This was how the season ended last year. He spent the first game of the Tournament on the bench where he had to watch helplessly while they lost. Timm was pissed. He didn't want to watch his senior season—and high school hockey career—expire from the bench.

With almost twelve minutes still to play, Jefferson got a break: penalty, Eastview. But the Lightning four threw their bodies in front of shots, cleared the zone, and stopped Bernie at mid-ice. Tommy lost his skates—and the puck—in the corner of his end. Kelly Gilbert wondered, *When are they going to explode and get it done?*

With twenty seconds left in the powerplay, Jimmy broke free with the puck. The crowd rose. *Go, Jimmy!!!* He faked, Alamano hit his pads. Jimmy shot high, short side. Alamano's glove flicked up and snatched the puck out of the air.

Diane Saterdalen bit her upper lip. Her husband watched the action with one foot on the bench, his raised knee supporting his elbow, hand cupping his chin. He straightened at each whistle and shoved his hands in his pockets. She read frustration in his shoulders. She didn't want it to end this way for him. He could still pull it out. His teams had mounted more amazing comebacks. In the '81 Tournament quarterfinals, Grand Rapids went up 3–1 in the third, but Jefferson scored on a powerplay, then Steve Bianchi tied it with his historic goal. In the section quarterfinals that same year, '81, they had peppered the Blake goalie with shots but still trailed 2–3 going into the final minute. Jefferson's Dan Beaty tied the game with 0:43 to play. In '92, Jefferson trailed Cloquet by a goal in the Tournament semis until Nick Checco tied the game with 0:51 showing on the clock. They had won all three games in overtime. Could these boys prove themselves champions like those teams?

Sats tried to stay positive behind the bench, but mostly he was quiet. He didn't want to believe it was over until the final buzzer, but the later it got, the worse he felt. Still, it wasn't the worst he had felt. That was '83, when his team had lost only one game all year and was seeded first in the section but got upended by the lesser Minneapolis Washburn in the first game. That was the lowest he had ever felt after a loss. He had nine months to replay the game in his mind, haunted by mistakes and missed chances, plagued by second-guessing and what-ifs. Then, there had been the three consecutive section final losses to Rochester John Marshall in the late '70s. At that point, he had yet to take a team to the Tournament. Each year he got this close, only to get bumped off. Following those, this feeling was the worst. His '01 team had so much potential. The boys just weren't living up to it that Saturday afternoon.

Sats had shortened his bench to Duncs's and Bernie's lines, but Tommy was trying to win the game himself. He coughed up the puck in the neutral zone. He boomed a thirty-five–foot slapshot that Alamano stopped with his blocker. He had a pass picked off at center ice. Kelly Gilbert kept checking the clock above Jeremy. The red numbers grew smaller while the yellow numbers stayed the same: 0–2. *Is there still enough time for two goals?*

Whenever Eastview could, it dumped the puck out of its end. The Lightning interrupted the flow with three icings in less than a minute. Jefferson couldn't get its momentum. With the clock paused at 5:48, Bernie, Tommy, and Dillon replaced the Senior Line. One Jefferson student turned to his buddy, "If we don't score now, there's no way we're going to get another."

With an anxious look on her face and knots in her stomach, Nancy Barthel, Bernie's mom, walked down the steps and implored the cheerleaders in the front row to rouse the crowd and players back into the game. She was worried the boys had started to panic. The cheerleaders' own plans for State thinned. They put their mittens together: "We say number, you say one! We say blue, you say white! We say Jefferson, you say Jaguars!"

Bernie waltzed around a black jersey and burst into the Eastview end. He had Tommy with him on a two-on-one. He carried the puck in deep, tried to slip a pass to Tommy, but the lone Eastview D blocked his pass. The puck deflected harmlessly into the corner.

With 4:07 left, Eastview called timeout. Gibbons gestured emphatic instructions to his team. Duncs's line took the ice. The Jefferson cheerleaders and fans were on their feet. The Eastview side chanted, "East-view Pow-er!"

In the stands, Wes, the long-time Jefferson follower and self-appointed high school hockey expert, couldn't believe what he was witnessing through his thick glasses. Eastview had Jefferson figured out. They stuffed the middle of their zone, shoved the shooters to the outside. They thwarted Jefferson's speed and quickness by slowing down the game. They manhandled the white jerseys. Eastview played hungrier. Especially the kid from Fresno in the net.

In the broadcast booth above the Lightning net, Bobby Hanson, a Jefferson goalie who graduated in '87, told the Channel 14 audience, "I'm a little nervous up here."

Alamano snagged a soft shot by Nick. 3:06 left. Bernie's line came out. The Jefferson student in the stands turned to his buddy. "We're done with. This sucks."

Tommy figured it would take a miracle to tie it, but they had worked miracles before. Edina. Apple Valley. They could do it again. They had to.

Nancy noticed her son repeatedly looking at the clock. She remembered in Mites how he used to time his shots to go in at the last second. She wondered what was going through his mind. He had such huge hopes and dreams for this season. His grandparents in Arizona had already bought their plane tickets for the Tournament in two weeks.

From deep in his end, Bernie hit Tommy with a pass at mid-ice. Across the Eastview blue, Tommy tried to sneak the puck through the defenseman's legs and go around him, but he got stood up and turned over possession. Going the other way, Eastview got whistled offsides. Two minutes and twenty seconds to play.

Sats sent out the Senior Line. His bulldog speech had resonated with Nick. He believed fate had ordained they would win; Sats's words reinforced his belief. He was ready to deliver on his destiny.

Duncs banked the puck up the boards. Nick tried to pick it out of his skates. An Eastview defender drilled him with a double forearm shot. The puck squirted free, but the defender dribbled Nick's head a couple more times off the glass. He had Nick pinned underneath the Eastview section. The Lightning fans roared. Duncs and another Eastview player jumped in. The puck got tied up along the boards, and the linesman whistled the play dead. Nick skated away gingerly and adjusted his helmet. One minute and fifty-four seconds left.

Tears streamed down Karen's cheeks. Memories flooded through her. The boys shooting on her dressed in goalie gear in the basement. Pumping them up before tryouts with Jock Rocks. Getting lost on the way to unknown rinks. Driving a rental van to the Sarnia tournament through a snowstorm. Stowing the milk out in the snow. The boys playing knee hockey in the hotel. Last year's banquet when Nick was anointed an alternate captain. His goal against Edina.

Ever since Nick was in seventh grade, they had talked about the Tournament his senior year. Planned on it. He was such a graceful skater. She wasn't ready to not watch him play.

Adam tried to hit Nick breaking out of his end, but the pass eluded Nick's stick. Icing. Nick banged his stick against the ice. The Jefferson fans hushed.

Jefferson worked the puck into the Eastview end. Sats pulled Jeremy and sent out Bernie. Jeremy joined Timm on the bench where the pair could only watch. Tommy managed an off-balance shot on net, but Alamano went down for a routine save and gloved the puck as the Braemar announcer declared, "One minute remaining." The Eastview fans erupted in a mighty cheer. Some helmets slumped on the Jaguars' bench.

One minute left to play. Perhaps just one minute left in their high school careers. Just one minute left in their lives. Unless they could scavenge two goals.

Nick leaned on his stick laid across his knees. It would take a miracle.

Sats waited as long as he could to give his boys a rest. He let them line up for the faceoff to Alamano's left. Just as the linesman bent his knees to drop the puck, Sats called timeout. The players gathered at their benches and passed the water bottles.

The Eastview fans chanted, "East-view rocks it!" and "Overrated!" The Jefferson cheerleaders answered with, "Jaguars, Jaguars!"—*clap, clap, clapclapclap*.

Sats wanted Duncs to take the draw and pull it back to his right. Tommy would be there waiting to take the shot. They would hope for a tip or a screen.

"Matt Duncan is taking the biggest faceoff in his high school career," Bobby Hanson needlessly reminded the home audience.

Duncs's mind whirred. *This can't be it. Our season can't be over. We're losing. We've got to get a couple of goals here. Quickly.* He crouched and lowered his Sher-Wood to the red faceoff dot.

Tommy lined up just outside the circle off Duncs's right shoulder. Stick on the ice, he was ready to catch the puck and fire it. Just before the linesman dropped the puck, Tommy shifted a half step to his left. But not quite far enough. Duncs snapped the puck back, but it sailed by Tommy on the left. A right-handed shot, Tommy couldn't get his stick over to the other side in time to catch the puck. The fans groaned.

The thousand thoughts rushing through Duncs's head had distracted him. He thought Adam, a left-handed shot, stood behind him. Had he been, Duncs's draw would've been right on the mark. Adam would've been able to get off the shot. They might have gotten a tip or screen. Or a rebound. But Adam wasn't there.

The puck slid all the way back to the Jefferson end. With an Eastview forward in pursuit, Tommy raced back to retrieve Duncs's draw. He stopped behind his empty net to shake the Eastview forechecker and set up.

This is bad, Kelly thought. *Not just for the team, but for Tommy. He's going to lose a lot of exposure. That's going to hurt his chances with colleges, with Mr. Hockey.* He stood with his arms folded across his winter jacket. Next to him Mary wondered if Tommy would cry. She couldn't remember the last time she had seen her son cry.

Tommy skated the puck halfway out of the zone, then hit Bernie with a pass at the Jefferson blue line. Bernie skated to the center line and dumped the puck in. Alamano stopped the puck, and an Eastview defender wrapped it behind the net around the boards. Duncs picked off the clearing attempt and tried to center the puck to Jimmy waiting in the slot, but another Eastview defender knocked away his pass. Bernie, cutting into the center, caught the puck and, in one fluid motion, dropped it and swept a shot past Alamano top shelf. Goal, Jefferson!

Bernie jumped into Adam's arms. They twirled once, then Nick, Duncs, Tommy, and Jimmy joined them, and the six on the ice hugged as one. Tears spread down Nick's face. *We're going to do something miraculous.* Duncs couldn't help but think if his goal had counted in the second period, the game would be tied at 2–2. He tasted bittersweet tears.

Nancy jumped up and down, bounced her feet in jubilation. She put on her Jaguar paw and pumped it. She willed herself to believe that all things were possible. The band belted out the school song. Mary Gilbert clapped in time. Merrelyn wept happy tears. The cheerleaders hugged one another. Mothers scooped their daughters in their arms and swung them around. The fans could smile again. Except for Ryan Briese, Nick and Duncs's good friend whom Sats had cut. Either way, he lost. The Channel 14 camera caught him standing with his red NY hat turned backwards, his tan jacket open, his face serious. In the thick of the student section going nuts, he didn't clap, but watched.

Thirty-eight point three seconds remained on the clock.

Tommy felt better. He could breathe. They had scored before with that little left. Sats had reminded them before the game that they had scored four goals on Eastview with less than a minute remaining. Let Eastview score early; they would take the late goals, the ones that mattered most. All they needed was a goal to tie and force overtime. Then they would start over. Bernie's goal had given them a second chance.

Duncs lost the draw at center ice. Eastview moved the puck into the Jefferson end. Jeremy, back in the net, played the puck to the corner. Eastview sent it behind the net. Bernie picked the puck off the boards and hit Nick breaking across center ice with a perfect pass on stride. Sats waved Jeremy over to the bench. With twenty-three seconds left, Nick soared across the Eastview blue line faster than he had ever skated in his life with only one defenseman and the goalie to beat. The fans hit their feet again.

Karen stood but sat down again and clenched her eyes. *Just let it go in,* she prayed. *Give us one more little chance.* She waited. Listened for the crowd to tell her.

Mike Coffman watched the play unfold before him like a dream come true. He had scored big goals himself, like the night he beat

Bowling Green by knocking in a loose puck with only three seconds to play. This was Nick's chance to shine.

Going wide, Nick showed the puck to the defenseman, who committed, swung his stick at it, but missed when Nick pulled the puck back. *Now get it on net*, Nick thought.

Mike noted that Alamano hadn't set up properly for Nick's shot. *Five-hole!* Nick had scored on shots like that before.

Nick fired for the daylight between Alamano's legs.

It's in! Oh, my god! Mike expected to see the rubber stretch mesh at the back of the net, but Alamano butterflied to shut off the daylight. The shot jumped off Alamano's pad back out to Nick, but a sliding defenseman knocked the puck away before Nick could reload. The puck skipped into the corner. The crowd sagged. Karen sobbed. Duncs flipped a pass out front to Jimmy. Jimmy knocked it down with his glove but out of reach of his stick. The Eastview defense poked the puck clear, but Tommy, waiting between the hash marks, stopped the puck with his left skate and backhanded a shot on goal. His shot hit the Eastview defender and bounced high in the air. It hovered there a moment amidst a salute of desperate sticks before the Eastview defender swatted the puck clear of the zone. The Lightning fans started the countdown: "10, 9—" An Eastview player touched the puck at center ice, and the ref whistled a hand pass. The faceoff went back into the Eastview end with only 00:08.2 showing in red numerals. Jefferson, unbelievably, like a cat with multiple lives, had yet another chance.

Bobby Hanson, speaking perhaps for everyone in the building, exclaimed, "My heart is beating a mile a second."

Nick still believed. It would happen here.

Sats gave Adam instructions at the bench, and he relayed them to the others. Duncs crouched for the draw to Alamano's right. Nick, Adam, and Jimmy lined up in front of the net. Bernie poised along the boards. Tommy manned the point. Enough time remained for one final shot.

This time, Duncs knew Tommy waited behind him. He wanted to pull the faceoff back to him, but it was a bad drop. The linesman put the puck down off center. Duncs's swipe missed. The Eastview center grabbed Duncs's stick and tied him up. Duncs leaned into the center, and they twirled 180 degrees. The puck bounced, then sat still just off the dot. Precious seconds vanished. Jimmy scurried in and edged the puck to the boards where Bernie picked it up. With four seconds left, he sent the puck toward the net.

If the puck had eyes, it could sneak through, and the screened Alamano wouldn't see it. It could get tipped in by one of his teammates. Bernie sent it toward the net in desperation and on a prayer. But the puck deflected off a defender's skate into the far, empty corner. Impotent. No one near enough to retrieve it in time for a shot. Before the buzzer could even ring, an Eastview defender, then Alamano leaped in the air. They had beaten the mighty Jaguars. They had worked the miracle in their favor.

An Eastview defenseman punched Nick. "Fuck you!"

Unable to contain the hurt, anger, frustration, and bewilderment already spilling onto his cheeks, Nick spun and whacked him with his stick across the back of his legs. The refs had to separate them.

Finally two long, slow lines—one a limp white, the other a perky black—slid past each other for the final handshake. Sats caught and released Gibbons's hand in his own.

He walked off with his eyes to the ice, careful not to slip and fall.

The parents processed soberly to the Braemar lobby to wait for their boys.

The Jefferson students lingered in the stands, hushed and stunned. There would be no rematch with the Holy Angels in the section finals. They wouldn't paint their faces for the Tournament. They would have to scramble for tickets and get hassled for skipping school. This wasn't how senior year was supposed to end.

They couldn't help but think Bernie's goal, added to Duncs's, should've tied the game. The players would be coming back for overtime. *Sucks to have the refs decide the game.*

Connie Van Blarcum, the maverick Jefferson librarian and major hockey supporter, thought of the players. The Lightning had toppled Mount Olympus. *This is right out of a Greek tragedy. It will be the defining moment of their lives.*

Kelly Bergmann and Dave Daly watched the ice clear from the dashers in front of the Jefferson bench. In time, they would pick up the water bottles and collect the sticks for the last time. The Channel 14 broadcast signed off with the final image a wide shot of the two managers dangling their feet over the boards, the expanse of vacant ice spread before them. It was 2:35 in the afternoon.

First off the ice, Nick heaved the stick that had failed him into the corner. He plopped onto the wooden bench, ripped off his helmet, and buried his head in his jersey. He wasn't ashamed of the way he played. He had worked hard. He fought along the boards, never gave up. He couldn't figure it out. He played like the bulldog, but ended up the Doberman.

Timm threw his dry gloves and custom-designed mask to the ground. It was all over. He had watched his season die an excruciatingly slow death and hadn't been able to do a damn thing about it. Not a goddamn thing. *Goddammit!*

Tommy hung his head in the corner down the bench from Nick. He would never play with these guys again. They had worked so hard together to get back to the Tournament as seniors. He blamed himself for not scoring. Behind the tears singeing his eyes, he replayed his final chance, only this time, in his mind, he shifted the puck to his forehand and picked his spot. The game tied with ten seconds left. He pressed his hands to his face. This was worse than his nightmares.

Between them, Bernie doubled over, his hands inside his facemask. He had set out to make All-State; be named to the All-Tournament team; erase Jefferson's single season records for goals, assists, and points; record the school's best face-off percentage of all time; and win every game. Forget all of that. Bernie had taken more penalties than anyone on the team except Adam, not a proud statistic for a center in Sats's system. He had hurt his shoulder, taken a suspension. He had next year, but not with these guys. It would be like starting all over.

Duncs stood in the center of the rectangular room and leaned on his stick. His shoulders bobbed. He had been the team's clutch performer. He had come through when the other guys hadn't. He had pulled out wins against Grand Rapids, Duluth East, Edina, and Apple Valley, but not today. That second period no-goal haunted him. Nine times out of ten he would've made the first shot. Reviewing it in his mind, he saw the puck slipping through the five-hole. His team, parents, fans, even scouts—everyone—expected him to deliver. That was the most important situation he had faced. But he fell short. His shot blocked. Then his goal disallowed. That shot would keep replaying in his thoughts. Wake him up at night. For weeks. For years. Forever.

Duncs was too hurt and confused to pray. He didn't understand why they had lost. Why their season had crashed so suddenly. They had worked so hard. Everything he had worked for since he was five years old—over that quickly. He couldn't imagine hockey ever being as fun again. All year he had seen the happiness and smiles on his teammates' faces, but that afternoon all he saw was pain and suffering.

It hit him. Game over.

Eventually, Duncs sank to the bench, still clutching his stick in his gloved hand.

Nick didn't want to take off his jersey. He knew once he did, he would never put it back on.

Timm thought of his father's death. Someone with so much life left in him suddenly struck down. It wasn't right that this team wouldn't play again. That their season was suddenly over. They had done so many things together for the last time without realizing it—their last practice Friday, their last team meal at Perkins, their last talk at the green board, their last time lacing their skates. They had gone through the motions without appreciating the significance. He felt closer to the guys in this room than any other group on earth. But they would return to school Monday no longer a team, just a memory.

Sats leaned against the cinder block wall, his chin to his chest, lips pursed. There was no need to say, "Heads down."

The twenty boys and their coach sat like that for ten minutes or more. Their tears dripped onto the green-speckled black rubber flooring, the only sound their sniffles and a leaky shower faucet.

Kelly and Dave entered, their arms loaded with sticks. They gently laid them down, careful not to make noise, as though that irreverence would only intensify the pain. Kelly sat down on the lip of the shower stall. Dave removed his cap.

Finally Sats raised his chin and said, "Those things happen. Life isn't fair. But that makes us better people. You had a helluva season. Coach Thomas and I are very, very proud."

Snot filled the boys' mouths. They spat it bitterly to the floor.

Sluggishly, they began removing their helmets. Their faces were red, swollen. Tommy wiped his eyes on his jersey.

Duncs finally removed his helmet. He leaned his head back against the wall, and the tears started again. He rubbed his glove to his face. His other hand still held his stick.

They stripped off their equipment wordlessly and stuffed the pieces into their bags. Bernie, the first undressed, crossed the room to the sink and splashed cold water on his face. He gathered his bag and sticks, hugged fellow juniors Shavvy and Dillon, and shook Coach Thomas's hand.

At 3:07 P.M., over a half hour since the game—and their season—ended, Duncs let go of his stick. It plopped against the rubber floor mat. He took off his gloves, peeled off his jersey, unstrapped his shoulder pads. His fingers fumbled with the tape on his wrist. The tears stinging his eyes made it difficult to find a seam to pull.

Sats left and returned five minutes later. "Let's go, guys. Come on. Let's go, Nick." Nick still turtled his head in his jersey. He hadn't touched his skates.

Duncs balled up his brown socks and shoved them in his bag. He pulled on a gray Jefferson Hockey T-shirt, suddenly an alumnus of the program. He paused at the door to shake Thomas's hand, then placed his forehead on the coach's shoulder to cry again.

He wiped his eyes and returned to give Sats a hug.

"You're a helluva kid," Sats said, trying to keep himself together. "We'll talk about it back at school."

Duncs climbed the steps on the Eastview side up to the lobby where his parents waited for him. Steve Duncan's pride had not dimmed a watt. His son hadn't quit. He had played hard until the very end. Deb wrapped Duncs in a hug.

Karen hadn't waited for Nick. She thought it best he not see her so torn apart. She sobbed the whole way home. She left a message on his cell phone telling him how proud she was of him, how she wouldn't trade one minute of the countless hours she spent devoted to his hockey. *I love you.*

Nick saw Mike waiting for him. He walked over to his dad but couldn't look him in the eye. Mike stood in his brown leather jacket, blue jeans, and Doc Martens, hands on his hips. He tried to be sympathetic. "What happened?"

"We weren't looking at this game," Nick said.

"Too bad. That's what happens in life. If you don't pay attention to what's before you, you blow it. You guys blew it."

Merrelyn hugged Jeremy. She hugged Timm. Her eyes were red, her mascara splotched.

When Tommy spotted his mom in the lobby, he put his hand to his face, then sank his head into her shoulder. He sobbed so hard he couldn't breathe. She placed her hand behind his head. They remained frozen like that for a long moment.

Kelly Gilbert escorted Tommy outside with his arm around his son's shoulder.

Nancy searched for Bernie. She hadn't seen him sneak out a side door. She looked for him outside. Someone told her he was already on the bus. She wanted to climb aboard but knew that it was unforgivable for a mother to do so. She peered through the dirty windows, spotted a shape inside, and waved in case it was her son but then realized it wasn't. She recognized Bernie toward the front, his back turned to the window. She reached out to him with her thoughts. *Oh, honey, I'm here.*

Nancy drove home and called her parents in Arizona.

The ten-minute ride back to school seemed as long as the final ten minutes of the game. Jennifer Mellberg, the senior captain of the cheerleaders, covered her face with her white mittens. They had talked about staying at the Holiday Inn in downtown St. Paul for the Tournament, tailgating Wednesday night. Today canceled those plans.

The boys had time to recite in their heads a silent litany of what-ifs. What if they had taken Eastview more seriously, not looked ahead to the section final? What if Sats had emphasized more to them that this could be their last game? What if more guys had increased their intensity with ephedrine? What if none of them had used the supplement? What if they had lifted more during the summer, skated harder in practice? What if Duncs's goal had counted? What if they hadn't bitched on the bench? What if Bernie had scored earlier? What if Adam had been there to catch Duncs's draw? What if Nick had shot somewhere else, maybe top shelf? What if Tommy had gone to his forehand?

They could've been state champions.

But "what if" is a curse. A rotten way to live, constantly looking over your shoulder, pining to rewrite what had happened. You missed the moment. "What if" keeps one mired in the past, forever reliving the loss. "What if" can sink a kid.

In the far back of the bus, Duncs remembered his Aunt Diane. They had lost a hockey game, but at least he still had the chance to enjoy whatever else life had to offer. She didn't have that anymore. He pulled together the seniors around him—Nick, Tommy, B.J., Jimmy, Shacks—in a hug and said, "Thanks for growing up with me."

The boys emptied the bus and walked through the darkened cafeteria, their bags bumping against the plastic chairs.

Downstairs Sats gathered them for one final time in front of the green board, still chalked with his pregame notes: "We must play hard—have fun."

"Clean out your lockers. Take your white and blue jerseys home, wash them, and turn them in Tuesday."

He put his hands in his pockets. "Thanks for a helluva great season. When you have great kids, you start caring so much, you want to win so bad. One thing you better learn: life is not fair.

"It's a good thing you might learn that lesson when you're sixteen, seventeen, eighteen, when you're home with your mom and dad and have people to support you, because some don't learn that until they're older.

"I know it won't be easy to go to school Monday, but you've got each other."

They shuffled off to their lockers. Tommy stayed a moment on the bench after the others had walked off.

Sats made his way through the rows of lockers, saying a few words to each of his players. His eyes swelled when he reached Nick. They embraced. "It's been a pleasure coaching you," Sats said. "I'm going to miss you."

"Thanks," Nick said. "It's been a lot of fun."

Sats gave Bernie a quick one-armed hug.

When he hugged Tommy, his captain broke down again. Tommy doubled over in pain. Sats kept his arm on Tommy's back, bent over to whisper into his ear, "You're a good kid. You can be proud of your season."

Sats worked his way around the room, then joined Thomas in front of the coaches' office. They quietly critiqued the game.

The boys walked past them, up the stairs, through the darkened cafeteria, and out to their cars in the rain-slickened parking lot.

Tommy cleaned out his locker, hoisted his bag over his letter jacket, and repeated to Sats and Thomas on his way out, "Life's not fair. Not fair."

EPILOGUE

Monday sucked. Within the space of ten hours on Saturday, the boys had suffered a major upset and the girls' hockey team had won its first state championship. The first day back at school was tough to stomach.

One sympathetic female classmate baked cookies for the boys, but that didn't take the edge off what Tommy called his "shittiest day ever." Duncs couldn't handle it. He went home at 10:15; his mom called him in sick. Nick cut his last period study hall. Timm gutted it out. Mostly friends gave him space, but by the end of the day, he wanted to pop the next person who said to him, "Sorry. I can't believe you guys lost."

Tuesday the indignities continued. After Larissa Luther's stellar state tournament performance, the *StarTribune* named Timm's ex-girlfriend "Metro Athlete of the Week." The Minnesota Girls' Hockey Coaches Association picked three Jefferson girls (Larissa, Joccie Cookson, and Chrissie Norwich) for the All-State team; Sharon Cole and Ali Lehrke made honorable mention. Meanwhile, the Minnesota Minutemen narrowed its Mr. Hockey candidates list down to five finalists. Duncs and Tommy failed to make the cut. After school, the varsity Jaguars turned in their equipment.

Wednesday, the Jefferson administration staged a congratulatory assembly to honor the state champion girls' hockey team.

The week ground on.

———

Tuesday of the following week, the day before the Tournament began, Duncs walked into the attendance office where he worked as a teacher's assistant and picked up a copy of the *StarTribune*. He turned immediately to the back page, where the paper pictured its All-Metro team. Marty Sertich, the Roseville center who led the state in goals scored, smiled out at him, the Metro Player of the Year surrounded by the Boys' Hockey All-Metro Team. Duncs found his own name on the third team. Tommy hadn't even made that.

Yanked from the spotlight, Duncs suddenly understood what the poet William Stafford meant when he wrote, "The darkness around us is deep." Duncs and Tommy had been reduced from vying for the top honor in the state to being overlooked. There had been no Tournament this year; there would be no D-I next year. They had plunged fast and hard into the darkness.

———

Timm and Nick skipped class to crash the Tournament. Nick's mom had haggled with her siblings to secure the family tickets for her son. They were excellent seats, twenty rows up from the ice, but far from where Timm and Nick wanted to be for Thursday's quarterfinal game pitting Elk River against Eastview, the surprise Section 5AA champion. This was not how they had imagined their experience of the first Tournament played at the Xcel. The Cokes they sipped tasted bitter compared to the water they should have been chugging on the bench.

They took small satisfaction in watching Elk River end the Lightning's Cinderella run. The Elks had been unbeatable since losing to Jefferson in early December. Bolstered by transfer reinforcements—affidavits and all—they had pounded Moorhead 8–1 to win Coach Tony Sarsland his first state championship. Sats, who watched the final from the WCCO Radio broadcast booth as a color commentator, found that especially difficult to swallow.

Meanwhile in the Class A title game, two Catholic schools squared off, prompting Benilde–St. Margaret's coach Ken Pauly to joke, "Means God is Catholic." The reporters laughed, but not the parents who had signed the petition back in January complaining about the "large influx of young, skilled role players" stealing varsity spots. When the Red Knights won the crown, parents thought their boys should be accepting the gold medals instead of the six players new to Benilde–St. Margaret's that year.

One mother cheering the Catholic school's victory was Bobbi Hopkins, Dougie Stansberry's mom. She had known the grief of burying one son and relished the joy won by her other sons, Ryan and Ricky, who teamed to score the game-winning goal. Both boys had come of age in the Jefferson Booster program—Ryan had skated with Tommy and Bernie on the Magic Line—but selected the small private school because they did not want to play for Sats. When the final buzzer rang, Bobbi flung her hands in the air, and Ryan, the Red Knights captain, emptied an orange Gatorade cooler over Coach Pauly. Later, mother and sons would enjoy a quiet, happy moment together.

———

During the season, Karen Bender, the '01 Varsity Social Director, and her committee had spent countless evenings and weekends planning the Jags' annual team banquet. The Monday evening following the Tournament, they dressed up the Minnesota Valley Country Club as they would have for a wedding reception. A Jaguar ice sculpture drooled onto a blue cloth-covered pedestal. Blue and silver balloons decorated white tablecloths. In one corner, the seniors' parents had constructed shadow boxes with photographs and mementos for each graduating player. A large poster displayed photos of the boys as youths—guess who's who. Everyone put on a good face, but the occasion, like the season, hadn't turned out as expected. It had been the year without the Tournament.

After dinner, Sats stood against the backdrop of a snarling, green-eyed Jaguar banner beset by gold and silver stars—each inscribed with a different player's name and number—and handed out varsity letters and awards. All-Conference: Tommy Gilbert, Matt Duncan, Michael Bernhagen, and Adam Dirlam. All-Conference Honorable Mention: Timm Lorenz, Jeremy Earl, Jimmy Humbert, and Nick Coffman. The daughter of Bill Masterton, the North Star who had died from a head injury sustained at Met Center, presented the William J. Masterton Scholarship to the player who demonstrated the qualities "people came to love in my dad"—leadership, perseverance, desire, and sportsmanship—to Tommy Gilbert.

Tommy passed the traveling baby blue captain's stick to Adam Dirlam. The no-nonsense defenseman would lead the '02 squad with Nick Dillon and Jeremy Earl as his assistants. The boys posed for photographs in their suits and ties.

And that was it for the '01 varsity. Good night.

———

Nick Coffman convinced his mom to let him play juniors. One of only five players Tri-City Storm had protected in the draft, Nick left Tommy Gilbert's graduation open house early for the United States Hockey League team's tryout, thinking it was merely a formality for him and Duncs. Nick didn't get asked back. That left him pondering his future at his own open house two weeks later. The University of St. Thomas still wanted him, but Division-III was never the dream. Eventually he decided to attend the University of Minnesota–Mankato and play intramural hockey. Sophomore year he transferred to the University of Wisconsin, where his intramural team (which included Nick Dillon) won the A-level fall championship. He pledged Sigma Alpha Epsilon, declared an economics major, and returned junior year for another season of intramural hockey.

Matt Duncan broke up with Gianna not long after the Eastview loss and girls' championship. His disqualified goal continued to haunt him. The weekend following the state tournament, Duncs's Section 5 team won the Minnesota Great Eight, a showcase of high school seniors played before college and pro scouts, and his strong performance (3 goals, 3 assists) led the same squad to victory at the six-game national tournament. But that still wasn't enough to garner any substantial D-I invitations.

Duncs turned down a tepid offer from Colorado College, which fingered him as a fourth-line winger for the 2001–2002 season. "Think of it this way," Steve Duncan explained. "If you're in a business situation and you bring in two guys to do the same job, paying one $150,000 and the other $10,000, when push comes to shove, who's going to get the support, the ice time?"

He took a drag off his Old Gold. "They weren't committed."

The summer after graduation, Duncs headed to Kearney, Nebraska, for Tri-City's final tryout. Someone from the Storm's booster club met him at the hotel to carry his gear. Nearly 2,500 fans showed up for the scrimmages. Duncs signed autographs afterward. Girls aged thirteen to thirty waited for the players outside. People stopped Steve in restaurants when they spotted his USA Select 16 T-shirt and asked if his son played for the Storm. "You would think these kids were the New York Rangers," Steve said.

Despite the Tri-City coaches' pitch that Duncs would develop his game with the chance to secure that coveted scholarship, the promises never came true. He barely got any ice time. When he did play, opponents cross-checked him from behind and whacked the back of his legs.

A couple of months into the season, Tri-City traded Duncs to the Chicago Steel. He roomed with Tommy, but he didn't start getting regular shifts until midseason. His confidence slumped. He wanted to quit.

He decided to give the USHL one more shot and returned to Chicago in the fall. He left after two weeks. "I could tell it wasn't going to work out," he said. "I didn't want to put in another year in that league."

He enrolled spring semester at Gustavus Adolphus College, a D-III school in St. Peter, Minnesota, where he played the remainder of the hockey season. Jefferson teammates Eric Lindquist and Cory Gilbert joined him on the Gustavus varsity for the '03–04 season, when Duncs scored nine points (1 goal, 8 assists) and had a +4 rating in 19 games. He returned to Gustavus in the fall.

Saturday, June 22, 2002, **Tommy Gilbert** gathered his family and some friends around the television where he had watched the state tournament so many times before, this time to catch the 2002 NHL draft. Tommy's "family advisor"—"He's an agent," Tommy explained, "but we can't call him that because it's illegal to have an agent under NCAA rules"—had received a tip that Tommy would be drafted in the first three rounds that day. When the ESPN2 coverage ended, they followed the draft selections on the Internet, but Tommy didn't see his name called the first day.

He spent the night at a buddy's house and was driving home the next morning when his family advisor reached him on his cell phone. Early on the draft's second day, the Colorado Avalanche selected Bloomington Jefferson's Tommy Gilbert in the fourth round (129th overall). The '01 Stanley Cup champions had been one of the top two teams he had hoped would pick him. "That was a really cool feeling," he said.

It capped off a year of cool feelings. After the disappointing end to his high school career, with no attractive offers forthcoming from D-I schools, Tommy wondered what would've happened if Sats had let him play defense senior year. The D-I coaches calling him knew Tommy as an offensive defenseman. He had wanted to go to the University of Minnesota, but that offer never came. Instead Tommy went to Chicago, where he got tagged a "top prospect" and became a USHL All-Star defenseman. His stock bounced back. He accepted a scholarship to the University of Wisconsin for the 2002–2003 season. The U.S. National Team invited him to try out for the team that would play in the World Junior Olympics. Then Colorado drafted him.

Tommy finished his sophomore season at the University of Wisconsin with 6 goals and 15 assists. His +17 rating was third best on the Badgers. The Edmonton Oilers claimed him on waivers from the Colorado Avalanche.

Timm Lorenz finished his Minnesota high school hockey career with the thirteenth best goals against average in the state (1.79) and a .903 save percentage. He sent out dozens of hockey résumés, tried out with teams from the USHL, the North American Hockey League, and the American West League, but nothing panned out. He finally landed a spot on the Bridgewater, Massachusetts, Bandits of the obscure Eastern Junior Hockey League, where he posted a 2.30 GAA on a .500 team, but he found it difficult to adjust to the mediocrity. "I've never been on a team that didn't win all the time," he said.

The next summer he was back pounding the pavement. At a tryout with the Chicago Steel, Timm was one of forty-eight goalies. Nobody noticed him. He wound up back in Bridgewater for another season.

He also survived an awful scare with his mother. Merrelyn had returned to their home in Colorado but missed Debbie Earl and her other Jefferson hockey friends. In January, less than five years after a heart attack had taken his dad's life, Timm fielded a call in Massachusetts, two thousand miles away, that his mother had suffered a heart attack. She pulled through, but after several bypass surgeries, she had another heart attack that summer. By the time Timm reported to Bridgewater for his second season, Merrelyn's condition seemed to have stabilized with the right mix of medication, diet, and exercise. In hindsight, he realized how golden those two years in Minnesota with his mother had been. Two seasons with the Bridgewater Bandits convinced Timm to try Division III hockey. He enrolled at Saint John's University in Collegeville, Minnesota, coached by '80 Miracle team member John Harrington. Timm couldn't crack the varsity lineup, so after a discouraging season on the bench, he decided to transfer to the University of Denver. He planned to try out for the hockey team even though he knew his chances were slim to none. After five years of playing hockey else-where, he wanted to be closer to home.

Jimmy Humbert and **Brian Johnson** teamed up at the D-III Augsburg College, where, in the first two months, they scored more points on the junior varsity than anyone had scored at Augsburg in an entire season. They both were skating on the varsity by the end of the year. **Bryan Shackle** went from playing four sports (soccer, football, golf, and hockey) at Jefferson to none at the University of Minnesota. He declared an architecture major and focused on his music.

After getting cut his senior year, **Ryan Briese** played for the Jefferson Jr. Gold. He scored twenty-two goals (tops on the team), forty points, and became a team leader. In only its fourth loss of the season, the Jefferson Jr. Gold came up short, 0–1, to Eden Prairie in the championship final. Two years after graduation, he was working at a car dealership and playing late-night pickup hockey.

Larissa Luther became the only female hockey player in history to win the Minnesota state high school girls' championship and an NCAA title when her UMD Bulldogs captured the 2002 national championship. After her All-Tournament goalie stint for the Jaguars, Larissa was back to playing defense, where she was named to the NCAA All-Tournament team and scored a clutch powerplay goal in the semifinal game.

Sarah Kraft declared a mass communications major with a concen-tration in public relations at the University of Wisconsin, where she occasionally played open hockey and watched former Jefferson team-mates Joccie Cookson and Sharon Cole skate for the Badgers. **Kendra Ottum** had offers from three D-I schools to play hockey but accepted a soccer scholarship at the University of Wisconsin–Green Bay. She returned home after a season, complaining that D-I soccer was "too much of a job." In **Gianna Gambucci**'s senior season, Jefferson lost 7–1 in the state tournament semifinal to South St. Paul, which ended the city's jinx and became its first state hockey championship. Gianna pledged the Delta Gamma sorority at Arizona State University her first year and decided to take some time off from hockey.

The man who seemed in line to be the next Minnesota hockey coaching legend, Duluth East coach **Mike Randolph**, was fired in April 2003, the month after he made his eighth state tournament appearance in fifteen years. While winning two Class AA state championships, finishing runner-up three times, and accumulating a 308–83–10 record at East, Randolph rubbed some parents the wrong way, including Duluth East principal Laurie Knapp, who made the decision not to renew Randolph's annual contract. Seven years ago, Randolph cut Knapp's son, then a sophomore, from the varsity team, though Knapp told the *Star Tribune*, "We're past that." Randolph's ouster renewed the Minnesota State Hockey Coaches Association's campaign for legislation that would give coaches tenure similar to teachers and due process. At present, schools are not required to provide reasons for terminating a coach upon expiration of his contract, and coaches have no recourse to answer critics. A subsequent state investigation confirmed the district's finding that the booster club had mismanaged funds from a Christmas wreath sale. A persistent grass-roots campaign to reinstate Randolph reshaped the school board. One year after Knapp fired Randolph, she urged the school board to stand by that decision. It voted 5–2 to give Randolph his job back. He begins the 2004–05 season as the new old hockey coach at Duluth East.

––––––––

A week after his penultimate season had ended, **Tom Saterdalen** spun his perspective on the Eastview loss. Sats wished Tommy had played bigger, but was gratified to have watched Nick, Duncs, and Jimmy grow up over the season. He felt bad for them and Timm, Bryan, and B.J. "I've got next year, the seniors don't," he said, leaning back in his office chair. He had one more shot before retirement to win that elusive, unblemished title.

Sats took comfort in the belief that everything happens for a reason. It reassured him to have struck upon the reason for this year's bitter, abrupt end. "The reason this happened is because it is going to help us win the state title next year," he said. Next year, his last, they wouldn't lose the section finals—too many guys returning from this year's team, remembering how it felt post-Eastview, wouldn't let it happen.

Michael Bernhagen picked No. 13 for his senior season. He thought he could defy superstition, but his luck with Sats went from bad to worse. In the handshakes after the Elk River game, an Elk player tweaked Bernie's tender thumb. Bernie slugged him in the face mask. The officials assessed Bernie a game misconduct. Sats drew up a behavior contract: do this, this, or this, and you sit.

Bernie violated the contract several times, and Sats benched him each one. The poet's play lagged well behind his potential. Finally, Bernie ran out of second chances. Sats organized another intervention. This time, it was for keeps. Mid-February, with two games left in the regular season and the Jaguars in third place in the Lake Conference, the captains—Adam, Jeremy, and Dillon—sat Bernie down and told their classmate they didn't want to play with him anymore. "He took his disrespect to a new level," Adam explained.

Bernie was finished as a Jaguar. He shrugged it off. In an odd way, he seemed relieved. He didn't have to fight anymore. He didn't have to perform. He had his afternoons free. He said he was done playing hockey. When he headed off to the University of Minnesota–Duluth, he brought only his skates and a stick but at the last minute decided to play intramural hockey in the fall.

Bernie transferred to the University of Minnesota for his sophomore year. He enrolled in the Carlson School of Management, declared a business major, and made the Dean's List. The Bloomington-based Buck's Furniture team enlisted Bernie to play on a line with Jeff Saterdalen. In April 2004, the unlikely matched pair led Buck's Furniture to its eleventh Senior Elite men's national championship. Bernie planned to walk on at the University of Wisconsin, but decided not to after the coaches told him he was a long shot to make the team. He returned to the University of Minnesota and Buck's Furniture for his junior year.

Sats turned sixty during the 2001–2002 school year and became eligible to take advantage of a favorable Bloomington school district retirement plan. In his thirty-eighth and final season, each Lake Conference opponent honored the long-time coach during his farewell visit to their rink. At BIG, members from past Jefferson

330 • Blades of Glory

teams returned home for a pregame retirement celebration where the mayor of Bloomington read a special proclamation.

Sats still believed in the reason for last year's Eastview loss, but it looked like Bernie might have spoiled the party. In the section semi-final at Braemar Arena against Minnetonka, the Skippers jumped to a 2–0 lead in the first period. The fathers smoking outside during intermission complained that the boys weren't moving their feet. When the score was still 2–0 after the second, Karen Rysavy shook her head. "Déja vu," she said in the lobby of the same rink where the boys had broken down her son's junior year.

Jeff Saterdalen and his sister Paige consoled their mother, Diane. "Tom wasn't optimistic when he left home," she said. They all knew this could be his last game, the end of his career. She dabbed moist eyes.

Sats returned to the bench for the third period with his face betraying none of the emotion churning under his sweater. He remained stoic even after Brad Peterson scored a powerplay goal to pull the Jaguars within one. The clock ticked down on Sats's career with his team, which had struggled all year to score, unable to put another goal on the scoreboard. He had three minutes left on his thirty-eight years.

Then, Adam, in his own end, spotted Peterson at the Minnetonka blue line and threaded a perfect pass through the defense. The junior wing who had matured into the team's leading scorer raced in alone, flipped the puck over the goalie's shoulder, and tied the game with 2:54 to play. Sats lived!

With a minute-and-a-half left in the game, Adam stepped around a Skipper sliding to block his shot, unleashed a wrister through traffic on net—and in! 3–2, Jaguars! Sats whistled in delight.

During heads down in the dressing room, Sats sobbed. "I've been around a long time, but you go far when you've got great kids," he shouted through his tears.

The '02 Jaguars got to ride the caravan once again to Mariucci. This year, though, there would be no section final rematch with Holy Angels. The MSHSL had realigned the sections, ostensibly to lump schools together by proximity, but league officials couldn't explain why they had split Bloomington down the middle, leaving Bloomington Kennedy in 5AA and moving Bloomington Jefferson to 6AA, a potentially tougher section including Eden Prairie, Edina, Wayzata, and Buffalo. Holy Angels remained in 5AA.

Jeremy started the section final against Buffalo. After two years of rotating with Timm, Jeremy had become the Jaguars' top goaltender his senior year. He made twenty-two saves, including two big ones in the third period. Jefferson won 3–1 and headed to the Tournament for the fifteenth time in Sats's twenty-nine years at Jefferson.

The coach raced out onto the ice to celebrate. When he neared the crease, he slipped—and Jeremy was there to make his biggest save of the night. He steadied Sats, and the two hugged.

————

Tom Saterdalen's farewell tour reached its climax at the 2002 Tournament. At the Tournament banquet Wednesday night, the coaches of the other seven AA participants each took a turn at the microphone toasting Sats.

The Minneapolis *StarTribune*, the St. Paul *Pioneer Press*, *Minnesota Prep Sports*, *Minnesota Hockey Journal*, *The Minnesota Score*, and the Tournament's official program featured articles about Sats's storied career coming to a close in Tournament City. The television and radio crews all mined him for his thoughts. Ironically, the Jefferson player that graced *Score*'s cover was the school's best ever—and the one the captains had kicked off the team a month earlier: Bernie.

Spotting Sats walking his team down West Seventh for a pregame meal Thursday afternoon, passersby stopped to wish the Jaguars coach good luck in that evening's quarterfinal game against defending champion Elk River. Sats admitted he was nervous. Jeremy had provided exceptional goaltending, but his team had trouble scoring all season. Peterson had stepped up, scoring twenty-two goals and forty-seven points, but this year's Jaguars missed the firepower of Duncs, Tommy, and now Bernie.

Still, Sats claimed he didn't worry about what he couldn't control. If he had done his job and prepared his team, he slept well. "I slept great last night," he said.

————

In the carpeted Xcel dressing room before the game, Shavvy stalled while his teammates dressed. He strutted around the spacious room bare-chested, his jeans slipping off his hips. Adam tried to get him into a game mood. "You do this for fun, right?" Shavvy smirked. "I do this for pussy."

"It just ain't working out, is it?" Peterson quipped.

A tournament official poked his head in the door. "Six minutes."

Sats paced the length of the dressing room, composing his pregame remarks. He wore gray slacks and a new beige sweater. He walked out of the dressing room, down the hall, then returned. "I hope you guys play a little pissed off tonight. I'm going to let you in on a few things that get me going..." He walked out, returned, and walked out again without a word.

He returned and whistled sharply. "How do you guys feel about a guy who doesn't think you're good enough, a guy who plays his No. 2 goalie against you?"

Elk River coach Tony Sarsland planned to start Dusty Hall, the Buffalo transfer, rather than his top goalie, Brent Solei.

"You know how I feel about those three guys who came in?" Sats referred to the three Buffalo transfers: Hall and the Birkeland brothers, Barnabus and Judah, whom Sats called "Judas."

"It pisses me off. You know what I stand for."

If they didn't, the stacked headline of the *Pioneer Press* article, written by Sats's tennis buddy Mike Fermoyle, should have made it abundantly clear: "Loyal to the end: Tom Saterdalen built the boys' hockey program at Bloomington Jefferson into a state power by standing by his players. The Jaguars have rewarded him with fifteen trips to the state tournament."

"It's not right," Sats said, pacing among the orange peels. "I hope you make a stand for that tonight. Have a good time, but play with an edge."

He stopped and looked up. "You know what else pisses me off? Did you hear Sarsland's comment last night [at the Tournament banquet]? He said Jefferson in '93 had one of Minnesota's four best teams ever. He put two of his own up there. Shit, they couldn't hold our jockstraps. It pisses me off.

"Heads down."

The cameraman shooting the season highlight video panned the room with Sats standing in the center, head bowed. The red numbers on the digital clock in the corner ticked off the seconds until game time.

"Focus on every single faceoff," Sats shouted. "Play forty-five minutes and another forty-five if we have to. We're not going to stop until we come out of here with a win. Guts out! Balls out!"

Their first meeting with Elk River early in the year at BIG— when Bernie punched an opponent in the post-game handshake— had been brutal. Van B got head-butted, and an Elk River player went down with a concussion. "They were out for blood," said Amber, the trainer. "It was my busiest game of the year."

Jefferson had squeaked by with a 2–1 win. This time, inspired by the pregame speech, Jefferson came out hard and applied early pressure. Sats matched lines with Sarsland. The Elks didn't get a shot on goal until four minutes and thirty seconds into the period. Soon after, when Jeremy made a big save on a breakaway, the fans wearing Columbia blue chanted, "We've got Jeremy"—*clap, clap, clapclap-clap*—"We've got Jeremy."

Two minutes into the second period, during a scramble in front of the Elks' net, Cory Gilbert spied the loose puck over his shoulder. The junior wing who had scored just six goals all season whirled and backhanded the puck past Hall to spot Jefferson to a 1–0 lead. It was the kind of quick, tough goal from down low that his older brother had been so adept at scoring.

Tommy's phone started to ring in Chicago. Friends at the game and friends watching on TV reported that Cory had scored. "He has scored more state tournament goals than you," they teased. Tommy felt a mixture of sibling rivalry and brotherly love. "I'm always jealous when someone else scores," he admitted later. "But, at the same time, I had never been happier for him."

Leaning over the dashers, Sarsland channeled Bobby Knight, spewing urgent instructions to his team, but the Elks couldn't beat Jeremy. The puck bounced dangerously in front of the Jaguars' net, yet in scramble after scramble, Jeremy came up with acrobatic saves.

At 10:32 of the third period, Peterson scored the clincher on a powerplay, picking up a deflected puck at the Elk River blue line, charging in alone, and deking the goalie with a sweet shimmy of his stick. Play roughened in the final minutes, but not to the point where Amber needed to make an appearance. The Jaguars survived the first round with a 2–0 victory.

In the dressing room after a quick heads down, Sats shouted, "Hey, you guys played together because you stayed together. You stuck it to the guys from Buffalo!"

Sats paused to meet with the media throng. Relieved by the win, he explained Jefferson's uncharacteristic scoring woes. "All of my other scorers are on other teams—two (Tyler Hirsch and Zach Parisé) are at Shattuck, two (Kevin Rollwagen and Matt Kaiser) are on the other team." He wouldn't even say Holy Angels' name. Then he was whisked away to a television interview with Jeff Grayson.

The Channel 9 sportscaster asked if Sats had been talking with the kids about this being his last go round. "This isn't about Tom Saterdalen," Sats replied. "This is about Jefferson and those kids. It's our senior class. Our senior class is unbelievable. I went to their Bantam banquet when they were in ninth grade. Nick Dillon and Jeremy Earl were captains of that team. I told them if you stick together, you'll be rewarded. These kids have stayed together, and they've been rewarded."

———

Jefferson played Hill-Murray in the second semifinal Friday. In the dressing room, they watched the Holy Angels–Roseville game on the TV mounted in the corner. The score was tied 3–3 in the second. Sats walked in. "Hey, guys, why don't you turn it off—that game has nothing to do with us."

They knew the other semifinal had everything to do with them. Especially when they heard the cheers repeated for Holy Angels throughout the third, and the Stars dispatched the favored Roseville 6–3 to gain a spot in the championship game. The Jaguars were on a collision course to meet up with the Stars. Sats and Trebil would play out their rubber match on the Big Stage.

Win that one, and Sats would achieve the ultimate vindication. He would put an end to the murmurs of him owing his success to Trebil's grooming. He would prove that homegrown talent could beat the Metro All-Stars. He would go out on top—Ted Williams homering in his final at-bat—winning his last game, never again to be defeated, immortalized as a champion. That would be a huge cherry on top of his career.

But lose that one, and he would go out with his tail between his legs, mumblings, "uncle" to his nemesis. A loss like that could forever tarnish Sats's success and bloody his ego.

After the pregame heads down that Friday night, Sats reached into his pocket and unfolded a piece of paper. "I found this in my room after breakfast," he started and read the letter to "Coach Sats and the Jags," which concluded, "Remember that hard work beats talent when talent doesn't work hard. Mark Parrish, '95." Sats choked up a little reading the final line.

"Guys, he would leave it on the ice every time. Work hard!"

They tried, but didn't have a chance. Two minutes into the game, Hill-Murray beat Jefferson goalie Ben Corbett on the first shot, a soft wrister over his blocker. Five minutes later, the junior goalie, still beset by jitters, gave up a fluke goal when a centering pass caromed off his stick into the net. The offensively challenged Jags, who had relied on defense and goaltending to win, suddenly found themselves down a steep hole, trailing 2–0.

In the stands, Jefferson fans criticized Sats's decision to start his second-string goalie in the team's biggest game to date. Nothing against Ben, a promising junior with a 1.50 goals against average, but he had played only eight games all year. Jeremy had two years of Tournament experience; Ben had none. Jeremy was a senior, an alternate captain, and, most significantly, he had the hot hand. Coming off his spectacular performance Thursday night, he would give the team confidence. Instead, Sats went with his backup who, before the period ended, let in another goal—a tip that might have eluded Jeremy as well—the Pioneers' third goal on seven shots.

Cornered by Channel 9 after the first period, Sats told the television audience that his team falling behind wasn't the goalie's fault— or his, the coach's, for starting him. "We made a commitment to Corby," he said. "We're not second-guessing ourselves. They're beating us to loose pucks. If we clear the zone, they never get the chance to put a shot on goal. Everybody sees the goalie as the last person, and that's not always true. Two of their goals, all we have to do is chip it out, and we're out of the zone."

That didn't stop some cynics in the press box from speculating that Sats was afraid to face Holy Angels, who clearly had the stronger team that year.

To open the second, Jeremy led the way out of the dressing room; Corbett took a seat at the far end of the bench. But the damage had been done. Jeremy couldn't make up the 3–0 deficit. He limited the Pioneers to one goal over the next two periods, until they put one in at the final buzzer. The Jaguars failed to score, going down 5–0. In the game's waning moments, Sats grit his teeth, his expression that of a man asked to identify a friend at the morgue.

He still had one more game left on his career, but it was tomorrow's third place game against Roseville instead of a shot at a final championship.

The Jaguars came off the ice in tears. Sats had little to say to them. Following heads down, he said, "Okay, I'll talk to you guys after your showers about tomorrow." He would tell them what color jerseys to wear and cover the post-game awards logistics. He ducked into the bathroom for a moment of solitude before he faced the press.

"Right before the Buffalo game [the Section 6AA final], we told Jeremy and Ben that Jeremy would play the Buffalo game and the first game of the Tournament, then Ben would play the next game because he'd been playing so well," Sats explained.

"Wasn't it tempting after the way Jeremy played last night to go with him?"

"Not if you're honest with kids," Sats said. "You can't go back on your word. Then you're a liar."

———

Hill-Murray took on Holy Angels in Saturday night's 2002 Class-AA Championship, the first ever AA final between two private schools. The Catholic school dominance (earlier in the day Catholic Totino-Grace won the Class-A championship) exposed the recent rise in private school strength and stirred resentment among the public school sector. While the Zamboni smoothed the surface for the opening faceoff, a vocal contingent in the upper deck seats led by boys in black Roseville sweatshirts castigated the final pairing: "Pub-lic schools!" *clap, clap, clapclapclap* , "Pub-lic schools!"

The green Hill-Murray student section answered from the lower bowl, "You're not here!"

Coming into the game on a nineteen-game winning streak, Trebil's all-stars beat Hill-Murray with their speed, stickwork, slick wide-ice passes, and disciplined systems. Sats's former lieutenant won his first high school title. The Stars' junior wing Kevin Rollwagen, a product of the Jefferson Booster Program, was named the No. 1 star of the game for setting up the game-winning goal and scoring the clincher on a great individual effort.

When asked afterward about the way Catholic schools dominated this year's Tournament, Trebil downplayed the significance of the Academy of Holy Angels' Catholic identity and instead emphasized the primacy of his hockey program—the very thing his critics had com-plained about a year earlier. "I don't know why it's a big deal there were three Catholic schools, except that it was a little bit of an oddity that it happened to line up that way," Trebil told reporters. "We would prefer to be thought of as just a hockey team and not labeled in that fashion. We're just a hockey team. I don't see any significance in it myself."

Jefferson's game against Roseville earlier Saturday afternoon proved an anticlimactic end to Sats's career. A scant crowd freckled the Xcel's forest-green seats. The arena was so quiet that way up in the press box you could hear Sats whistle his line changes. No one cared about third place.

The only interest was in the historic occasion of Sats's final game, the last one of his thirty-eight–season, 959-game career. He wore two small microphones clipped to his Columbia blue sweater—one for a local television station's evening news broadcast, the other for the highlight video. He would be the Minnesota Hockey Coaches Association's pick for Class AA Coach of the Year, an obvious senti-mental choice but also a legitimate selection because of how far he had brought this year's group.

Sats entered the game with 545 career victories at Jefferson, more than any other Minnesota hockey coach save Willard Ikola and Larry

Ross, but 546 proved one too many. With Roseville up 2–0 after the second period, Sats tried to rouse his boys. "The fourth line's the only line working hard," he shouted at them in the dressing room. "We can win this game. Anybody who thinks we can't win this game, stay here."

He walked out, then came back, paced a lap, and walked out. With the red numbers in the corner showing one minute until the third started, Sats returned, strode quickly across the dressing room, and wrote on the white board, "11 vs. 2."

"What's that mean?" he asked. "Jeremy?"

"They're ranked No. 2, we're ranked No. 11," Jeremy answered.

"Right. You can go out there and show them something. It's not for me. It's for you." His voice rose. "You've got to care about each other. You've got to go out there and block shots for each other. You've got to skate hard for each other. You've got to work hard for each other." Veins ridged the sides of his face. "It's not about the coaches—it's for you."

But Roseville, clearly the better team, outplayed Jefferson in the third. Late in the game, Sats watched intently, hands in his pockets. He checked the clock: 1:59. He wasn't ready to concede defeat. He said nothing for the microphones.

Jefferson staged a fifteen-second flurry in front of the Roseville net. Sats's eyes followed the action closely, his mouth open, but the Jags couldn't score.

With 0:21.4 showing, Sats called timeout and diagramed a play. The Jefferson band played Beethoven's Ninth.

Sats stood on the bench, leaned forward with one foot on the boards. "Ice, ice," he shouted when Roseville dumped the puck out of its end. The linesman obliged Sats by calling icing. Jefferson got a faceoff in the Roseville end with 0:08.9 left in the game, with 0:08.9 left in Sats's career.

The puck dropped. Sats shouted. Van B shot. The goalie gloved it. Five point one seconds to go.

Bernie transferred to the University of Minnesota for his sophomore year. He enrolled in the Carlson School of Management, declared a business major, and made the Dean's List. The Bloomington-based Buck's Furniture team enlisted Bernie to play on

ABOUT THE AUTHOR

A native Minnesotan, John Rosengren developed an early love for hockey. He learned to skate as soon as he could walk and gained intimate knowledge of the game as a player, referee, and fan. He still plays—though a little more slowly—once a week with other aging players and cheers the hometown Wild.

An award-winning writer, Rosengren writes frequently about the drama that plays out in sports. His work has appeared in more than seventy-five publications, including *Maximum Golf, Men's Health, Reader's Digest, Self, Sports Illustrated,* and *Tennis.* He earned a master's degree in creative writing from Boston University. He lives in Minneapolis with his wife, Maria, and their two children.

a line with Jeff Saterdalen. In April 2004, the unlikely matched pair led Buck's Furniture to its eleventh Senior Elite men's national championship. Bernie planned to walk on at the University of Wisconsin, but decided not to after the coaches told him he was a long shot to make the team. He returned to the University of Minnesota and Buck's Furniture for his junior year. Sats bit his lower lip, shoved his hands in his pockets. The puck dropped. Time expired.

Before the awards ceremony, MSHSL tournament director Skip Peltier shook Sats's hand. The two had clashed over the years, but Peltier sounded sincere when he said, "Great career." Sats looked grateful for the gesture.

The P.A. announcer saluted Sats. The fans, swelling for the final to be played next, applauded. Sats raised his right hand to acknowledge them and blinked back a few tears. He turned a game puck over and over in his hands. Coach Thomas put his arm around Sats's shoulders.

After the awards, Sats headed to the dressing room, but a group of kids on the railing begged him to autograph their programs, tickets, and magazines with his picture. He stopped and signed them all.

"Heads down."

The emotion hung thick in the Jaguars' dressing room.

"Guys, that was a nice effort." Sats started to cry. "It has been a great career. I've had so much fun. I want to thank you guys." He paced across the orange peels. "You guys went through a lot. The captains took a stand. I'm proud of you.

"We get on your ass a little sometimes because we want to get a lot out of you. Remember that with your kids someday. Ask a lot of them, but don't put pressure on them. They'll give a lot back. That's what has been our success here."

He made his way around the room and shook each player's hand. He pulled a white hankie out of his pocket, blew his nose.

The players stripped, showered, and finally left. As usual, Sats was the last one out. He pulled a leather jacket off a hook, took off his Jaguars Hockey warmup, and replaced it with the leather jacket. He walked out and closed the door.

For the last time in his thirty-eight–year career, Sats left the build-
But his legacy lingered.